India and the G20

India and the G20: Legacy and Prospects for Multilateralism Amidst a Polycrisis

CFA
Centre for Financial Accountability

YODA PRESS
79 Gulmohar Enclave
New Delhi 110 049
www.yodapress.co.in

India and the G20: Legacy and Prospects
for Multilateralism Amidst a Polycrisis

ISBN 978-93-82579-20-5

Edited by Sonal Raghuvanshi
Illustrated by Soumik Lahiri
The moral rights of the author have been asserted
Database rights reserved with YODA PRESS (maker)

Cover art is the copyright of prole.info
Cover design by Anirban Bhattacharya

This publication has been prepared by the Centre for Financial Accountability with the support of the Heinrich Böll Stiftung, Regional Office, New Delhi. The views and analysis contained in the publication are those of the author(s) and do not necessarily represent the views of the foundation.

Editors in charge: Ishita Gupta, Neha Madhusudan and Arpita Das
Typeset in Minion Pro, 10/12
By MSourcing
Published by Arpita Das for YODA PRESS First edition published in 2022, Second edition in 2023
Printed in India

Table of Contents

Acknowledgement

This book is an endeavor of the Centre for Financial Accountability and has come to fruition because of the support of the Heinrich Böll Stiftung, Regional Office, New Delhi.

We are grateful to all the research fellows and authors featured in this book for their valuable analysis. We thank them for their engagement and patience despite the constraints and immediacies of the COVID-19 health emergency. We would also like to thank the 20 anonymous reviewers for taking the time and effort necessary to review the manuscript. We sincerely appreciate all valuable comments and suggestions, which helped us to improve the quality of the manuscript. We would also like to commend Soumik Lahiri for wonderfully illustrating all the essays.

We would also like to thank Professor Prahbat Patnaik and Professor Patrick Bond for their constant guidance and authoring the foreword and afterword, respectively. The research fellowship and the book has greatly benefited from the conversations with Joe Athialy and Anuradha Munshi and their unwavering support.

We are also grateful towards our publisher, Yoda Press for materializing this. We particularly thank Ishita Gupta and Arpita Das for believing in the project and navigating the course towards the publication and Neha Madhusudan for the copy-edits. Special thanks to prole.info for the cover art and Anirban Bhattacharya for cover design.

We would finally like to thank Sonal Raghuvanshi who not only edited this book but also coordinated the research fellowship. We acknowledge her for patiently following up with each author at all stages, as well as liaising with Yoda Press.

Centre for Financial Accountability

Foreword

India's assumption of the Presidency of the G20 opens up immense possibilities for a democratic intervention in world economic affairs. What such an intervention should look like is discussed in the various papers brought together in this volume.

India's Presidency is also occurring at a crucial moment in the history of the world economy. Inflation is currently raging everywhere, even in the advanced capitalist world, including the United States which has substantially raised its interest rates. The Federal Reserve Board has increased the Federal Funds Rate from 0.25 per cent on March 1, 2022, to as much as 4 per cent by the first week of November 2022; some expect it to be raised even higher, to a whopping 6 per cent in the near future.

This increase in rates has led to a flight of finance from the rest of the world to the US, notwithstanding the fact that other countries too have raised their interest rates along with the US, and because of this inflow of finance into the US, the dollar has appreciated vis-à-vis virtually all major currencies of the capitalist world with the exception of the Russian rouble. India for instance has not only raised its interest rates substantially to match the increase in US rates, but has even run down its foreign exchange reserves by over USD100 billion, or nearly a sixth of its total reserves, between March 1 and end-October; yet it has been unable to prevent a substantial depreciation of the rupee, by more than 10 per cent over this period.

There has been a good deal of discussion on the prospects of a global recession arising from this pervasive increase in interest rates, and the mass unemployment that this would give rise to. The generation of such mass unemployment however should cause no surprise, for unemployment is the main weapon that capitalism uses against inflation, as it both reduces excess demand pressures and also weakens the bargaining strength of the workers, because of which they are unable to defend themselves and thereby bring inflation to a halt.

For the third world, however, there is an additional danger looming large, namely, the near impossibility of servicing its current external debt. The hardships to the people that this can cause is illustrated by the example of Sri Lanka which till the other day was considered a 'middle income country'. Therefore, for a large swathe of countries across the world, there is a real danger of their drowning under the burden of external debt.

There are a number of reasons why such a fate is imminent. First, we are entering a period when the availability of external finance for third world countries will be severely limited so that, let alone servicing external debt, even meeting current account deficits on the balance of payments will pose a severe problem. Second, with the rise in interest rates, whatever external finance does become available, whether from private or from official institutional sources, will be much more expensive than before, so that even if external debt is allowed to be rolled over, it will still entail a far heavier burden on the borrowing countries. Third, since the bulk of this debt is denominated in dollars, the depreciation of third world currencies vis-à-vis the dollar implies that the burden of debt in local currency will be greatly enhanced. The people will be saddled in effect with an even heavier debt-burden because of currency depreciation. Fourth, the impact of the world recession will mean that exports from the third world will suffer both in volume terms, and, in the case of primary commodities, also in terms of prices; this means that most third world countries will face the additional problem of a wider current account deficit, quite apart from the greater difficulty of financing such deficits. Therefore, most such countries are staring at the terrifying prospects of a real economic collapse.

The typical preoccupation in such a situation of the advanced capitalist world, and of institutions like the World Bank and the IMF dominated by them, is with the interests of the creditors, with how to ensure that they get back the money they had lent, or resources of an equivalent order of magnitude. To this end, debt renegotiations are carried out which impose draconian 'austerity' measures on these countries with seriously adverse implications for the lives of the common people, a fact illustrated by a host of cases, from Greece a few years ago to Sri Lanka and Pakistan today.

This approach however is both practically and ethically flawed. It is practically flawed because an economic collapse of several third world countries will simultaneously jeopardize the security and well-being of the advanced countries themselves; for a start, it will increase the scale of attempted immigration into the latter. It is also ethically flawed because while 'getting one's money back' may be the dominant consideration within the existing rules of the game, these rules themselves are weighed heavily against the people of the third world. For instance, the exchange rate depreciation brought about by the whims of a bunch of financial speculators who cause an outflow of finance has the effect of raising a country's debt-burden even in dollar terms, though it bears no responsibility for such a rise. There is little ethical justification for this.

India's Presidency of the G20 gives it a unique opportunity to intervene on behalf of the third world, to act as a tribune of the third world people, and break with the purely commercial approach of ensuring that the lenders get their money back, even if in the process, millions are pushed into destitution.

The G20 till now has been a club of the advanced capitalist countries, even though some third world countries have got admission to this club. This was evident in 2008, for example, when the then President of the U.N. General Assembly, Father Miguel d'Escoto Brockmann of Nicaragua, had wanted, in the wake of the financial crisis, an international conference, with the participation of all the member states of the United Nations, to discuss and establish a new world economic order. But a G20 meeting convened shortly after Brockmann had set up a Commission to make recommendations on what such an order should look like, and scuttled his attempt, though Brockmann had the support of most of the third world countries. India's Presidency of the G20 should be used to thwart advanced countries' attempts to ride roughshod over the third world peoples' interests.

The danger that currently threatens the people of the third world must be urgently assessed and steps taken to prevent it. To discuss what these steps should be, a Commission for discussing the problem of third world external debt and making recommendations on how to cope with it, must be set up forthwith. Such a Commission should not consist of the usual coterie of financiers, bureaucrats and Fund-Bank officials, but rather should have representation from eminent public intellectuals, including from the debtor countries themselves. India can use its Presidency of the G20 to move in this direction.

Prabhat Patnaik
New Delhi, 2023

Preface

The beginning of this book can be traced back to the G20 Research Fellowship launched by the Centre for Financial Accountability in 2021. For what was an early start to a critical examination of the G20 framework, and more specifically, India's Presidency of the G20, the compendium has come a long way. The aim of the fellowship was to bring together researchers representing different disciplines and methodological approaches. The final cohort came out to be a vibrant mix of voices including senior academics, trade unionists, activists, and young research scholars who try to look at India's G20 Presidency from a people's perspective. This book is a compilation of select manuscripts prepared during the term of the fellowship.

Policy choices made by governments and international institutions throughout the last few years have fallen woefully short of protecting people from the impact of multiple crises. Eruption of proxy wars, spiraling inflation, sky-rocketing energy bills and fuel prices, severity of sovereign debt, the struggle with actual resources, and the hoarding of critical technology while the viral pandemic was swallowing the world whole spelled disaster for so many across the world, and continues to do so even now. And especially as central banks tighten monetary policy, several of the climate-vulnerable, lower income countries are already facing a series of financial shocks and are on the edge of a financial abyss.

While the existing mess, semi-paralysis and inaction in the official G20 summits might hold the ground as the leaders show very little imagination and commitment, clearly, the idea would still be to put together broken pieces and further push timelines for action. This situation, however, is neither desirable nor sustainable for we are nearing a crisis of an unimaginable scale on multiple fronts. It goes without saying that India's G20 Presidency in 2023 is occurring at a crucial moment in the history of the world economy; it is important to ask as to what India's role would be sitting on this high table. More so is the need for research and advocacy that is not afraid of asking the difficult questions or presenting analysis that might not necessarily be comfortable to the mainstream narratives. All the papers in this book attempt to provide a much needed grounded analysis of the G20 framework by focusing on particular sectors and issues. Given the diversity of voices, some papers in this collection also provide valuable insights into why and how progressive and radical movements participate in a process that they do not recognize as legitimate in the first place.

Credits are due to all the authors, the illustrator and all the reviewers and experts for helping us bring out the book with so much grace. We hope that such a review of issues acts as a great reference material for students, academics, researchers and activists alike, in both India and abroad. And even when they do not agree with the views articulated in this collation, we hope that they would, nonetheless, find it useful for organizing their own thoughts.

This book is our sincere attempt to urge the international community to address the confluence of economic and environmental disasters ravaging the third world and rise up to the challenge of assessing and taking steps to prevent it.

Sonal Raghuvanshi
New Delhi, 2023

Digitization at the G20 and Beyond

Anushka M.

INTRODUCTION

This essay is an attempt to map and critique the governance and regulation of digital technologies by the G20. While the interest of the group has been marked across various communiques (Blueprint for Innovation and Growth, 2016; Communique 2016, 2017, 2021) and mapped out by researchers (Barnett, 2018; Kirton and Warren, 2018), the present focus takes a step towards analysis of this new domain of interest. It seeks to dig deeper into the reasons for the G20's interest in the digital economy, emboldened by the efforts of its sister institutions. Further, the essay focuses on what the impact of such discussions can be on domestic agendas and as global templates for other international organizations (IOs), along with a case study of digital financial inclusion as an area influenced by G20 precepts and powers. This area assumes greater significance for India as it assumes the G20 2023 presidency and continues to churn out new experiments and innovations, infusing the digital and daily lives of people as a matter of policy (for instance, E-RUPI, Digital India, etc.).

It is important to lay down the contours of technologies that would be covered by the research i.e., emerging technologies in the digital domain which are facilitated by the internet. The time span covered here derives from but excludes technologies such as telecommunications or the internet. The essay is structured to first enquire about the need to globally govern emerging technologies, followed by a mapping to show the solidification of a similar position across multiple global fora which may not be representative of interests of developing nations. The last section focuses on the case study of financial inclusion, as modified by fintech to serve as an example of what kind of future awaits. It concludes with a need for careful monitoring and engagement to develop and centre appropriate priorities of developing countries, which must be shaped at the local, regional and global level for any marked shift in the discourse.

IS TECHNOLOGY A GLOBAL PUBLIC GOOD?

The governance of the internet started with the establishment of the paradigm of the need not to govern or regulate it. Unlike most areas where global institutions have been created and the role of governments is predominant, 'the Internet is a field where the private sector and civil society each have a role as important—or sometimes more important— than governments' (Mathiason, 2009).

The history of internet regulation is a patchwork of global standard setting organizations (not represented by states but stakeholders), private corporations who find a seat in such organizations, and general international conventions that guide domestic policies in the domain of the internet. It is a battle for occupying the void and vacuum. If global governance is involved in the regulation of global public goods, the first step is to devolve the kind of goods that are being governed. This exercise of devolution can enable the choice of an appropriate governance mechanism. In the Information and Communication Technologies (ICT) domain, standards and security are known to be dealt with as global commons (Murphy, 2010). Increasingly, AI governance and data flows are also pitched as issues of emerging technologies which require action from the global community first (de Oliveira, Heseleva, and Ramos, 2020). However, what constitutes a global public good and how it should be distributed are deep and contentious questions (Bodansky, 2012).

Before one can embark on any discussion related to the global governance of digital technologies, generally, and in the realm of the G20 specifically, one must establish the need for such kind of governance. While there are increasing calls for technological global governance, that too, sooner than later (Fay, 2019), the first step is to discuss the reasons for the need for overarching action at the international level. The importance of technology is not a given.

It is increasingly recognized that the internet impacts our social, political and economic lives and rightly so. Any naysayers have been compelled to take notice, especially with the global inflexion point in the form of the COVID pandemic. There is a vast body of research which establishes and recognizes a link between technologies and economic growth and livelihood (OECD, 2017; Hernandez et al., 2016). At the same time, it is also noted that the positive and negative effects do not impact the various regions of the world equally or similarly (Maiti et al., 2020). Against this background, what criterion determines the kind of regulation (i.e. global governance) which should apply to technologies?

This question assumes importance because global governance (through the G20 or the other major representative IOs) would establish common principles and norms that would dictate the actions by states, domestically and internationally (Hughes and Wilkinson, 2003). The state actors differ muidely, across the social, economic, political, cultural and any other dimension that can be thought of. If the benefits of technology are not equally distributed and global governance is thought of as the means to secure a prosperous future for all, surely the structural mechanisms should be such which can ensure this form of equity (United Nations, Global Governance and Global Rules for Development, 2014). The global call for regulation is marked by a disdain for national regulation, which characterizes the latter as a form of nationalism that will fragment globalizing attempts. It supposes that 'the demand for digital sovereignty, which seeks a balance between protection and collaboration, risks both undermining multilateralism and leading to "digital nationalism"' (Jessop 2011; Morse and Keohane 2014; Jelinek, Kerimi and Wallach, 2020).

Global governance is a complex system understood in many ways, through a focus on multiple attributes. A few comprehensive understandings are provided here as it is one of many sites, in which struggles over wealth, power, and knowledge are taking place (Murphy, 2000). James N. Rosenau emphasizes the role of private transnational associations, linking the strong evidence of the growing empowerment of such groups to the material attributes of contemporary globalization.

A summary of these two characterizations is provided in TWAIL scholarship, which suggests that

> In principle, intergovernmental organizations offer a site for deliberative equality as national delegations engage in lawmaking with equal formal power. In practice, that equality in deliberation is not achieved, which creates challenges for invention of innovative practices to ensure the participation, influence and pragmatic local knowledge from states in the Global South. Global regulation of the financial sector, for example through the Financial Stability Board or G-20, similarly suffers from asymmetries of input and power in both global rule-making and international surveillance of national economies and transnational flows of capital. The global governance system is more than the sum of the institutions that produce regulations; it is about the interplay and the relationship between these institutions, and their embedding in a normative order. It selects inputs from actors inside and outside of the system and allocates responsibility to institutions on different political levels. (Benson and Zürn, 2019)

Individualized technology in the form of personalized infrastructures might as well be private goods, but the underpinning infrastructure such as connectivity, networks (for e-commerce, social media) are best provided as public goods to unleash their full force. In the domain of ICTs, it is necessary for all global governance institutions to first identify the global public goods as well as the nature of publicness which requires such all-encompassing solutions before they can be deliberated upon.

G20'S FOCUS ON TECHNOLOGY: A SITE FOR CROSS POLLINATION

There are several powerful IOs and multilateral fora where technological governance is being discussed and helmed. These are the Organisation for Economic Cooperation and Development (OECD), the World Trade Organization (WTO) and multiple United Nations (UN) agencies. G20 as an informal governance mechanism is not the first or only one of them. This part of the essay explores the choice of G20 as the appropriate forum to govern technology, along with its potential to determine the agenda in a particular direction.

An Overview of an Imbalanced Structural Setup

Officially, the mandate of the G20 can be said to be designed with a focus on economic growth and financial stability, to be an institution for global financial governance (Kirton, 2020). With these objectives in mind, what is it that permits the G20 to permeate its operation to that of technology?

While the G20/T20 (Group of 20/Think20) research understands it as an 'informal and crisis response-driven institution', it nevertheless advises it to step up to assume a larger role for regulation of emerging technologies such as AI and Big Data (Jelinek, Kerimi and Wallach, 2020). Some point to its compliance track record and annual summits which are more than what can be said for any other international or multilateral institution (Kirton, 2020). While its representativeness is lauded, the vast majority of developing countries are excluded. The G20 represents a continuation of a pattern that could be called 'elite multilateralism', a framework that raises serious concerns about representativeness, inclusiveness and accountability (United Nations, 2014). It is a mix of multistakeholderism and multilateralism. There is significant consternation with respect to the lack of representativeness of the G20, not only in terms of the members involved (or not involved) but the process which allows certain interests to be represented over others. It is known to be an elite club, with a disproportionate representation by private business interests and powerful lopsided IOs. Thus, any framework for technology must be sufficiently thought through and analyzed with the necessary criticality of the background against which it is embedded.

The G20 has started to focus on the topic of the digital economy. While all social or political aspects are linked, to each other and to the economy and vice versa, these links provide an entry point for the exercise of jurisdiction by the G20. For a type of institution that suffers from a legitimacy crisis of sorts (Slaughter, 2019), this devolution exercise is imperative.

The legitimacy crisis arises, also in part, due to its composition beyond nation states. The non-state composition of the G20 includes representatives from the IMF and World Bank (Kirton, 1999), Financial Stability Board (FSB) (as established by the G20), ILO, OECD, UN and the WTO (International Organisations, n.d.). Further, the Inter-Agency Group on Economic and Financial Statistics (IAG) dealing with the Data Gaps Initiative comprises of: Bank for International Settlements (BIS), European Central Bank (ECB), Eurostat International Monetary Fund (IMF, Chair), Organisation for Economic Co-operation and Development (OECD), and the World Bank. The FSB Secretariat participates in the IAG meetings.

With such a composition and reach, the cross pollination of thought processes, narratives and agendas become important to note for consistency across the positions of a state and the challenge that lies ahead to carry out any change in policy positions. The invitation and inclusion of more powerful and imbalanced IOs to assimilate and influence policy positions has entailed into a 'network relation-

ship' between the G20 and other IOs, the original sites of global governance (Slaughter, 2019); (Kelly and Cho, 2012). This is not to say that the agenda is sourced from one place alone. Instead, it is the constant interaction with multiple fora with the same line of ideas (not the same idea), thought processes and policy priorities which provide the template for future interactions. This interaction can be understood as an ostensible effort to democratize policy making. It shapes a narrative which is constantly reinforced by equally or more influential global IOs and vice versa. These IOs and the participants in the network assume different roles which complement each other, ranging from broad principles or guidelines to treaties which eventually shape domestic governance. This 'network coordination' uses 'frameworks or blueprints' that take advantage of pre-existing network dynamics resulting in specific 'end products or regulatory prototypes' (Kelly and Cho, 2012). Similarly, the impact of working groups, various tracks and other events is also circumspect. An example of a structural overlap of this setup is the Trade and Investment Working Group (TIWG). It allows G20 officials to draw on key international organizations to prepare the ground for discussions and decision-making by leaders on trade matters, including defining a work programme and/or action plan and creating mechanisms to hold each other accountable for progress in implementing what is agreed. The TIWG includes representatives of the OECD, UNCTAD, the World Bank as well as the WTO. It was the TIWG's deliberations that helped prepare the ground for the launch of plurilateral discussions on e-commerce, investment facilitation and other policy dimensions of digital trade in the WTO, illustrating that the G20 has been able to influence the launch of initiatives on subjects that could not be addressed on a multilateral basis in the WTO (Hoekman and Wilkinson, 2021).

Impact of the Structural Setup

While the structure blurs the boundaries between the formal and informal mechanisms for final decision making, the following part provides a broad overview of the way the discussion around digitalization and emerging technologies has shaped across the IOs enumerated above and the G20. The aim is to point to necessary overlaps which gives a strong indication of the narrow policy space available for all member countries across the field of international policy making.

A shopping list of topics have been discussed under the umbrella of digitalization at the G20. Its policy mandate covers the use of data in policy making (Blueprint for Innovation and Growth, 2016; Communique, 2016, 2017, 2021). Substantively, it wants to devote greater financial resources to digital infrastructure like broadband connectivity as part of investment in infrastructure (Blueprint for Innovation and Growth, Communique, 2016), promote wider use of cross border digital currencies and encourage fintech growth through financial inclusion (Communique, 2021). The 2021 Declaration has announced the creation of a Digital Economy Working Group, subsuming the Digital Economy Task Force (DETF). A broad-based group with multi stakeholder representations, it calls for specific engagement with representatives from G20 engagement groups, notably the B20 task force on digitalization, to express their views.

The myriad cross-referencing of approaches and recommendations serves to strengthen the position developed in an alternative forum which is not representative of G20 members but still must be accepted and negotiated upon by all of them. For instance, the G20 has taken a visible lead in financial inclusion through its endorsement of Principles for Innovative Financial Inclusion in 2010. The World Bank has built upon these principles to guide the digitization process of financial inclusion. It recognizes regulatory primacy 'but in partnership with the private sector' (World Bank, Bill and Melinda Gates Foundation and Better Than Cash Alliance, 2014).

The OECD Going Digital Project also covers a multitude of topics such as Artificial Intelligence, Digital Consumers, Labour Markets etc. The recommendations and research under each head has not been equally influential but many strands of work have been noted and endorsed for and by the entirety of the G20. The 2021 Declaration commits 'to implement trustworthy Artificial Intelligence (AI) and to commit to a human- centred approach, as decided in 2019 under the Japanese G20 Presidency, guided by the G20 AI Principles, drawn from the OECD Recommendations on AI.' Similarly, it seeks to source policy guidance from the OECD on consumer protection through the 'OECD's Global Recalls portal and other existing tools and guidelines to protect consumers.' It also depends on the 'OECD's AI Policy Observatory to improve evidence for MSME policies related to AI and nurture the understanding of the role played by different actors, including large firms, business associations, academia, national and local governments as well as international organisations.'

In the domain of digital identity, the World Bank and the OECD have shaped the narrative which is boosted by the involvement of the G20, as the G20 Collection of Digital Identity practice, has been developed in collaboration with the OECD

(Declaration of G20 Digital Ministers, 2021). Most international organizations dealing with trade, commerce and its policy have taken cognizance of e-commerce in one form or the other (such as UNCITRAL Model Law on Electronic Commerce, WTO Work Programme on Electronic Commerce established at the Second Ministerial Conference, 1998 and OECD Action Plan for Electronic Commerce). The Second Ministerial Conference of the WTO in 1998 adopted the Declaration on Global Electronic Commerce. It led to the establishment of a Work Programme on E-Commerce. The Work Programme required the General Council, the Council for Trade in Services, the Council for Trade in Goods, the Council for TRIPS, and the Committee on Trade and Development, to review, examine and understand the implications of e-commerce in the domain of the WTO. The Work Programme provides a useful starting point to understand the contours and types of services in the context of e-commerce. These are:

a. the provision of Internet access services themselves, meaning the provision of access to the net for businesses and consumers;
b. the electronic delivery of services, meaning transactions in which services and products are delivered to the customer in the form of digitized information flows;
c. the use of the Internet as a channel for distribution of services, by which goods and services are purchased over the net but delivered to the consumer subsequently in non-electronic form.

According to the Council on Trade in Goods, goods traded online are still covered under GATT disciplines such as the Agreement on Implementation of Article VI, GATT, 1947, (Anti-Dumping Agreement), Agreement on Subsidies and Countervailing Measures etc. In the context of e-commerce, the members of the WTO (1999) have agreed that further clarification and discussion on the definition of services is required. It has categorized e-commerce as follows:

i. electronically conducted transactions combined with physical delivery of goods; in this case the traditional GATT commitments would apply;
ii. trade in goods related to electronic commerce (e.g. computers); also in this case, the traditional GATT commitments would apply;
iii. sale of carrier media such as CD's or tapes, which contain digitalized information (e.g., software or music); the question of content of the carrier media would relate to customs valuation questions;
iv. digitalized information transmitted by electronic means, i.e. electronic transmissions.

The Council for Trade in Services has also highlighted that the commitments on distribution services under the GATS include electronic distribution, meaning the right to offer and sell goods on the Internet. If the goods ordered have to be imported, the importation will be subject to whatever tariff bindings and other GATT obligations are applicable.

At the WTO now, the research and regulatory work has moved beyond e-commerce to include emerging technologies such as AI, IoT, Big Data analytics, Blockchain etc. which impact cross-border trade and digital trade. Launched in 2019, the Joint Statement Initiative on E-commerce (JSI) lauded the G20 summit in Japan for the boost to the work being done at the WTO. Even within this initiative, the list of covered areas under discussion is broad and includes spam, source code, open government data, trade facilitation in goods, services market access, electronic signatures and authentication, and online consumer protection (World Trade Organization, 2020). The JSI was designed to be a plurilateral agreement at the time, with limited participation by developing countries. It is feared that it will circumvent the promise of multilateralism even in a global forum like the WTO, with detrimental effects for developing countries which will be in the position of acceptors (United Nations Conference on Trade and Development, 2021). The final text of the JSI is not out in the public domain yet and its consistency or similarity of positions with the G20 programmes remains to be seen. However, there are many Free Trade agreements, being negotiated by the US and EU (to some extent) which clarify the preference for unrestricted cross-border data flows (Gao, 2021). This preemptive and costly action by powerful Global North states/regions is seen as an attempt to thwart commercial competition with other powerful states as well as a way to establish common positions across regional setups (Meissner, 2019). The express overlap of G20 policy positions and directions with research output and recommendations of the OECD hits hard at the notion of representativeness of the G20 because all developing country members of the G20 are not OECD members and are not even externally consulted to result in such recommendations. The OECD is notoriously understood as a rich man's club from the perspective of developing countries and many nations of the Global South. Thus, this convergence across a futuristic area has the potential to lead to a very entrenched position that can be hard to shake off unless the developing members form broad based coalitions.

Potential for Contested Multilateralism to Break the Bind

The notion of contested multilateralism is increasingly absent from the international regime complex of the Bretton Woods system that includes the G20 and governs technology (Morse and Keohane, 2014). Even within the G20, the developing nations have sufficiently diverse positions which do not lead to an effective change of agenda (Gnath and Schmucker, 2012). However, the BRICS as one forum where India is also a member can be a useful comparator, especially to develop its strategy for the upcoming presidency. The BRICS nations are a part of the G20, although they were invited to create a hub structure of all members (Cooper and Stolte, 2020). With a solid yet distinct institutionalization of the voices of developing countries, it is useful to map any directions of contested multilateralism, if any, in the G20 for the digital agenda.

At the G20 Summit in Osaka, the BRICS group (Brazil, Russia, India, China and South Africa) stressed the role that data play in economic development for emerging economies and re-emphasized the need for data sovereignty. India did not sign the Osaka Declaration on the Digital Economy that kickstarted the 'Osaka Track'—a process whereby the 78 signatories agreed to participate in global policy discussions on international rule-making for e-commerce at the World Trade Organization (WTO). This was a continuation of India's sustained efforts opposing the e-commerce moratorium at the WTO. The importance of cross-border data flows in spurring the global economy found its way into the Final G20 Leaders Declaration which India signed (Basu, 2019).

At the same time, the BRICS summit has not released a common position on digitalization beyond digital health in view of the pandemic and the need to foster digital tools as equitable public goods (BRICS Joint Statement on Strengthening and Reforming the Multilateral System, 2021). With its express focus as the voice of the *'Rest'* (Cooper and Stolte, 2020), it expresses its belief in the multilateral system but with the need for greater representation and equity (BRICS Joint Statement on Strengthening and Reforming the Multilateral System, 2021). It is hoped that these principles can translate into cogent positions which can be negotiated and agreed upon at the larger G20 forum as it represents the greater globalized world in which the developing world finds itself, especially in the domain of technology.

A Possible Future Trajectory

The possibility of entrenched positions take a tangible shape when they influence the investment decisions and developmental strategies of MDBs (Soederberg, 2013). Soederberg has traced the financial instrument of securitization that was created as financial inclusion strategies were adopted by states of the Global

South. In the same vein, this section identifies the elements which could make for instruments in the future, given the unstoppable pace of finance and technology.

The World Bank highlights the role of MDBs to partner with the governments, the private sector, and development partners in the direction of digitizing payments, a requirement which should become more prominent in the agenda of governments (Klapper and Dorothe, 2017). The 2021 Summit of the G20 further recognized that 'there is a need to stimulate financing and optimize the domestic environment to attract investments in digital infrastructure', an issue which is focussed upon in the work of the G20 Infrastructure Working Group (Casalini, Taku and Lopez-Gonzalez, 2021). Similar is the focus of the World Bank to provide financing which can help close the digital divide to fully benefit from the Digital Development revolution (Digital Development, n.d.). The 2021 DETF has suggested a linkage of financing for MSMEs with an AI component, diverting the financial distribution to enhance digitalization. It provides the options and intentions as highlighted below:

- Improving MSMEs' financing for AI-related intangible assets (skills, data, software, process innovation, organizational changes), e.g. through sharing evidence on the cost-benefits of AI for different types of MSMEs, better collateralizing of intangible assets, and supporting access to alternative sources of finance, such as angel investors, venture capital, equity crowdfunding and private equity.
- Providing public schemes to encourage the participation of private investors in financing AI investments in MSMEs through public kick-start programmes and risk-sharing and mitigating mechanisms with private partners.
- Strengthening public-private support for early stage and venture capital, and facilitating the use of intellectual property by start-ups, spin-offs and MSMEs as collateral. Equity investments in start-ups could be combined with R&D support schemes (e.g., grants, tax credits) within broader innovative acceleration schemes that strengthen the link between research and industry and encourage joint technology development between academia, industry and government

The WTO 2021 Report also focuses on financing for digital MSMEs to boost trade and include MSMEs in the digital economy. This is largely premised on bridging the information asymmetry between the funders and the seekers using digital tools. It unravels the potential of the digital footprint of MSMEs which can be or should be easily gauged in this era to identify good risk for financial needs (Patel and Ganne, 2020). This leads to the observation that the financial logic when applied to digitalization can treat this new force much the same way. The financing priorities and development agendas indicate a need for rapid industrialization to digitize as many domains as possible. For developing countries, with huge developmental needs and populations, the direction that financing can take needs to be predetermined before it can be usefully taken up.

THE APPARATUS FOR FINANCIAL INCLUSION: A CASE STUDY

> *For advocates, financial inclusion is a means through which to access 'modern' eco-nomic citizenship by smoothing consumption cycles. For critics, it is better under-stood as a set of practices that create hierarchical relations based on debt, justified through the supposed need to expand marketization and individualism. (Clarke, 2019)*

The focus areas identified above and the questions answered become a vital input to contextualize the precepts which underlie domestic policies and laws. As digitalization increases, the specific contributions of G20 global summit governance to the domestic regulatory space becomes interesting to note. The topic of 'financial inclusion' (FI) is chosen as a case study here because the G20 endorsed the G20 Principles for Innovative Financial Inclusion (GPFI) in 2010. Further, FI is perceived as an important developmental requirement and there is now a recognition to enhance financial inclusion by digitalization (Clarke, 2019). The GPFI were drafted by the Access through Innovation Sub-Group of the G20 Financial Inclusion Expert Group, which involved three key implementing partners—the Alliance for Financial Inclusion (funded by the Bill and Melinda Gates Foundation), the Consultative Group to Assist the Poor (CGAP), and the World Bank Group's private financing arm, the International Finance Corporation (IFC) (Soederberg, 2013).

The discourse around financial inclusion is dominated by lending and credit provision which has the potential to fuel instability and debt traps for people (Clarke, 2019). FI is also integral to the process of financialization. Digital FI, on the other hand, is usually 'the process that starts with populations which are neither part of the digital realm nor the financial realm.' (Jain and Gabor, 2020). Working towards it, the complementary institutions of the G20 have been busy for quite a while. For example, the World Bank laid out a blueprint in 2014 to be taken up in future G20 summits, to leverage the digital potential for financial inclusion through innovations in payments and remittances, built upon biometric systems and data histories. Similarly, in 2016 it suggested that digital credit and lending, largely for small individual loans, furthers financial inclusion (Hwang and Tellez Merchan, 2016). This assertion read against the experience of countries like India would present a macabre contrast, to say the least. It is a form of lightly regulated digital lending which has led to a spate of suicides in India, especially during the pandemic. This is more so because domestic civil society groups have unveiled a sinister chain of events as means to implement the global policy frameworks, starting from demonetization to state-led development of fintech to provide financial services to the unbanked (Singh, 2019; Jain and Gabor, 2020). It has rendered a situation where these policy steps are considered so uninspired by reality that they are assessed more as ends than means to resolve a specific issue. There is also academic recognition of the idea that digitalization is a way to direct information flows and these flows as constructed can lead to greater risk and volatility. Any regulatory measures to then take care of these gaps also end up producing different kinds of risk (Campbell-Verduyn et al., 2019).

The Impact of these Services Through 'Innovation'

The digital divide in India is such that more than 400 million people have no access to the internet, with a high representation of women and rural communities (2020). On the other hand, approximately 190 million people in India are estimated to be 'unbanked', a massive 11 per cent of the world's unbanked population (World Bank, 2021). Financial inclusion of underbanked people and MSMEs, as part of the development agenda, is ostensibly a victory gained by the addition of developing countries to the G20. However, the unconnected and unbanked are service and policy takers. Global tech firms use financial inclusion as an entry-point in finance, leveraging Global South concerns with the 'unbanked' dating back to the promotion of, and hype around, microcredit initiatives (Jain and Gabor, 2020).

Driven by increased internet access and demand for retail loans, it is projected that the business value of digital lending in India will exceed USD 1 Trillion by 2023 (Shah, Roongta and Avadhani, 2018). Since a large proportion of Indian citizens did not previously have access to formal credit, new business models are emerging that are increasingly dependent on 'digital exhaust' to inform lending decisions. In other words, businesses are looking to analyse data, both held by the banks of potential borrowers, and generated as a by-product of a borrower's digital transactions to predict repayment behaviour. This model is not new. Kenya's M-Shwari has used 'alternate data sources' such as mobile phone recharge transactions to serve as the basis for loans since 2012 (Cook and McKay, n.d.). Lenders have traditionally scrutinized the financial history of prospective borrowers, but often through ad hoc arrangements involving sharing of login information and 'screen scraping' practices. The 'Open Banking' movement aims to streamline this process, by enabling 'enhanced market capabilities' through 'collaborative banking models which share consumer data through APIs' (Oakes and Brodsky, 2017). By creating standards for sharing of information such as the 'Payments Service Directives' (PSD2) in the EU and 'Open Banking Standard' in the UK, it intends to facilitate sharing of information between financial institutions with the consent of the citizens involved. With citizen consent, the envisioned ideal is that these standards will

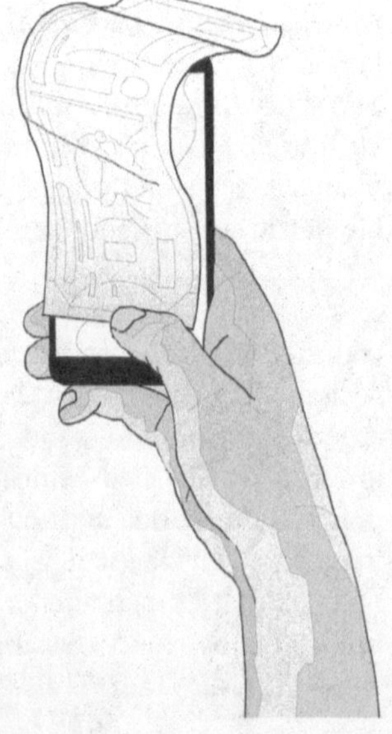

lead to more secure forms of sharing data that enable greater access to a range of financial services. These services would include money management, insurance or lending to be delivered through 'innovative' startup driven applications in the fintech ecosystem.

Recently, India has proposed to implement a similar model to facilitate increased, consent-centric data sharing across sectors such as health, telecommunications, and finance, through the Data Empowerment and Protection Architecture (DEPA) (IndiaStack, n.d.). In the finance sector, DEPA has been implemented through the Account Aggregator (AA) framework to enhance financial inclusion through credit access (Reserve Bank of India - Notifications, n.d.). In a manner similar to the Open Banking framework, DEPA envisions API standards to be made available as public digital infrastructure to facilitate the sharing of transactional information to enable services such as access to credit on the basis of transactional information instead of traditional collateral (which has sometimes been referred to as 'flow based credit'). Citizens are required to consent to this sharing of information. The consent is framed in a manner that is 'granular, revocable, auditable, and secure'. Non-banking Finance Companies (NBFCs) can use these APIs to deliver new, more customized lending products to citizens. DEPA proposes the creation of a new business entity called 'Consent Managers' to help manage user consent and facilitate data sharing. These entities are responsible for ensuring that user consent is gathered as per the established principles, and to 'empower' and 'protect' citizens while they share their information to access services. It proposes the regulation of Consent Managers through Self-Regulatory Organizations (SROs), with an explicit role imagined for 'Sahamati', a collective of AAs in the finance sector that will 'provide procedural and best practice guidelines for all participating institutions, support organisations to adopt and go live, and continue to foster innovation in protecting data rights' (Sahamati, n.d.). The relevant data from telecom, education, or jobs will also be routed through Consent Managers in the future, forming 'alternate data sources' to inform financial decisions.

These innovations, interesting and positively impactful for some segments of society, are still centred around the capitalist logic and understanding of finance. This underpinning is sought to be further entrenched, using the means of digitization. It is facilitated by the equally sticky nature and speed of technologies. The solutions are complex to design and to use. For a country with a very distinct usage of the internet (through shared mobile phones) and a populace burdened with digital illiteracy, the success of these solutions is yet to be proven. Additionally, the amalgam of powerful international bodies with lopsided representations, domestic power holders which replicate power dynamics internally and technology and capital providers, uses sufficient resources to legitimize the use of such technologies. However, the direct communicative connections are seemingly hard to establish between these three elements which could shape domestic discourse and greater clarity for people to truly choose to partake in the promises of the new dawn of technology. Further, using the essential and palatable goal of financial inclusion, a layered and nuanced discussion takes a backseat due to the dire need and urgency to resolve such problems for the vulnerable populations of developing nations.

CONCLUSION

This research employs a broad brush stroke to paint a picture of continuity in digital development at the global level, rife with all the latent and patent inequities of such a regime. Because technological development has not been uniform for all G20 members, the interests and priorities are naturally distinct. However, these dissimilar priorities do not surface in the final declarations as more than asides and exceptional references. This status quo is bolstered by the lack of a bloc level position on the digital economy by developing nations as the domestic trajectories are very different. Technological development is a rapidly evolving and a dynamic space which must be carefully understood and engaged with by all parties. The most curious space to watch out for is the change in decision making for investment, aid and support priorities by multilateral development banks which has been touched upon here. As India assumes the presidency for 2023, and its digital economy being of interest to all powerful players, domestic and global, it is a highly opportune time for many changes of interest.

REFERENCES

Barnett, Sophie. 2018. "G20 Governance of Digitization, 1999-2017." POL495 Independent Study. University of Toronto.

Basu, Arindrajit. 2019. "India's Role in Global Cyber Policy Formulation." *The Centre for Internet and Society*. November 13. Accessed August 20, 2021. https://cis-india.org/internet-governance/blog/lawfare-arindrajit-basu-november-7-2019-indias-role-in-global-cyber-policy-formulation.

Benson, R., and Zürn, M. 2019. "Untapped potential: How the G20 can strengthen global governance." *South African Journal of International Affairs*, pp. 549–562. doi:https://doi.org/10.1080/10220461.2019.1694576.

Bodansky, D. 2012. "What's in a Concept? Global Public Goods, International Law, and Legitimacy." *European Journal of International Law*, pp. 651–668. doi:https://doi.org/10.1093/ejil/chs035.

BRICS. 2021. "BRICS Joint Statement on Strengthening and Reforming the Multilateral System." Accessed August 20, 2021. https://brics2021.gov.in/brics/public/uploads/docpdf/getdocu-22.pdf.

Campbell-Verduyn, M., Goguen, M., and Porter, T. 2019. "Finding fault lines in long chains of financial information." *Review of International Political Economy,* pp. 911-937. doi:https://doi.org/10.1080/09692290.2019.1616595.

Casalini, Francesca, Taku Nemoto, and Javier Lopez-Gonzalez. 2021. "Mapping Commonalities in Regulatory Approaches To Cross-Border Data Transfers." *OECD Trade Policy Papers,* p. 248. doi:https://doi.org/10.1787/ca9f974e-en.

Clarke, C. 2019. "Platform lending and the politics of financial infrastructures." *Review of International Political Economy,* pp. 863–885. doi:https://doi.org/10.1080/09692290.2019.1616598.

Cook, T., and McKay, C. 2015. "How M-Shwari Works: The Story So Far." *Access to Finance Forum: Reports by CGAP and Its Partners.*

Cooper, A. F., and Stolte, C. 2020. "Insider and Outsider Strategies of Influence: The BRICS' Dualistic Approach Towards Informal Institutions." *New Political Economy* 25 (5): 703–714. doi:https://doi.org/10.1080/13563467.2019.1584167.

Declaration of G20 Digital Ministers. 2021.

Digital Development. n.d. Accessed August 20, 2021. https://www.worldbank.org/en/topic/digitaldevelopment.

Fay, B. n.d. "Global regulatory collaboration is essential in the digital era." *ORF.* Accessed August 2, 2021. https://www.orfonline.org/expert-speak/global-regulatory-collaboration-essential-digital-era/.

Fay, Robert. 2019. "Digital Platforms Require a Global Governance Framework." *Centre for International Governance Innovation.* October 28. https://www.cigionline.org/articles/digital-platforms-require-global-governance-framework/.

G20. 2016. 2016 Hangzhou Summit. *G20 Blueprint on Innovative Growth.* G20 Information Centre. September 5. Accessed at http://www.g20.utoronto.ca/2016/160905-blueprint.html

G20. 2016. "2016 Hangzhou Summit Communique".

G20. 2017. "Hamburg G20 Leaders' Declaration".

G20. 2021. "G20 Rome Leaders' Declaration".

G20 Information Centre. 1999. *What is the G20?* Accessed August 19, 2021. http://www.g20.utoronto.ca/g20whatisit.html.

Gao, H. 2021. "Data regulation in trade agreements: Different models and options ahead." In Smeets, M. (Ed.) *Adapting to the digital trade era: Chal-*

lenges and opportunities. p.322–335. https://ink.library.smu.edu.sg/sol_research/3351/

Gnath, K., and Schmucker, C. 2012. "The Role of the Emerging Countries in the G20: Agenda-Setter, Veto Player or Spectator?" Edited by C. Herrmann & J. P. Terhechte. *European Yearbook of International Economic Law (EYIEL)* (Springer Berlin Heidelberg) 3: 667-681. doi:https://doi.org/10.1007/978-3-642-23309-8_21.

Hernandez, K., Faith, B., Prieto Martín, P., and Ramalingam, B. 2016. "The Impact of Digital Technology on Economic Growth and Productivity, and its Implications for Employment and Equality: An Evidence Review." IDS Evidence Report IDS Evidence Report;207, IDS. https://opendocs.ids.ac.uk/opendocs/handle/20.500.12413/12659.

Hoekman, B., and R. Wilkinson. 2021. "Trade, the G20 and the EU: Soft Power for Greater Policy Coherence?" January. https://respect.eui.eu/wp-content/uploads/sites/6/2021/04/Hoekman_Wilkinson_EU_G20_policy_coherence_Respect.pdf

Hughes, S., and Wilkinson, R. 2003. *Global Governance: Critical Perspectives.* Routledge.

Hwang, Byoung Hwa, Tellez Merchan, and Camilo Andres. *The proliferation of digital credit deployments (English).* CGAP brief Washington, D.C.: World Bank Group. http://documents.worldbank.org/curated/en/830661467994632311/The-proliferation-of-digital-credit-deployments

IndiaStack. n.d. *About Data Empowerment and Protection Architecture (DEPA).* Retrieved August 20, 2021.

International Organisations. n.d. *G20.org.* Accessed August 19, 2021. http://g20.org.tr/about-g20/g20-members/international-organisations/.

Jain, S., and Gabor, D. 2020. "The Rise of Digital Financialisation: The Case of India." *New Political Economy* 25 (5): 813–828. doi:https://doi.org/10.1080/13563467.2019.1708879.

Jelinek, Thorsten, Kerimi, Danil and Wendell Wallach. 2020. "Coordinating committee for the governance of artificial intelligence." *G20 Insights.* Accessed August 19, 2021. https://www.g20-insights.org/policy_briefs/coordinating-committee-for-the-governance-of-artificial-intelligence-2/.

Jessop, Bob. 2011. *The SAGE Handbook of Governance.* London: SAGE Publications Ltd. https://doi.org/10.4135/9781446200964.

Kelly, C., and Cho, S. 2012. "Promises and Perils of New Global Governance: A Case of the G20." *SSRN Electronic Journal.* doi:https://doi.org/10.2139/ssrn.1907845.

Khasru, S. M., Mahmud, K. M., and Nahreen, A. 2017. The G20 Countries Should Assume Leadership of the Forced Migration Crisis and Mitigate the Deficiencies of the Existing Governance System. Accessed October 17, 2022. https://www.g20-insights.org/wp-content/uploads/2017/03/The-G20-Countries-Should-Assume-Leadership-of-the-Forced-Migration-Crisis-and-Mitigate-the-Deficiencies-of-the-Existing-Governance-System.pdf

Kirton, John. 2020. *The G20's Global Governance Centrality.* November 18. Accessed August 19, 2021. http://www.g20.utoronto.ca/analysis/201118-kirton-odi.html.

Kirton, John, and Warren, Brittaney. 2018. "G20 Governance of Digitalization." *International Organisations Research Journal.* 13. 16-41. 10.17323/1996-7845-2018-02-02.

Klapper, Leora and Dorothe Singer. 2017. "The Opportunities and Challenges of Digitizing Government-to-Person Payments." *The World Bank Research Observer* 32 (2): 211–226.

Maiti, D., Castellacci, F., and Melchior, A. 2020. "Digitalisation and Development: Issues for India and Beyond." In *Digitalisation and Development: Issues for India and Beyond,* edited by F. Castellacci, and A. Melchior D. Maiti, 3-29. Springer. doi:https://doi.org/10.1007/978-981-13-9996-1_1.

Mathiason, John. 2009. *Internet Governance : The New Frontier of Global Institutions.* Routledge Global Institutions. London; New York: Routledge.

Meissner, K. L. 2019. "Cherry picking in the design of trade policy: Why regional organizations shift between inter-regional and bilateral negotiations." *Review of International Political Economy.* . https://www.tandfonline.com/doi/abs/10.1080/09692290.2019.1625421.

Mishra, Saurabh, and Ejaz Ghani. 2020. "Closing the digital divide." *The Financial Express.* https://www.financialexpress.com/opinion/closing-the-digital-divide/2126724/.

Morse, J. C., and Keohane, R. O. 2014. "Contested multilateralism." *The Review of International Organizations* 9 (4): 385–412. https://doi.org/10.1007/s11558-014-9188-2.

Murphy, C. N. 2000. "Global governance: Poorly done and poorly understood." *International Affairs (Royal Institute of International Affairs 1944-)* 76 (4): 789–803. doi:10.1111/1468-2346.00165.

Murphy, Tara. 2010. "Security Challenges in the 21st Century Global Commons." *Yale Journal of International Affairs* 5 (2). Accessed August 20, 2021. https://www.yalejournal.org/publications/security-challenges-in-the-21st-century-global-commons.

Nations Unies. 2014. *Global governance and global rules for development in the post-2015 era: Policy note*. United Nations. Accessed August 19, 2021. https://www.un.org/en/development/desa/policy/cdp/cdp_publications/2014cdppolicynote.pdf.

Oakes, Liz, and Laura Brodsky. 2017. "Capitalizing on the potential benefits of open banking." McKinsey. September 5. Accessed August 20, 2021. Capitalizing on the potential benefits of open banking | McKinse. https://www.mckinsey.com/industries/financial-services/our-insights/data-sharing-and-open-banking.

OECD. 2017. "Key Issues For Digital Transformation In The G20." OECD, Berlin. Accessed August 2, 2021. https://www.oecd.org/g20/key-issues-for-digital-transformation-in-the-g20.pdf.

Patel, Deepesh, and Emmanuelle Ganne. 2020. Blockchain & DLT in Trade: Where Do We Stand?. Trade Finance Global and World Trade Organization. November.

Ramos, Vincent Jerald, Kateryna Heseleva, and Alan Ichilevici de Oliveira. 2020. "Towards a Multilateral Consensus on Data Governance." *G20 Insights*. Accessed 19 August, 2021. https://www.g20-insights.org/policy_briefs/towards-a-multilateral-consensus-on-data-governance/.

Reserve Bank of India—Notifications. n.d. Accessed August 20, 2021. https://www.rbi.org.in/Scripts/NotificationUser.aspx?Id=10598&Mode=0.

Sahamati. n.d. *Sahamati—Collective of the Account Aggregator Ecosystem*. Accessed August 20, 2021. https://sahamati.org.in/.

Shah, Alpesh, Roongta, Prateek, and Shashank Avadhani. 2018. *Digital Lending A $1 Trillion Opportunity Over The Next 5 Years*. Mumbai: The Boston Consulting Group. Accessed 19 *Digitization*. https://image-src.bcg.com/Images/BCG-Digital-Lending-Report_tcm9-197622.pdf.

Singh, J. P. 2019. "Development finance 2.0: Do participation and information technologies matter?" *Review of International Political Economy* 26 (5): 886–910. doi:10.1080/09692290.2019.1616600.

Slaughter, S. 2019. *The Power of the G20: The Politics of Legitimacy in Global Governance*. Routledge.

Soederberg, S. 2013. "Universalising Financial Inclusion and the Securitisation of Development." *Third World Quarterly* 34 (4): 593–612. doi:10.1080/01436597.2013.786285.

United Nations Conference on Trade and Development. 2021. *What is at Stake for Developing Countries in Trade Negotiations on E-commerce?: The Case of the Joint Statement Initiative*. United Nations. doi:10.18356/9789210056366.

World Bank, Bill and Melinda Gates Foundation and Better Than Cash Alliance. 2014. *The Opportunities of Digitizing Payments.* Washington, DC: World Bank. Accessed August 10, 2021. https://documents1.worldbank.org/curated/en/188451468336589650/pdf/903050WP0REPLACEMENT0Box38 5358B00PUBLIC0.pdf.

World Trade Organization. 1999. *Work Programme on Electronic Commerce.* Council for Trade in Goods.

World Trade Organization. 2020. *Negotiations on e-commerce continue, eyeing a consolidated text by the end of the year.* Accessed August 12, 2021. https:// www.wto.org/english/news_e/news20_e/ecom_26oct20_e.htm.

BANK
BANK

Platform-mediated Finance: Summary of Attendant Risks and Policy Responses

Beni Chugh

THE G20'S FOCUS ON BIGTECH PLATFORMS: THE BACKGROUND

This essay has been written ahead of the Indian Presidency of the G20. It attempts to persist in the thought leadership provided by earlier presidencies in conceiving of digital financial inclusion, the role of platforms in enabling it and a taxonomy for discussing regulatory priorities. In 2016, the G20 set out the High-Level Principles for Digital Financial Inclusion, which recognized the role of platforms in reducing transaction costs, lowering barriers to access across participants and sustainably supporting small-ticket size transactions. While that conceptualization of platforms related almost entirely to their role as utilities or infrastructures and the G20 encouraged governments to invest in such infrastructure, the role and nature of platforms in finance has evolved since then (GPFI, 2016). The most notable shift has been the participation of BigTech platforms[1] in finance and a tendency for fintech and traditional financial players to evolve into platforms. Subsequent G20 publications note these shifts. The Task Force 8 during the T20 Summit, shepherded by Saudi Arabia, made a salient contribution to the policy discourse on regulation of BigTech. They vividly describe that all policy priorities in the context of BigTech can be marshalled along three axes—capital access, market structure, and consumer experience (Task Force 8 International Financial Architecture, 2020). Capital access refers to BigTech's ability to direct capital towards underserved populations, riding on their alternative data processing capabilities; market structure refers to the efficiencies but also the ensuing risks of domination, restriction of consumer choice and potential manipulation of consumers' decision making that could tip markets and raise competition concerns; and, consumer experience captures the advantages and risks that BigTech presents for consumers. Of the advantages, financial inclusion of those typically excluded is the most noteworthy, while protection of personal data surfaces as the key customer protection risk. In 2021, Task Force 9 indicated the risks that BigTech platforms could pose for financial services and the ecosystem. These include evolving into gatekeepers of the economy and raising privacy and competition concerns (Task Force 9 International Finance, 2021). Here we hope to unpack these risks of BigTech-mediated formal finance, but also more broadly, digital platform-mediated finance. We attempt to tease out how these risks are

---

[1] The BIS defines BigTech as 'technology companies with established presence in the market for digital services' (Frost et al., 2019).

realized and summarize emerging policy responses both globally and in India, while bringing out how platforms could benefit India; who is characterized by low usage of formal financial services; and how regulators in India and elsewhere are responding to the three key risks that arise from platforms—competition risks, financial risks and risks of data protection.

INTRODUCTION: THE DRIVERS OF PLATFORMS

Platforms are increasingly becoming mediators of many parts of our lives and finance is no exception. In India, the nexus of digital financial infrastructures,[2] the deepening reach of smartphones[3] and the falling costs of data[4] have precipitated a reconfiguration of the financial sector. Digital financial infrastructures, designed to be interoperable with other infrastructures and with non-financial tech companies (hereafter, 'tech companies'), are facilitating a *modularization* of financial services.

Modularization refers to the unbundling of the value chain of financial services into individual processes or modules which are then provided by specialized tech companies (Nishanth and Madhu, 2017). This results in the same financial service to be provided through different combinations of entities and processes (Chugh, 2019). It also allows the separation of the core financial activity such as transfer of payments, acceptance of deposits, or underwriting, from ancillary services such as communicating payment orders, loan origination, repayment collection, etc. This allows unregulated entities such as tech companies to provide ancillary services, even as the core financial activities are hosted by regulated entities. Modularization opens the pathways to disintermediation[5] of traditional, regulated financial entities.

The entry of tech companies in the financial value chain lays the foundation for platform-mediated finance. We borrow the BIS's definition of platforms, i.e., 'digital platforms that operate in multi-sided markets, using big data to match different groups of customers (e.g. users and providers)' (Croxson et al., 2022). Platformization here refers to both—the evolution of fintech and traditional companies into platforms and the entry of BigTech platforms into finance. In the Indian context, the former would refer to entities such as Paytm, that started out

---

[2] India's digital financial infrastructure consists of modular, open-source architectures that comprise three layers—identity, payments, and data-sharing. These work simultaneously to facilitate digital financial transactions (Stanley, 2020).

[3] India adds approximately 25 million smartphone users every quarter (Abbas, 2021).

[4] India has one of the lowest data prices in the world, at $0.68 per GB (Inc.42, 2021).

[5] Disintermediation in financial services refers to the replacement of regulated intermediaries by technology (Chugh, Raghavan and Singh, 2019).

as a provider of a single financial product but now connects consumers to several financial markets such as credit, insurance, investment and facilitate non-financial services such as booking tickets or even slots for COVID-19 vaccinations (Livemint, 2021). It would also include traditional banks whose functions now seem to have been reduced to maintaining customers' accounts. Their growing reliance on fintech providers to acquire, solicit, and service customers are turning banks into platforms that provide the utility of operating accounts and safekeep customers' money (and data) until they decide to move it (Mukherjee, 2021). The latter would apply to very large technology companies making a foray into financial services, such as Google Pay.

Platformization of finance is closely entangled with the data-intensive nature of tech companies. This data-intensive character is in turn facilitated by a deepening reach of smartphones and falling costs of data. As more parts of our lives migrate online, more data about our daily lives is generated. This data can be used multiple times to generate insights relevant to contexts other than those in which it was generated. For instance, when a food delivery platform enables food delivery, it is also collecting data on which dishes are popular in which parts of the city and during which part of the day (or night). This helps them expand into other allied businesses such as cloud kitchens where they curate menus with restaurants or may even run restaurants to plug the gaps between supply and demand (Velayanikal, 2020). This expansion into allied services is facilitated by the *economies of scope* exhibited by data, i.e., data generated in the context of one service provides information on the supply chain of the service, enabling single service providers to offer newer services (Schepp and Wambach, 2016; Stigler Research Centre, 2019; Stanley, Prasad and Singh, 2021). The rise of platforms can also be attributed to *network effects* activated by data. The more users a platform has, the more attractive it becomes for other users to join. This is typical of social networking sites or messaging services that are not interoperable.[6] These are *direct network effects* (Parker, Petropoulos and Alstyne, 2020; Stanley, Prasad and Singh, 2021). Network effects also operate across markets, where the more

---

[6] Interoperability typically constitutes two dimensions—the ability of systems to exchange information with each other and in a usable format (Diallo et al., 2011). The lack of interoperability between different systems would imply that users would be forced to use the system with the largest user base, allowing them to transact with the widest set of users. For instance, if wallets were not interoperable, then every customer would prefer the wallet with the largest set of users. Where interoperability exists, the dividend of network effects is realized at the level of the economy instead of at the level of a service provider (Parsheera, Shah and Bose, 2017).

users join a platform, the more lucrative it becomes for more providers to join in, in turn making it even more attractive for more users to join. This is at play in ride-hailing services or even app-store platforms such as the Google Play Store. As the number of app-users on the platform increases, it is more attractive for more app developers to join the platform. These are *indirect network effects* (Schepp and Wambach, 2016; Stigler Research Centre, 2019; Stanley, Prasad and Singh, 2021). Network effects ostensibly imply that digital businesses have an inherent tendency to grow big and that there are no ceilings on the scale or lifespan of the platform, as long as the core service provided by the platform continues to be relevant. Given that services such as finance are likely to remain relevant for longer, platforms that provide financial services (such as the stock exchanges) are likely to be more resilient and have a greater longevity than those that facilitate social interactions, for instance.

This section discussed how platforms in finance come to be and how platforms operating in other sectors foray into financial services. We discuss the rise of platforms in finance in the context of the Indian financial system and then summarize the opportunities presented by the rise of platforms in finance and their attendant risks. These risks are typical of platforms that operate in finance but are accentuated in the case of larger platforms. Finally, we conclude with an overview of emerging policy responses.

RISE OF PLATFORMS IN FINANCE: SPOTLIGHT ON INDIA

Platforms in financial services bridge (at least) two sides of a market. This could take the form of bringing together lenders and borrowers, insurers and prospective insureds, or payment processing entities like banks, and consumers such as merchants and individual consumers. This section discusses select platforms that mediate financial services in India.

Globally, it appears that payments serve as an entry point for several platforms. In fact, facilitating payments appears to be a well-worn strategy for BigTech players (Frost et al., 2019). Intuitively, it would appear that initiating activities with payments allows platforms to build trust with the consumers (Boissay et al., 2021). For platforms that have a presence in the real economy for instance, e-commerce or food delivery, embedding payments in their businesses increases convenience and enhances consumers' experience. In India, the rise of payments platforms is also explained by the creation of digital financial infrastructure, designed to be interoperable with tech companies, such as the UPI.[7] UPI-enabled payments are growing at an astronomical rate with over 4 billion transactions realized in

---

[7] UPI i.e., Unified Payments Interface enables real time, direct to bank account payments. See more here: https://www.npci.org.in/what-we-do/upi/product-overview.

the month of January 2022 (NPCI, 2022). Curiously, though vibrant, the UPI platform appears to be dominated by a few big, non-financial players (third party app providers or TPAPs),[8] with over 96 per cent of the market (by volume) being claimed only by three players,[9] all of whom are platforms (Mundhra, 2022a; Chugh, 2020). We turn to this feature in a later section.

It is increasingly common for payments platforms to distribute a wider range of financial and non-financial services, as seen in the case of leading TPAPs in India. Most TPAPs in India distribute credit products. They act as an intermediary between licensed entities, authorized by the Reserve Bank of India (RBI) to lend, and the users of their payments services. Google Pay, for instance, allows financial service providers, including lenders to set up *spots*—a digital storefront on its app. This is also true of non-BigTech platforms such as Paytm. While many platforms begin as distributors of financial services, some also graduate to partnering with regulated entities to inform financial decisions. For instance, e-commerce giant, Amazon, offers a 'Buy-Now-Pay-Later' (BNPL) product through its lending arm, Amazon Pay India Pvt Ltd, in association with NBFCs (such as Capital Float) and banks (AmazonPay). Its agreement with one of its partner banks states that Amazon Pay India Pvt Ltd 'acts as a service provider to source retail customers for offering of BNPL Facility from IDFC FIRST', (IDFC First Bank, n.d.). This suggests that over time, as platforms observe financials more closely, they can directly contribute to the design of the financial product. Further, some lenders also resort to using psychometric tools to understand the prospective borrower's ability and willingness to pay (Arráiz, Bruhn, and Stucchi, 2018). While the discussion so far points to how non-credit platforms foray into credit, the 'Peer-to-Peer lending' (P2P Lending) business model is predicated on a platform. P2P platforms act as marketplaces that connect prospective borrowers with prospective lenders (Reserve Bank of India, 2021). Similarly, the Trade Receivables Discounting Systems (TReDS) is a platform that provides working capital loan-like facilities to MSMEs. It is a bill discounting facility that realizes immediate payments for MSMEs, against invoices of their future receivables (The Hindu BusinessLine, 2021).

Another instance of a regulator-facilitated platform is the Insurance Web Aggregator Model of the Insurance Regulatory and Development Authority of India (IRDAI) (Insurance Regulatory and Development Authority of India, 2019). Insurance Web Aggregators collect information across insurance products and help consumers compare price and product features. Again, they do not play an active role in either designing or underwriting the insurance product but are important

---

[8] TPAPs, i.e. third party app providers are service providers who participate in UPI through Banks. See more here https://www.npci.org.in/what-we-do/upi/roles-responsibilities.
[9] PhonePe leads the UPI market in India, followed by Google Pay and Paytm. In March 2022, PhonePe claimed 46.9 per cent transactions, Google Pay claimed 33. 7 per cent of all transactions, and Paytm accounted for 15.6 per cent of all transactions (by volume) (Mundhra, 2022).

distribution intermediaries. In the investment space, there are several platforms that facilitate brokerage of stocks, mutual funds, commodities and currencies (The Tribune, 2021). While these platforms merely digitize the existing broker model, many are known to cost less than traditional brokers, on account of lower transaction costs (Agarwal, 2022). These brokerage platforms also partner with payment apps that act as a pathway to the platform. Not just new age brokers, but traditional entities such as banks also tie up with payment apps to offer investment products. Recently, Google Pay offered a spot to Equitas Small Finance Bank, to offer fixed deposits to non-account holders (Agrawal, 2021). While permissible under the extant RBI regime, this partnership is being closely examined by the RBI. Though the arrangement does not appear to create prudential risks, there are potential risks associated with competitiveness. We bookmark it here and turn to it in a later section.

It appears that it is most common for platforms to act as distributors of financial services while only a few participate in the financial activity and partake in financial risks. To reiterate, the discussion in this section is only illustrative in nature, and by no means an exhaustive account of all platforms that mediate financial services in India. The economic forces of economies of scope, network effects and economies of scale operate on all these platforms, however, these forces appear to have a stronger impact on larger platforms. These economic forces result in a host of efficiencies in the financial sector, we discuss them next.

OPPORTUNITIES PRESENTED BY PARTICIPATION OF PLATFORMS IN FINANCE

The data-intensive nature of platforms allows them to capture and generate vast swathes of personal data of consumers. This helps overcome economic frictions such as information asymmetry and high transaction costs, easing the supply of formal finance. Specifically, platform-mediated finance can:

1. Expand the reach of formal finance to include new-to-banks and otherwise thin-filed consumers: Formal financial markets are fraught with information asymmetries. Lenders do not have complete information of the borrowers' willingness and ability to pay, making it hard to price risk. Therefore, the interest rate in the market reflects the average risk, and funds remain idle at equilibrium (Stiglitz and Weiss, 1981). Regulated institutions such as banks default to extensive documentation, collaterals, and long relationships to overcome information asymmetry between themselves and the borrowers. This raises the barriers to entry for new borrowers who do not have a history of an extensive engagement with formal finance or assets to offer as collaterals (Chugh and Raghavan, 2019).

Platforms help reduce information asymmetry in financial markets (Dvara Research, 2020). First, unlike financial markets, platforms, especially those that already have footprints in other digital or real markets, are designed to *include* and *not exclude* consumers. For instance, onboarding messaging services or a food delivery platform does not require a KYC, collateral, or any proof of net worth. Platforms are designed to serve both those who are in the fold of formal finance and those who operate outside it. Second, sophisticated credit risk modelling allows financial platforms to infer financial information from seemingly non-financial information. As merchants interact with the platform, it begins to build intelligence on them. The platform becomes sensitive to the volume of demand that the merchant caters, its popular products, geographical spread of consumers etc. (Peermohamed, 2017). All these factors help platforms piece together a rich profile of the merchant, with very little contribution from financial information. Merchants' relationship with the platform offers insights that make up for their lack of a relationship with formal financial institutions such as banks. By passing these insights to a regulated entity, platforms enable them to serve those who have been excluded or underserved traditionally. In India, Paytm for instance, started as a UPI-based payment app but now also distributes loans of partner banks and NBFCs. Estimates suggest that a sizeable proportion of its borrowers are new to credit, i.e., their first loan is facilitated by their relationship with Paytm (ICICI Securities, 2022; Karthik, 2021). While it is common to think of data as money, payments apps have been successful in converting money that flows through transactions into data and memory about the consumer's financial circumstances (Westermeier, 2020).

2. *Improve the product fit:* Platforms can improve product fits on two counts. First, they understand the prospective borrowers, their needs and their financial abilities better than formal financial institutions who may not have as much visibility of their cash-flows or cyclical needs. For instance, food delivery platforms have a granular understanding of the demand for restaurants, the revenues they generate and the potential to scale up, making it easier to facilitate loans to them (SH, 2017; Bajaj Finserv Markets, n.d.). These loans are likely to be more risk-sensitive (Jagtiani and Lemieux, 2017)), better timed (International Finance Corporation, n.d.), and potentially of a more appropriate ticket size than traditional loans.

Second, these loans are likely to have lower transaction costs both in terms of time and money (Frost et al., 2019). Network effects and the use of AI and ML reduce the costs of assessing credit worthiness of an additional borrower. Low transaction costs are manifest in lower ticket sizes. For instance, in India, reports suggest that the average size of personal loan has reduced from Rs 2.4 lakh in 2017 to Rs 1.5 lakh in 2021. More than a fifth of these loans are below INR 10,000.

(Chugh, 2021). Add to that, fully digitized processes imply that the turn-around-time of the loan is markedly lower than traditional loans.

Clearly, platforms have the potential to improve the quality of financial solutions available to the consumer. However, their effect on overall welfare remains ambiguous, given their attendant risks, which we discuss next.

RISKS POSED BY PLATFORM-MEDIATED FINANCE

The growth of platform-mediated finance presents a set of risks. Some of these risks are familiar to financial regulators such as operational risks and risks to consumer protection. However, platforms also pose a fresh set of challenges, such as risks from abuse of dominance, misuse of personal data or even new kinds of systemic risks. This section unpacks risks posed by the participation of platforms in finance:

1. Risks to competitiveness of the financial sector: It appears that the same economic features (network effects, economies of scope and scale) that allow platforms to reduce transaction costs and reach a wider set of consumers could also entrench their dominant positions. The three features operate together to: (i) Induce concentration, i.e., it is beneficial for one firm to capture the market because network effects imply that each additional user increases benefits for the whole consumer base (Bruno and Sand-Zantman, 2020) and; (ii) Foreclose competition, because early entrants create larger databases with exclusive property rights. Any new entrant would have to incur significant economic and/or time costs to access comparable datasets (Schepp and Wambach, 2016). This results in *tipping* the market in the favour of one provider. Observers of the digital space note that competition in digital markets is often for the *entire* market and that digital markets often lend themselves to winner-take-all outcomes (Stanley, Prasad and Singh, 2021).

This can have potentially grave consequences for the financial sector. First, a dominant position of the platform positions it as a gatekeeper of the sector. The platform can unlevel the playing field by arbitrarily denying space to providers. The case of Google Pay partnering with Equitas serves as a useful context. While the partnership does not appear to raise prudential concerns, it is worth examining it from the perspective of competitiveness. Google Pay being a private entity could reject a similar partnership with competitors of Equitas Banks. This would have the effect of Equi-

tas gaining from the dominance of Google Pay, on the back of private contracts. Second, platforms, especially BigTech platforms are dominant in other markets beyond the financial sector. This gives them access to deep pockets to subsidize products and outlast venture funded, fintech platforms. This is manifest in India's UPI market. The three leading players incur significant losses in their UPI business, due to the reward driven nature of the businesses (Chugh, 2020). Participants often rely on captive capital and other businesses to keep up operations (Tyagi and Vardhan, 2020). This creates barriers of entry for other participants but also raises concerns about the competitiveness among the incumbents. Unless providers distinguish themselves on the quality of user experience, it is likely that the one with the deepest pockets emerges dominant.

2. Financial risks: Platform participation in finance can create new sources of financial risks. First, dominance or even concentration among a few platforms could create concentration risks. Most platforms enter into private agreements with regulated entities for providing ancillary financial services. Given most platforms do not partake in the financial activity itself, they are rarely subject to reporting requirements that apply to regulated entities. Therefore, there is little visibility of the operational risks they create for the regulated entity and the ability of the regulated entity to absorb them. The RBI recently observed that digital partners who originate, underwrite loans or collect repayments for regulated entities induce operational risk in the system and do not have the safety of regulatory capital to fall back on, should the risks materialize (Reserve Bank of India, 2021).

Matters get even more complicated due to the convoluted corporate structure of these platforms. For instance, a platform that is a loan originator for a regulated entity could invest in that entity through its other business arms, raising a fresh set of governance concerns.[10] Further, the convoluted corporate structure of platforms, with their subsidiaries engaged in ancillary financial services and non-financial services can be a potential source of risk. The interaction of several ancillary services within the same group entity could raise risks that remain uncovered by regulation (Restoy, 2021). Finally, the activities of a platform may be fraught with conflicts of interest. For instance, platforms exert a high degree of control over their participants and have a higher ability to enforce sanctions in instances where the participants default on loan repayments. For instance, platforms could downgrade or blacklist merchants in case they default and these sanctions could be costlier to merchants, incentivising them to clear debt (Bank for International Settlements, 2019). This creates concerns for consumer protection in financial services, in cases of over-indebtedness or cases of genuine defaults.

---

[10] Amazon Pay Pvt Ltd ties with Capital Float to offer Buy-Now-Pay-Later services. Amazon is also a leading investor of Capital Float (Khatri, 2018). It is unclear if this investment allows Amazon to exert any influence on the credit business of Capital Float but these transactions within group companies are worth investigating further.

3. Risks to and from personal data: While exclusive control over personal data imparts market power, it also raises concerns for consumers' privacy. There is growing evidence that low-income users value their privacy. Dvara Research's (upcoming) work on privacy preferences of low-income individuals suggests that users are unwilling to share financial information, such as the value of assets owned, with financial service providers. Further, most individuals are wary of sharing information because they consider it personal. In another study, respondents unanimously protested the prospects of sharing their location data or their search history, indicators that are rather routinely collected by platforms (Dalberg, Dvara research and CGAP, 2017). In this context, the ethics of platforms collecting consumers' deeply personal information over the course of the transaction remain questionable.

These concerns are further amplified for digital migrants, unfamiliar with the nuances of data. Harm from data is hard to anticipate, establish and attribute (Prasad, 2021). In 2018, news reports suggested that data from the Aadhaar database was being sold for a small sum (The Tribune, 2018). It is hard to predict who all may have purchased the data and how that data was sold forward. Further, it is quite hard if not altogether impossible to determine whose data got leaked and how that might be misused in the future. Low-income, newly online individuals feel ill-equipped to manoeuvre the digital landscape, challenge providers' practices and identify or seek compensation for harms that arise from a compromise of their personal data (Dalberg, Dvara research and CGAP, 2017). This raises fresh concerns about data governance of platforms. A lapse in data governance could offset the gains made from financial inclusion.

EMERGING POLICY RESPONSES

There is a growing consensus that financial regulators must contend with these multifarious challenges, to leverage the benefits of platform-mediated finance while addressing its attendant risks. This section unpacks some policy responses being considered by regulators globally:

1. Addressing competition risks through conduct and caps on market share: The first source of market power is the platform's gatekeeping position. It gives an unregulated entity the potential ability to decide the rules of engagement for regulated, financial entities. This could distort the choice set available to the consumers who would have to incur significant search costs to identify providers beyond those who are allowed, favoured and advertised by dominant platforms. This raft of powers brings the platform closer to an infrastructure than a private marketplace. Several jurisdictions are considering or enforcing regulations to check these powers of platforms. For example, China enforced the *Guidelines for antimonopoly in the platform economy* in 2021 (Government of China, 2021). The

Guidelines use a number of factors to determine dominance of a platform such as the control that the platform exerts over the market, its financial and technical resources, in addition to the market share. They also present a series of impermissible actions, which could be construed as abuse of dominance. These include selling goods at unfairly high prices or buying goods at unfairly low prices, treating similar counterparties differently or denying transacting with counterparties without justifiable reasons (ChinaBriefing, 2020). Similar measures are also set out in the EU's proposed *Digital Markets Act* (European Commission, 2021). The Act requires platforms to treat similar vendors similarly, allow vendors to port across other competing platforms, and design platforms to be interoperable. Similarly, the *Report of the Digital Competition Expert Panel* (Digital Competition Expert Panel, 2019) calls upon the Competition and Markets Authority of the UK to designate *strategic market status* to platforms that could potentially be gatekeepers and subject them to an escalated code of conduct.

In December 2020, the NPCI capped the share of TPAPs operating on UPI to 30 per cent. Ostensibly, the regulation intends to prevent any single player from becoming too large and abusing dominance or creating systemic concerns. The participants whose market shares exceeded 30 per cent at the time of notification would have up to two years to comply with it (Chugh, 2020).

2. *Addressing financial risk through licensing and self-regulation:* The bulk of financial fears associated with platforms' participation in finance arise from the lack of transparency about their functions. In India, RBI's Working Group on Digital Lending recommends that all service providers who provide ancillary services to regulated entities (i.e., lending service providers) must be regulated by Self-Regulatory Organizations (SROs). It further advocates that consumer protection obligations must be imposed on lending service providers (Reserve Bank of India, 2021). While these recommendations cover all lending service providers, they are particularly relevant for platforms, given the role they perform in facilitating digital credit.

Several jurisdictions are considering virtual banks that could use online-only channels to provide banking services. Countries such as China, Hong Kong, Singapore, among others, have issued virtual bank licenses even as others mull over them. It could provide a pathway for large platforms to systematically participate in financial services while allowing regulators to oversee their operations (Zamil and Lawson, 2022). However, the success of these banks in terms of meeting policy objectives is predicated on a risk-proportionate regulatory regime.

3. *Enforcing data protection safeguards for preserving privacy and competitiveness:* Several jurisdictions have put in place data protection laws to set bounds on the use of consumers' personal data. The EU's General Data Protection Regime sets out conditions for processing Europeans' personal data (Intersoft Consulting, 2016). Similarly, India has been considering a data protection legislation that enforces well-established principles of data protection and also sets out obligations for those who process users' data. The current version of the Data Protection Bill (2021) refers to data processors as data fiduciaries and they are expected to account for users' best interest when processing their personal data (Joint Parliamentary Committee on The Data Protection Bill 2019, 2021). China enforced its Personal Information Protection Law in November 2021, which emphasizes rights of data principals (the natural persons to whom the personal data relates), obligations of data processors and controllers while processing personal data (Peng and Sha, 2021). A common thread running across these legislations is the emphasis on data minimization, a well-established data protection principle that emphasizes not collecting more data than what is needed and not predicating the provisioning of the service on the access to avoidable data. This implies that platforms cannot deny services to users if the users do not wish to share data that is not necessary to provide the service. This could significantly change the way platforms conduct business currently. There is also a rising trend of legislation aimed at protecting data in the financial sector. EU's Payments Service Directive 2 sets out obligations for payment service providers when processing users' personal data (European Commission, 2015). Recently, amidst growing privacy and data quality concerns arising from unregulated entities' access to credit information companies, the RBI set out criteria for entities that would qualify to ping credit information companies (Reserve Bank of India, 2022). These entities would further be regulated by the Credit Information Companies (Amendment) Regulations, 2021, that set out the data protection principles applicable in relation to credit information such as access control, necessity, data retention (Government of India, 2005).

Several legislations also contemplate measures to prevent multisided platforms to wield significant market power from their control over data. The proposed Digital Markets Act, for instance, proposes that platforms should not merge data collected from different business entities (European Commission, 2021). Similarly, the Chinese Guidelines appear to ban any use of data between the platform and its counterparts that forecloses competition (Government of China, 2021). The Competition Commission of India recently observed that the sharing of data between two subsidiaries—Facebook and WhatsApp—could have exclusionary effects (In Re: Updated Terms of Service and Privacy Policy for WhatsApp Users, 2021). Additionally, there is a growing support for data portability between the platform and its participants. This could be crucial to maintain vertical competitiveness. Legislations also emphasise data portability in the financial sector. In 2017, the UK's competition authority prescribed Open Banking for nine major banks. Open Banking enables consumers and Small and Medium-sized Enterprises (SMEs) to share their bank and credit card transaction data securely with trusted third parties (Competition and Markets Authority, UK, n.d.). Since then, the open banking ecosystem has expanded to include more than 200 entities. Similarly, India created a special class of entities called Account Aggregators that allows for consent-based porting of data among financial sector participants (Reserve Bank of India, 2021).

4. Move towards an activity and entity-based approach to regulating platforms, especially BigTech: Several central banks are expressing the need to devise a combination of activity and entity-based regulatory instruments to regulate platforms, especially BigTech. These concerns arise from the central banks' core mandate of 'adequately monitoring and, as appropriate, applying prudential standards to all aspects of the business conducted by the banking group worldwide', including the 'ability to identify and act upon risks posed by unregulated activities within the group to the regulated entity or to financial stability' (Restoy, 2021; Basel Committee on Banking Supervision, 2016). It appears that covering for individual activity-based risks would still leave the group company, and by extension, the financial system vulnerable to risks that arise from interconnectedness of within-group entities. This intuition appears deeply rooted in the learnings of the sub-prime crisis (Restoy, 2021). The Chinese central bank recently enforced regulations for financial holding companies. The regulations require any entity that holds two or more financial institutions and satisfies specific size thresholds to apply for a license. The objective of the regulation appears to ensure adequate risk buffers both at the level of individual entities and at the level of the group, indicating greater risks due to greater interconnectedness within the group companies. Again, these have enhanced significance for platforms but especially BigTech platforms that might operate in more than one financial sector (People's Bank of China, 2021; Carstens et al., 2021).

Table 1: Summary: Risks Associated with Platform-Mediated Finance and Emerging Policy Responses	
Competition Risks	**Emerging policy responses**
■ Abuse of platform's gate-keeping position with the effect of distorting the markets	■ Enforcing stricter conduct obligations on dominant platforms that prevent: a. Overcharging consumers/underpaying suppliers (Government of China, 2021) b. Discriminating between comparable counterparties (Government of China, 2021) (European Commission, 2021) c. Supporting interoperability with competing platforms (European Commission, 2021) ■ Enforcing caps on market share to prevent dominance (National Payments Corporation of India, 2020)

■ Dominance arising from control over rich personal data	■ Discouraging exclusive control over data by: a. Encouraging data portability (European Commission, 2021) b. Disallowing platforms to merge data across businesses (European Commission, 2021)
Financial Risks	Emerging policy responses
■ Operational risks arising from the participation of unregulated platforms in financial services	■ Risk-proportionate regulation: a. Licensing of platforms when they provide ancillary financial services (Reserve Bank of India, 2021) b. Allowing the creation of virtual banks (Hong Kong Monetary Authority, 2022; Monetary Authority Singapore, 2020) c. Regulating at the level of the consolidated group, in addition to individual activity (People's Bank of China, 2021)
Risks from data protection	Emerging policy responses
■ Incursions on consumers' privacy from widespread collection of personal data	■ Enforcing data protection legislations with a focus on: a. Data minimization, informed, granular and withdrawable consent, privacy by design, algorithmic accountability (Joint Parliamentary Committee on The Data Protection Bill, 2019, 2021; Peng and Sha, 2021) b. Regulating the use of financial data (European Commission, 2015; Reserve Bank of India, 2022)

CONCLUSION

Preceding G20 discussions emphasize that platforms could entrench dominant positions, influence consumers to opt for financial instruments they might not need or use consumers' personal data in a manner that violates their privacy and exposes them to further harm. These factors could diminish consumer welfare, potentially off-setting the welfare gains that arise from efficiencies of platform-based finance. This essay summarizes emerging policy actions that have either been enforced or are being considered, in response to these risks. Authorities appear to be addressing risks of abuse of dominance by creating guidelines that prevent platforms from abusing their gatekeeping positions, prohibit merging datasets across businesses, place caps on their sizes and support interoperability among competitors. Data protection is becoming a crucial consideration for central bankers, with many investigating abuse of data by platforms. Finally, there is a move to regulate platforms involved in ancillary financial services and also applying regulation at the group level to counter the risks that emerge from the interconnectedness among the different business arms of platforms.

REFERENCES

Abbas, Muntazir. 2021. India's growing data usage, smartphone adoption to boost Digital India initiatives: Top bureaucrat. *The Economic Times.* October 9. Accessed March 2022. https://economictimes.indiatimes.com/news/india/ indias-growing-data-usage-smartphone-adoption-to-boost-digital-india-initiatives-top-bureaucrat/articleshow/87275402.cms

Agarwal, Mehak. 2022. Lower taxation costs': Here's what Zerodha's Nithin Kamath expects from Budget 2022. *Business Today.* January 17. Accessed March 2022. https://www.businesstoday.in/union-budget-2022/markets/ story/lower-taxation-costs-heres-what-zerodhas-nithin-kamath-expects-from-budget-2022-319332-2022-01-17

Agrawal, Amol. 2021. Equitas-Google Pay deal reflects confluence of banking and fintech. *MoneyControl.* September 24. Accessed March 2022. https:// www.moneycontrol.com/news/opinion/equitas-google-pay-deal-reflects-confluence-of-banking-fintech-7499181.html

AmazonPay. n.d. *Amazon Pay Later- Loan Agreement.* https://www.amazon.in/ gp/help/customer/display.html?nodeId=G4GX8HKMGKLXZ5QP

Arráiz, Irani, Bruhn, Miriam and Stucchi, Rodolfo, 2018. "Psychometrics as a Tool to Improve Screening and Access to Credit." IDB Publications (Working Papers) 7266. Inter-American Development Bank.

Bajaj Finserv Markets. n.d. *Swiggy partners with PM's AtmaNibhar Nidhi to bring over 36,000 street food vendors online.* Accessed March 2022. https://www. bajajfinservmarkets.in/loans/business-loan/articles/swiggy-partners-pm-atmanibhar-nidhi.html

Bank for International Settlements. 2019. *BIS Annual Economic Report.* Basel: BIS.

Baruzzi, Sofia. 2020. China Releases Anti-Monopoly Guidelines for its Platform Economy. *China Briefing.* December 16. Accessed March 2022. https:// www.china-briefing.com/news/china-releases-anti-monopoly-guidelines-for-its-platform-economy/

Basel Committee on Banking Supervision. .2016. "Guidance on the application of the Core Principles for Effective Banking Supervision to the regulation and supervision of institutions relevant to financial inclusion." September. Accessed March 2022. https://www.bis.org/bcbs/publ/d383.pdf

Bhalla, Kritti. 2021. As Telcos Push For Higher ARPU, India No Longer Has The World's Cheapest Mobile Data Plans. *Inc.42.* April 13. Accessed February 2022. https://inc42.com/buzz/as-telcos-push-for-higher-arpu-india-no-longer-has-the-worlds-cheapest-mobile-data-plans/

Boissay, F., Ehlers, T., Gambacorta, L., and H. Song. 2021. *Big techs in finance: on the new nexus between data privacy and competition.* Basel: Bank for International Settlements.

Bruno, J., and W. Sand-Zantman. 2020. "The Economics of Platforms: A Theory Guide for Competition Policy." Accessed March 2022. https://www.cesifo. org/en/publikationen/2020/working-paper/economics-platforms-theory-guide-competition-policy

Carstens, A., Claessens, S., Restoy, F. and H. S. Shin. 2021. *Regulating big techs in finance.* Basel: Bank for International Settlements.

ChinaBriefing. 2020. *China Releases Anti-Monopoly Guidelines for its Platform Economy.* December 16. https://www.china-briefing.com/news/china-releases-anti-monopoly-guidelines-for-its-platform-economy/.

Chugh, B. 2019. Financial Regulation of Consumer-facing Fintech. *Dvara Research.* September. Accessed March 2022. https://www.dvara.com/research/wp-content/uploads/2019/09/Financial-regulation-of-consumer-facing-fintech-in-India-status-quo-and-emerging-concerns.pdf

Chugh, B. 2020. Caps on third party app providers in UPI: Missing the woods for the trees?. *Dvara Research.* December 1. Accessed March. https://www.dvara.com/research/blog/2020/12/01/caps-on-third-party-app-providers-in-upi-missing-the-woods-for-the-trees/

Chugh, B. 2021. Fintech in India: Can the trust stack up? *ORF.* November 27. https://www.orfonline.org/expert-speak/fintech-in-india-can-the-trust-stack-up/

Chugh, B. and Raghavan, M. 2019. The RBI's proposed Public Credit Registry and its implications for the credit reporting system in India. *Dvara Research.* June 18. https://www.dvara.com/research/blog/2019/06/18/the-rbis-proposed-public-credit-registry-and-its-implications-for-the-credit-reporting-system-in-india/

Chugh, B., Raghavan, M., and A. Singh. 2019. "Primer on Designing Optimal Regulation of Financial Services." April 5. Accessed March 2022. https://papers.ssrn.com/sol3/papers.cfm?abstract_id=3569432

Competition and Markets Authority, UK. n.d. Open Banking UK. Accessed March 2022. https://www.openbanking.org.uk

Croxson, K., Frost, J., Gambacorta , L., and T. Vallet. 2022. "Platform-based business models and financial inclusion." *BIS Working Papers.* January 10. https://www.bis.org/publ/work986.htm

Dalberg, Dvara research and CGAP. 2017. *Privacy on the Line.* Chennai: Dvara Research.

Diallo, Saikou Y., Herencia-Zapana, Heber, Padilla, Jose J., and Tolk, Andreas. 2011. "Understanding Interoperability." In *Proceedings of the 2011 Emerging M&S Applications in Industry and Academia Symposium (EAIA '11).* Society for Computer Simulation International, San Diego, CA, USA, pp. 84–91.

Digital Competition Expert Panel. 2019. *Unlocking digital competition Report of the Digital Competition Expert Panel.* London: HMTreasury.

Dvara Research. 2020. *Regulating data-driven finance: Conference Proceedings.* November. Accessed March 2022. https://www.dvara.com/research/wp-content/uploads/2020/11/Conference-Proceedings-from-the-Fourth-Dvara-Research-Conference-2019.pdf

European Commission. 2015. *DIRECTIVE (EU) 2015/2366 OF THE EUROPEAN PARLIAMENT AND OF THE COUNCIL.* November 25. Accessed March 2022. https://eur-lex.europa.eu/legal-content/EN/TXT/PDF/?uri=CELEX: 32015L2366&from=EN

European Commission. 2021. *Proposal for a REGULATION OF THE EURO-PEAN PARLIAMENT AND OF THE COUNCIL on contestable and fair markets in the digital sector (Digital Markets Act).* December 15. Accessed March 2022. https://eur-lex.europa.eu/legal-content/EN/TXT/PDF/?uri= CELEX:52020PC0842&from=en

Evans, D. S., and R. Schmalensee. 2013. "The Antitrust Analysis of Multi-sided Platform Business." National Bureau of Economic Research. February. Accessed March 2022. https://www.nber.org/papers/w18783

Frost, J., Gambacorta, L., Huang, Y., and H. S. Shin. 2019. BigTech and the changing structure of financial intermediation." Working Paper, Bank for International Settlements. April 8. Accessed March 2022. https://www.bis.org/publ/work779.pdf

Ghosh, I., and A. Ranade. 2020. "A Trilemma and a Possible Solution: Can Payments Banks Succeed?". *Economic and Political Weekly.* April 11. Accessed March 2022. https://www.epw.in/journal/2020/15/special-articles/can-payments-banks-succeed.html

Government of China. 2021. *UNCTAD Intergovernmental Group of Experts on Competition Law and Policy "Competition Law, Policy and Regulation in the Digital Age" Roundtable.* UNCTAD.

Government of India. 2005. "THE CREDIT INFORMATION COMPANIES (REGULATION) ACT, 2005." Accessed March 2022. https://legislative.gov.in/sites/default/files/A2005-30.pdf

GPFI. 2016. "G20 High-Level Principles for Digital Financial Inclusion." https://www.gpfi.org/sites/gpfi/files/G20%20High%20Level%20Principles%20for%20Digital%20Financial%20Inclusion.pdf

Hong Kong Monetary Authority. 2022. Virtual Banks. March 01. Accessed March 2022. https://www.hkma.gov.hk/eng/key-functions/banking/banking-regulatory-and-supervisory-regime/virtual-banks/

ICICI Securities. 2022. *Equity Research: One 97 Communications.* February 18. Accessed March 2022. https://economictimes.indiatimes.com/photo/89715918.cms

IDFC First Bank. n.d. List of Digital Partners. Accessed March 2022. https://www.idfcfirstbank.com/content/dam/idfcfirstbank/footer/adlp.pdf

In Re: Updated Terms of Service and Privacy Policy for WhatsApp Users. S.M. Case No. 01 of 2021 (The Competition Commission of India 2021). 2021.

Insurance Regulatory and Development Authority of India. 2019. "Insurance Regulatory and Development Authority of India (Insurance Web Aggregators) Regulations, 2017." October 30. Accessed March 2022. https://www.irdai.gov.in/ADMINCMS/cms/Uploadedfiles/Regulations/Consolidated/Web%20Aggregators%20Regulations-2017-After%20Amendment-May%202020.pdf

International Finance Corporation. n.d. "MSME Digital Finance: Reselience & Innovation durng COVID-19." Accessed March 2022. https://www.gpfi.org/sites/gpfi/files/documents/5_IFC-SMEFF%20Report_MSME%20digital%20finance_Resilience%20and%20Innovation%20during%20COVID-19.pdf

Intersoft Consulting. 2016. General Data Protection Regulation :GDPR. Accessed March 2022. https://gdpr-info.eu

Jagtiani, J., and C. Lemieux. 2017. "Fintech Lending: Financial Inclusion, Risk Pricing, and Alternative Information." Working Paper. July 19. Accessed March 2022. https://papers.ssrn.com/sol3/papers.cfm?abstract_id=3005260

Joint Parliamentary Committee on The Data Protection Bill 2019. 2021. *Report of the Joint Parliamentary Committee on The Data Protection Bill 2019.* December 16. Accessed March 2022. https://www.medianama.com/wp-content/uploads/2021/12/17_Joint_Committee_on_the_Personal_Data_Protection_Bill_2019_1.pdf

Karthik, Hamsini. 2021. SBI Cards growth nears pre-Covid level on higher spends, new card sourcing. *Business Standard.* January 26. Accessed March 2022. https://www.business-standard.com/article/companies/sbi-cards-growth-nears-pre-covid-level-on-higher-spends-new-card-sourcing-121012501075_1.html

Khatri, Bhumika. 2018. Amazon Backs Capital Float With $22 Mn In Series C Funding. *Inc42.* April 24. Accessed March 2022. https://inc42.com/buzz/amazon-backs-capital-float-with-22-mn-in-series-c-funding/

Livemint. 2021. Paytm users can book vaccine slots on the app: Details here. *Livemint.* June 14. Accessed March 2022. https://www.livemint.com/

technology/tech-news/paytm-users-can-book-covid-19-vaccination-slots-on-app-details-here-11623664591432.html

Monetary Authority Singapore. 2020. *MAS Announces Successful Applicants of Licences to Operate New Digital Banks in Singapore.* December 4. Accessed March 2022. https://www.mas.gov.sg/news/media-releases/2020/mas-announces-successful-applicants-of-licences-to-operate-new-digital-banks-in-singapore

Mundhra, Laxitha. 2022a. PhonePe Maintains Lead In UPI With 49% Market Share In Jan 2022, WhatsApp At 0.02%. *Inc42.* February 9. Retrieved March 2022, from Inc42.com: https://inc42.com/buzz/phonepe-maintains-lead-in-upi-with-49-market-share-in-jan-2022-whatsapp-at-0-02/

Mundhra, Laxitha. 2022b. UPI Txn Value Of PhonePe, Google Pay Declines Marginally In February 2022. *Inc42.* March 8. https://inc42.com/buzz/phonepe-google-pay-upi-volume-declines-marginally-in-february-2022/

National Payments Corporation of India. 2020. *NPCI/UPI/OC-97/2020-21: Guidelines on volume cap for Third Party App Providers (TPAPs) in UPI.* Mumbai: NPCI.

Nishanth, K., and Madhu S. 2017. Designing Regulations for a Rapidly Evolving Fincancial System - Financial Systems Design Conference 2017. *Dvara Research.* October 20. Accessed March 2022, from https://www.dvara.com/research/blog/2017/10/20/designing-regulations-for-a-rapidly-evolving-financial-system-financial-systems-design-conference-2017/

NPCI. 2022. *UPI Product Statistics.* February. Accessed March 2022. https://www.npci.org.in/what-we-do/upi/product-statistics

Parker, G., Petropoulos, G., and M. V. Alstyne. 2020. *Digital platforms and antitrust.* Brussles: Bruegel.

Parsheera, Smriti, Shah, Ajay and Avirup Bose. 2017. "Competition Issues in India's Online Economy." *SSRN Electronic Journal.* 10.2139/ssrn.3045810.

Peermohamed, Alnoor. 2017. "Swiggy taps customer data to help restaurants scale up." *Business Standard.* June 10. Accessed March 2022. https://www.business-standard.com/article/companies/swiggy-taps-customer-data-to-help-restaurants-scale-up-117060900965_1.html

Peng, Alice, and Shirley Sha. 2021. China: The first Personal Information Protection Law (PIPL) in China. *Mondaq.* October 15. Accessed March 2022. https://www.mondaq.com/china/data-protection/1121892/the-first-personal-information-protection-law-pipl-in-china

People's Bank of China. 2021. *PBC Officials Answer Press Questions on Trial Measures on Regulation of Financial Holding Companies.* September 9. Accessed

March 2022. http://www.lawinfochina.com/Search/DisplayInfo.aspx?id=2 8068&lib=news&keyTitle=&keyCTitle=

Prasad, S. 2021. "Understanding harm from personal data processing activities and its challenges for consumer protection." *RGNUL Student Research Review Journal.*

Reserve Bank of India. 2021. October 5. *Master Direction- Non-Banking Financial Company - Account Aggregator (Reserve Bank) Directions, 2016 (Updated as on October 05, 2021).* October 5. Accessed March 2022. https://www.rbi. org.in/Scripts/NotificationUser.aspx?Id=10598

Reserve Bank of India. 2021. *Master Directions - Non-Banking Financial Company – Peer to Peer Lending Platform (Reserve Bank) Directions, 2017 (Updated as on October 05, 2021).* October 5. Accessed March 2022. https:// www.rbi.org.in/Scripts/BS_ViewMasDirections.aspx?id=11137

Reserve Bank of India. 2021. *Report of the Working Group on Digital Lending including Lending through Online Platforms and Mobile Apps .* Mumbai: Reserve Bank of India.

Reserve Bank of India. 2022. *Eligibility criteria for entities to be categorised as Specified User under clause (j) of Regulation 3 of the Credit Information Companies (Amendment) Regulations, 2021.* January 5. Accessed February 2022. https://rbidocs.rbi.org.in/rdocs/content/pdfs/Eligibility05012022.pdf

Restoy, F. 2021. *Fintech regulation: How to achieve a level playing field.* Basel: Bank for International Settlements.

Schepp, N.P., and Achim Wambach. 2016. "On Big Data and Its Relevance for Market Power Assessment." *Journal of European Competition Law & Practice, 7 (2):* 120–124.

SH, Salman. 2017. Swiggy ties up with Indifi technologies to offer loans to restaurants. *Livemint.* October 12. Accessed March 2022. https://www.livemint. com/Companies/giZfHu9aa7PSGBQgNTbtCL/Swiggy-partners-Indifi-to-launch-Capital-Assist-programme.html

Stanley, S. M. 2020. A review of BIS' paper on The Design of Digital Financial Infrastructure: Lessons from India. *Dvara Research.* June 23. Accessed January 2022. https://www.dvara.com/research/blog/2020/06/23/a-review-of-bis-paper-on-the-design-of-digital-financial-infrastructure-lessons-from-india/

Stanley, S. M., Prasad, S., and A. Singh. 2021. *A Primer on Competition in the Digital Economy.* Dvara Research.

Stigler Research Centre. 2019. *Stigler Committee on Digital Platforms, Final Report.* Chicago: Chicago University.

Stiglitz, J. E., and A. Weiss. 1981. "Credit Rationing in Markets with Imperfect Information." *American Economic Review,* 393–410.

Task Force 8 International Financial Architecture. 2020. "POLICY BRIEF BIG-TECH COMPANIES: AN INCLUSIVE AND GLOBAL REGULATORY FRAMEWORK IS NEEDED." https://www.g20-insights.org/wp-content/uploads/2020/11/T20_TF8_PB3.pdf

Task Force 9 International Finance. 2021. "Policy brief THE EMERGENCE OF NEW MONIES AND THE NEED TO PREPARE THE FINANCIAL SYSTEM FOR THE DIGITAL AGE." September. https://www.g20-insights.org/wp-content/uploads/2021/09/TF9-THE_EMERGENCE_OF_NEW_MONIES_AND_THE_NEED_TO_PREPARE_THE_FINANCIAL_SYSTEM_FOR_THE_DIGITAL_AGE.pdf

The Hindu Business Line. 2021. 'Mandatorily participate in TReDS platform for settling bills'. October 29. Accessed March 2022. https://www.thehindu-businessline.com/info-tech/mandatorily-participate-in-treds-platform-for-settling-bills/article37224899.ece

The Tribune. 2018. Rs 500, 10 minutes, and you have access to billion Aadhaar details. January 5. Retrieved March 2022. https://www.tribuneindia.com/news/archive/nation/rs-500-10-minutes-and-you-have-access-to-billion-aadhaar-details-523361

The Tribune. 2021. Top 4 Best Mobile Trading Platforms in India. November 29. Accessed March 2022. https://www.tribuneindia.com/news/brand-connect/top-4-best-mobile-trading-platforms-in-india-343083

Tyagi, Gaurav, and Jai Vardhan. 2020. G-Pay India's profit surges 6.5X to Rs 33 Cr in FY20; 80% revenue comes via reimbursements. *Entrackr.* December 7. Accessed March 2022. https://entrackr.com/2020/12/google-pay-indias-profit-surges-6-5x-to-rs-33-cr-in-fy20/

Velayanikal, Malavika. 2020. Will Swiggy cloud kitchen model transform dining?. *Livemint.* October 4. Accessed March 2022. https://www.livemint.com/news/business-of-life/swiggy-s-cloud-kitchen-model-is-set-to-transform-dining-11601824832719.html

Westermeier, C. 2020. Money is data: The platformization of financial transactions. *Taylor & Francis,* 2047–2063.

Zamil, R., and A. Lawson. 2022. *Gatekeeping the gatekeepers: when big techs and fintechs own banks – benefits, risks and policy options.* Basel: Bank for International Settlements.

Financial Inclusion and SDGs in G20: Accelerating Entrepreneurship and Creating Jobs in Post-Pandemic Economic Recovery

Prativa Shaw

INTRODUCTION

Expansion of Financial Inclusion (FI) in the country through suitable financial products like savings, credit, insurance, payments and remittances helps the most excluded and unbanked individuals and Micro, Small and Medium Enterprises (MSMEs). According to the assessment of the Reserve Bank of India (RBI), FI is successful in terms of improving overall economic growth, and accomplishing a more extensive development agenda. Billions of people have been benefitting solely through an advanced mode of payment that spurs inclusive growth. Through these improved facilities of credit, FI creates more opportunities for women entrepreneurs to enhance their productivity. With the enhancement of accessibility of finance, individual saving and investment habits improve which, in turn, make people more independent, even in a short-run liquidity crisis. In fragmented economies, money and investment are complemented with increasing return of money. This raises desirability to store it and makes it easier to accumulate capital to take opportunities of lumpy investments (McKinnon, 1973), and access to formal savings instruments would enhance the return on money.

FI helps to mobilize domestic resources and create more stability in the financial system as the model supports banks and cooperatives, and micro-finance institutions in extending financial service delivery to unreachable and marginalized societies (UNDP, 2014). The principles for innovative FI provide guidance to foster the safe and sound adoption of innovative, technology-driven, low-cost financial service delivery models. It was estimated that the use of digital technology in delivering financial services has the potential to add up to USD 3.7 trillion to the GDP of emerging economies within a decade (Siddik and Kabiraj, 2020). Over the last decade, significant progress has been achieved. However, the financial inclusion gender gap in developing countries has remained low and unchanged since 2011. Women's contribution to economic growth is not only limited to building businesses but also managing their financial resources. The wider gap in financial inclusion, particularly among women, can be addressed through prioritizing inclusion and harnessing the potential of digital technologies for enhancing efficiency in the financial sector.

In this context, Agenda 2030 has highlighted the inter-linkages between FI and economic growth and recognizes the importance of promoting development-oriented policies for all through access to financial services. Since the inception of Agenda 2030, the G20 leaders have committed to ensuring collective action for the effective implementation of the Sustainable Development Goals (SDGs). The systemic and holistic development approach of the Agenda 2030 on 'Sustainable Development' was acknowledged in the 'G20 Action plan on the 2030 Agenda for Sustainable Development' during the Chinese Presidency in 2016 (G20 Leaders' Communique Hangzhou Summit, 2016).

Under the Seoul development consensus, G20 recognized Financial Inclusion (FI) as one of the main pillars of the global development agenda and

endorsed a concrete 'Financial Inclusion Action Plan' (G20 Leaders' Communique Seoul Summit, 2010). Also, the Saudi Presidency endorsed a 'COVID-19 Response and Recovery in Developing Countries' to build an inclusive and sustainable future for all (Saudi Presidency Communique, 2020). Over the last decade, with the establishment of the Global Partnership for Financial Inclusion (GPFI) by G20 Leaders at the Seoul Summit in 2010, FI has made substantial progress. As per the latest figure (GPFI Action Plan, 2020), around 3.8 billion people had access to formal financial services in 2018 (i.e., equivalent to 70 per cent of all adults) in comparison to the 51 per cent in 2011. This figure is notable. However, there is huge scope to bank the unbanked population in developing countries. Furthermore, there is a question of whether the progress has been made at the required pace with adequate quality or not.

The objective of this chapter is to evaluate the progress of Financial Inclusion in G20 Countries under the mandate of Agenda 2030. It aims to critically evaluate how financial delivery services would facilitate gender equality, and promotes harnessing the potential of the digital payment system. The chapter is divided into six parts, including introductory remarks and a conclusion, with a roadmap to accelerate women-led entrepreneurship to create jobs in post-pandemic economic recovery. The second section examines the impact of the COVID-19 pandemic and the importance of FI, particularly for women and youth. The third section highlights direct and indirect inter-linkages of SDG targets and FI for economic growth. The fourth section assesses the status of FI in G20 countries in terms of access, usage and quality of financial services in the categories of men, women, and youth. The penultimate section evaluates the progress of FI under the national monitoring framework of SDG indicators in India and the impact of key flagship programmes, which are aligned. The final section aims to conclude the analysis and presents a few recommendations for the policy-makers.

COVID-19 AND THE IMPORTANCE OF FINANCIAL INCLUSION

The ongoing COVID-19 pandemic has caused complex and multi-faceted health and socio-economic challenges, especially in developing countries. According to IMF estimates of October 2020, there is a loss of USD 3 trillion from global GDP due to continued deterioration of resources, loss of incomes, the collapse of export revenues, drying up of capital markets, etc., in order to deal with priorities in the health sector (Währungsfonds, 2020). The initial strict preventive measures like lockdown and social distancing have disrupted economic activities, leaving millions of jobless people, migrants, and students hard hit. In 2020, labour markets were also hard hit, particularly young workers and women. As per the UN, 255 million full-time jobs have been lost, which is approximately four times more than what was lost in the financial crisis of 2009 (ILO, 2021). Also, the World Bank has estimated that more than 150 million people have been pushed into poverty and hunger, plunging the world economy into the worst recession since the Great Depression of the 1930s, and putting years of development progress at high risk.

The COVID-19 pandemic threatens to reverse the progress of SDGs made in the last five years. The severe disruption of economic activities in the short run has compounded developmental gaps, particularly in terms of poverty, income and social inequalities, work participation among women, and high youth unemployment in Africa and South Asia. As per the World Bank, a total of 150 million people will be pushed to extreme poverty by 2021, majorly in middle-income countries.

The COVID-19 has deepened pre-existing inequalities; the UN reported 7.9 per cent layoffs at women-led businesses in comparison to the 4 per cent among men-led formal SMEs. Presently, around 1.7 billion adults in the world remain unbanked, especially women from the informal economy in developing countries. The SDG agenda seeks to address multidimensional poverty as many people are facing not only income poverty but also nonmaterial deprivations, such as poor health, lack of education, food insecurity and inadequate living conditions. The absence of financial inclusion for social protection and entrepreneurship would delay escape from multi-dimensional poverty and erode prospects of livelihood generation among women and youth (ADB, 2019).

The livelihoods of women and youth are severely impacted, with severe disadvantages caused due to fragmented social protection systems and lack of access to financial services (UNSGSA, 2020). As per the UN Women estimates, around 47 million more women and girls worldwide have fallen into poverty since the start of COVID-19. Most women in Micro, Small and Medium Enterprises (MSMEs) have closed their businesses in comparison to men (ibid.). To provide liquidity and combat financial crunches, most governments have utilized digital platforms to address the unprecedented situation. Over 200 nations have expanded their social protection system and integrated digital technology for improving payment systems (ibid.). The wider gap in financial inclusion, particularly among women, can be addressed through prioritizing inclusion and harnessing the potential of digital technologies for enhancing efficiency in the financial sector.

Narrowing the gender gap in FI could lead to positive impacts in the economy by increasing saving and consumption rates, lowering financial risks and costs, and facilitating new opportunities (Aportela, 1999). For example, the world has witnessed a remarkable success story of Kenya's M-PESA model, which lifted 2 per cent of the Kenyan population out of poverty (Suri and Jack, 2016). Kenya has made progress in expanding financial services like digital payment from 26 per cent in 2006 to 83 per cent in 2019, resulting in a significant dip in the financially excluded adult population to 11 per cent in 2019, while it was 17 per cent in 2016 (FINACCESS, 2019). Among the beneficiaries, women, the rural poor, and displaced people benefit the most from the use of digital and Fintech technologies as it serves as a gateway toward empowerment. At this juncture, the role of FI is very important to promote sustainable and inclusive growth, and build resilience across developing countries so that no one is left behind.

FINANCIAL INCLUSION AS A KEY ENABLER OF AGENDA 2030

Financial inclusion is a key enabler for a country's development path as it facilitates socially inclusive economic growth (Banwo, 2020) and helps youth make their own economic decision to escape poverty and reduce inequality (UN Youth, 2015). The significance of FI is well recognized in the global development blueprint under SDG Goal 8 on 'Decent Work and Economic Growth' and SDG 9 on 'Build resilient infrastructure, promote sustainable industrialization and foster innovation' with dedicated targets being that of 8.3, 8.10 and 9.3 (UN DESA, 2016).

List of Directly-linked Targets of SDGs on Financial Inclusion

Target 8.3: Promote development-oriented policies that support productive activities, decent job creation, entrepreneurship, creativity and innovation, and encourage the formalization and growth of micro-, small- and medium-sized enterprises, including through access to financial services

Target 8.10: Strengthen the capacity of domestic financial institutions to encourage and expand access to banking, insurance and financial services for all

Target 9.3: Increase the access of small-scale industrial and other enterprises, in particular in developing countries, to financial services, including affordable credit, and their integration into value chains and markets

Source: UN DESA, 2016

These targets directly place emphasis on the strengthening of financial institutions to bridge the gap of financial exclusion, and promote development-oriented policies. Further, they support and measure the access of affordable financial services for decent job creation and entrepreneurship, particularly for MSMEs. SDG targets of 8.3, 8.10 and 9.3 directly dovetail the aspiration of promoting access to financial services and strengthening the domestic institutional capacity to encourage and expand banking, insurance, and financial services for all (UN DESA, 2016).

FI would create a unique opportunity to effectuate local actions to ensure last-mile delivery services. Agenda 2030 does not explicitly encapsulate FI, but it captures the aspiration of the accessibility and availability of financial services. FI is predominantly placed as an enabler of other development goals. These include SDG 1 on eradicating poverty; SDG 2 on ending hunger, achieving food security and promoting sustainable agriculture; SDG 3 on profiting health and well-being; SDG 5 on achieving gender equality and economic empowerment of women; SDG 8 on promoting economic growth and jobs; and SDG 9 on supporting industry, innovation, and infrastructure (UN DESA, 2016).

The SDG goals are interconnected to each other such that they require convergence at all levels to draw impactful results. Localization of the SDGs is an agenda of central importance among policy-makers and countries/nation-states; they are the primary stakeholders to ensure the success of the 2030 Agenda for Sustainable Development. However, the importance of interconnectedness and multidimensionality under FI is periphrastically captured in SDG targets 1.3, 1.4, 2.3, and 3.8 with objectives to improve social protection systems and provide equal rights to economic resources through financial services, including microfinance (UN DESA, 2016).

SDG targets can be achieved only through fulfilling the desired results across multiple goals. For instance, targets 1.3, 1.4, 2.3, 3.8 and 5.a. outline the opportunity to improve national service delivery systems as well as enhance access to basic services. Further, SDG targets 1.4, 2.3 and 3.8 stress equal rights to economic resources and basic services through appropriate technologies and financial services, particularly microfinance. Target 5 captures the gender perspective of equal rights to economic resources for minimizing the financial exclusion gender gap (UN DESA, 2016). These interlinkages of the issues reflect that a silos approach would be insufficient for the success of the SDGs. Generally, government departments and agencies tend to work in silos, whereas the success of SDGs will not be possible until and unless inter-departmental strategies have been adopted.

PROGRESS MADE BY THE G20 COUNTRIES IN FINANCIAL INCLUSION: WOMEN AND YOUTH

The COVID uncertainty has introduced a negative impact on global remittance flows to low and middle-income countries, estimated to fall by 7 per cent to USD 508 billion in 2020 to further decline of 7.5 per cent to USD 470 billion in 2021 (UN 2021). Financial inclusion is the key to mitigating the negative impact of COVID and improving the well-being of society. There is huge scope to help marginalized sections of the society, including women, youth and SMEs.

Over the years, there has been some significant progress in deepening the financial market in developing countries. However, 1.7 billion adults, primarily in rural areas of developing countries, do not have access to formal financial services, and remain unbanked (UN, 2017). Despite the progress made in FI, globally, the gender gap in FI remains at 9 per cent, with 1 billion women financially excluded (World Bank, 2018). Given the socio-economic disparities and limited outreach of the banking sector in developing countries, policymakers need to intervene in the monitoring and evaluation process of banking outreach.

It has been acknowledged by G20 leaders and additional responsibilities have been assigned to GPFI to reflect current circumstances and address the crisis impact, and the post-crisis economic effects have been enlisted. In the Italy G20 Presidency 2021, the GFPI second plenary session was held on June 23–24, 2021, and members discussed the global partnership for FI and prioritized awareness of digital finance and protection from the risk of financial exclusion. Also, members placed emphasis on small-and-medium-sized enterprises and the barriers to accessing finance. The global SME sector is huge, representing 50 per cent of global GDP and about half of the world's employable population (UN, 2021). The severity of the pandemic has been felt by small businesses. Due to limited financial literacy and digital skills, however, the resilience of smaller businesses has been compromised.

The global agenda of reducing poverty and providing access to basic services among the poor will not be achieved without immediate action towards minimizing financial exclusion. At the macro level, FI supports sustainable and inclusive socio-economic growth for all by establishing means to create jobs, supporting SMEs and empowering women and youth. The low presence of women in leadership positions in the financial industry, the regulators, and in the new emerging Fintech sector need to be looked at (Trivelli et al., 2018). As per the latest statistics, less than 2 per cent of Bank CEOs are women, and less than 20 per cent of board member positions are held by women in the banking sector (IMF, 2017).

One of the most important elements in improving the mobility of resources for livelihood stability is access to financing. Smoother financial service delivery leads to improved prospects for self-employment. Youth entrepreneurs often face the challenges of access to capital and start-up funding, access to business development services, and sometimes, age restrictions to operate banking services independently. Furthermore, just 33 per cent of the world's youth are more likely to have a savings account than the adult population. This is mainly because many nations have age limitations for opening and managing savings accounts (UN Youth, 2015). Adults making or receiving digital payments increased from 35 per cent in developing economies in 2014 to 57 per cent in 2021 (Demirgüç-Kunt et al., 2022). Adults in high-income economies make or receive practically all types of digital payments (95 per cent) (ibid.). Borrowing from formal financial institutions among youth is also quite low at 6 per cent (UN Youth, 2015). Therefore, to promote entrepreneurship as a career for youth, we need to provide uninterrupted financial services to young people for sustainable livelihoods. Through FI, transfers of benefits become smooth and it is easy to create better returns on their savings and investment, and opportunities for self-employment. The increasing use of Fintech technology in digital financial services may have improved quality and availability for both providers and end-users.

MONITORING OF FI - KEY INDICATORS ADOPTED BY GPFI

One of the components of the SDG Agenda is to monitor and evaluate the progress of the country's development based on 169 targets. The monitoring and evaluation of SDGs are quite complex, and more than five years have passed but very little progress has been made. To do so, the Inter-Agency and Expert Group on SDG (IAEG-SDGs) has developed a global indicator framework with 231 unique indicators that was adopted by the UN General Assembly on Work of the Statistical Commission pertaining to the 2030 Agenda for Sustainable Development (UNSTATS). The global indicators are divided into three tiers—tier 1 indicators, with internationally established methodology and standards; tier 2 indicators, which are well-developed but data is not available; and tier 3 indicators, with no standard methodology that is being developed. Even after five years, some global indicators are in tier 3 classification, which require internationally established methodologies.

In order to examine the progress of FI, we have adopted G20 Financial Inclusion Indicators from the standard Global Partnership for Financial Inclusion (GPFI) indicators list (GPFI, 2016). These targets are analyzed based on a broad framework of access, usage and quality of financial services. They are comprehensive and follow the criteria of availability, sustainability, and robustness of data. The G20 leaders have formulated some indicators for monitoring FI in G20 member countries. The evolution of the FI indicator framework has been summarized in Table 1 a. GPFI has also developed a framework for FI indicators based on three dimensions and these indicator lists are finalized, but the availability of data at the disaggregated level remains one of the biggest challenges.

Table 2 presents the basic FI indicators for G20 countries for youth and women. In 2014, around 56.6 per cent of youth from developing countries, with age above 15 years had a bank account, while in 2017, these figures improved to 62.8 per cent. Only 48.9 per cent of the youth from developing countries had an active bank account in 2017. There is a huge gap in access to banking services between developed and developing countries for women. In 2017, only 45 per cent of women from developing countries held an active account whereas 86 per cent of those from developed countries had an active bank account (see Table 2).

Table 1. Evolution of Financial Inclusion Indicator Framework in G20

G20 Summits	Action towards FI
Cannes Summit 2011	G20 leaders agreed to the recommendation by the Global Partnership for Financial Inclusion (GPFI) to support global and national financial inclusion data efforts.
Los Cabos 2012	Endorsed the G20 Basic Set of Financial Inclusion Indicators
Russian Presidency	Endorsement of the Basic Set of Financial Inclusion Indicators
St. Petersburg Summit in 2013	Indicators on financial literacy and the quality of financial service provisioning and consumption were endorsed
Chinese G20 Presidency in 2016	New indicators were introduced to measure the use, availability, and quality of digital financial services
Japanese G20 Presidency	New indicators on savings for old age were introduced along with an update of several current indicators to include disaggregated data for various age categories
Source: Author compilation from G20 Summit Declaration of various years	

Table 2. Access to Basic Account in the Financial System

Countries	Account (%)						Active Account (%)					
	Youth (age 15+)		Female		Male		Youth (age 15+)		Female		Male	
	2014	2017	2014	2017	2014	2017	2014	2017	2014	2017	2014	2017
Developed	90.80	92.19	89.98	90.53	91.39	93.51	83.16	88.05	81.11	86.24	84.93	89.44
EU	88.59	90.09	88.27	89.35	88.94	90.90	83.28	85.76	82.70	84.72	83.89	86.85
Australia	98.86	99.52	99.04	99.20	98.67	99.85	97.05	96.64	96.42	97.41	97.72	95.83
Canada	99.10	99.73	99.20	99.85	99.00	99.59	97.60	98.09	96.60	97.21	98.67	99.03
France	96.58	94.00	95.47	91.29	97.79	96.98	88.76	89.66	88.46	87.28	89.07	92.27
Germany	98.76	99.14	99.44	99.20	98.05	99.08	92.78	94.40	92.16	94.13	93.42	94.69
Italy	87.33	93.79	83.16	91.62	91.87	96.14	77.07	90.79	68.39	88.70	86.51	93.07
Japan	96.65	98.24	97.02	98.06	96.24	98.46	92.19	94.15	92.99	93.21	91.31	95.27
Korea, Rep.	94.36	94.85	93.38	94.69	95.39	95.02	85.71	92.85	83.70	93.72	87.83	91.93
Russian Federation	67.38	75.76	70.19	76.13	63.80	75.30	51.47	68.21	53.60	68.67	48.76	67.65
Saudi Arabia	69.41	71.70	61.15	58.17	75.33	80.54	46.29	62.10	32.68	45.55	56.04	72.92

(Continued)

Table 2. (*continued*)

Countries	Account (%)						Active Account (%)					
	Youth (age 15+)		Female		Male		Youth (age 15+)		Female		Male	
	2014	2017	2014	2017	2014	2017	2014	2017	2014	2017	2014	2017
United Kingdom	98.93	96.37	98.65	96.07	99.22	96.67	95.90	93.70	94.64	92.99	97.22	94.45
United States	93.58	93.12	94.80	92.69	92.36	93.57	89.83	90.26	90.98	91.24	88.68	89.26
Developing	**56.56**	**62.81**	**53.27**	**60.03**	**59.84**	**65.63**	**43.70**	**48.90**	**39.68**	**45.40**	**47.75**	**52.46**
Argentina	50.20	48.71	50.85	50.76	49.46	46.47	43.45	42.56	42.96	43.42	44.01	41.62
Brazil	68.12	70.04	64.77	67.51	71.69	72.85	57.28	58.27	52.78	56.91	62.07	59.78
China	78.85	80.23	76.25	76.36	81.37	83.97	66.52	68.20	63.26	64.35	69.67	71.92
India	**53.14**	**79.88**	**43.13**	**76.64**	**62.76**	**83.01**	**29.86**	**41.34**	**19.64**	**34.88**	**39.69**	**47.59**
Indonesia	36.06	48.86	37.46	51.35	34.62	46.25	30.75	34.14	32.25	35.73	29.21	32.47
Mexico	39.14	36.93	38.90	33.29	39.40	41.10	27.91	29.41	25.64	25.12	30.34	34.31
South Africa	70.32	69.22	70.36	69.99	70.27	68.40	57.19	57.04	57.33	55.43	57.04	58.77
Turkey	56.68	68.59	44.46	54.29	69.16	82.99	36.62	60.26	23.56	47.38	49.95	73.24

Source: Global Findex Database, 2021

One of the major challenges for developing countries is to develop quality infrastructure in terms of road, railways, etc, as well as improve digitalization (Gurara et al., 2018), particularly in the area of transportation, digital connectivity, ICT and communication, and market accessibility, which restrain inclusivity and equal growth for all. Infrastructure indicators such as lower telecom density, lower road density, erratic power supply, poor availability of POS terminals, etc., had an adverse impact on banking penetration in developing countries (ibid.). Therefore, there is a need to saturate banking coverage for all and address the limitations of access to credit. Basic infrastructure for banking, like the number of ATMs per 100,000 adults, is quite low for India in comparison to other developing countries in the G20 grouping (see Table 3). In 2017, the total number of branches per 100,000 adults in developing countries was just 15, which was quite low in comparison to developed countries like Italy, Japan, and France. India and Indonesia had the lowest number of people using debit or credit cards in the grouping of developing countries represented within the G20. It may be the case that inadequate and untimely credits, along with procedural hassles from formal institutions, were some of the important reasons for the increased dependency on informal or non-institutional lending agencies.

Less than 30 per cent of the youth receive wages or government transfers into their formal channel of banking. Over the years, there has been no significant improvement in the gender gap in utilizing banking services for smooth transfer of subsidies or wages as shown in Figure 1. In the developing countries, only 22.7 per cent of females were receiving government transfers in 2014, which improved to 26.2 per cent in 2017.

IMPORTANCE OF FINANCIAL INCLUSION AND SDGS IN INDIA

While the banking services are in the nature of public goods, it is essential to provide banking and financial services to the entire population, particularly the underprivileged sections of society. Still, in India, moneylenders are the most frequently used source of loans for middle-class Indian households (RBI, 2017). In the last five decades, some major policy efforts have been made to improve the banking services in India. These actions include nationalization of banks, building robust banking networks of scheduled commercial banks, co-operative and regional rural banks, formulation of self-help groups, permitting BCs/BFs to provide doorstep banking services, etc. As per the World Bank indicators, India had 14.56 commercial bank branches per 100,000 adults in 2018, which is quite low in comparison to other emerging markets economies such as Australia, Russia, Canada, Brazil and Iran.

To deepen the overall financial services coverage, the Reserve Bank of India (RBI) drafted the National Strategy for Financial Inclusion for India 2019-24, under the

Table 3. Access to Basic Infrastructure for FI in G20 Countries

Countries	ATMs per 100,000 adults		Branches per 100,000 adults		Used a debit or credit card to make a purchase in the past year (% age 15+)	
	2014	2017	2014	2017	2014	2017
EU	77.18	76.10	30.53	26.97	66.38	71.79
Australia	164.93	162.01	29.11	29.61	89.52	90.00
Canada	221.20	227.82	23.94	21.48	92.86	95.32
France	108.07		38.00	35.86	81.40	85.13
Germany	123.39		14.55	12.89	82.08	86.74
Italy	92.41	92.40	50.79	44.62	57.86	78.17
Japan	127.49	127.77	33.89	34.03	59.48	68.69
Korea, Rep.	280.97		17.21	15.45	76.37	83.90
Russian Federation	185.32	163.93	37.02	29.22	40.65	45.64
Saudi Arabia	68.65	74.38	8.56	8.54	36.10	48.21
United Kingdom	129.50	128.13			93.24	89.19
United States			32.38	31.46	83.77	85.92
Developing	**61.13**	**63.35**	**14.80**	**15.17**	**28.23**	**28.31**
Argentina	58.84	59.39	13.13	13.42	35.06	31.67
Brazil	117.25	106.78	21.09	19.22	46.60	39.05
China	54.75		8.01		23.61	41.94
India	**17.80**	**22.07**	**12.87**	**14.72**	**11.11**	**12.33**
Indonesia	49.45	55.61	17.92	16.89	8.86	12.28
Mexico	48.83	53.53	14.86	14.13	21.70	16.37
South Africa	65.70	67.93	10.86	10.43	41.90	25.26
Turkey	76.47	78.12	19.64	17.39	37.03	47.55

Source: Global Findex Database, 2021.

aegis of the Financial Inclusion Advisory Committee, which would expand the scope of formal financial services availability, accessibility and affordability for all. Access to appropriate financial instruments creates opportunities for the poor to access mainstream financial services and products, invest in physical assets and education, improve livelihoods, reduce income inequality, and contribute to economic growth (RBI, 2008).

The current initiatives of financial inclusion through the Jan Dhan Yojana have enabled a sound policy framework to expedite the delivery of social safety

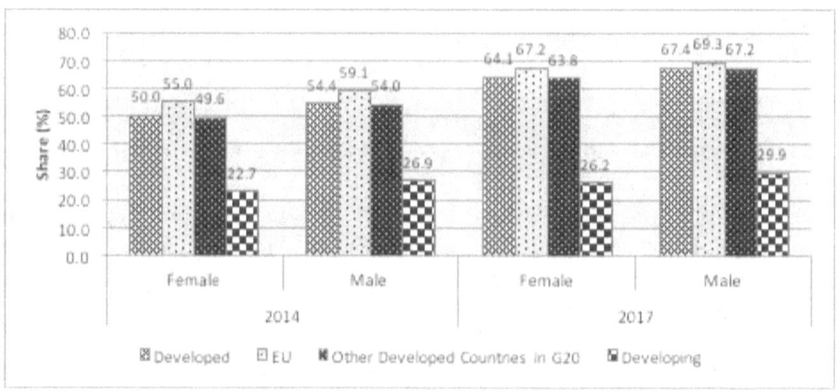

Figure 1. Received wages or government transfers into an account (% age 15+) in the year 2014 and 2017.

Source: Author compilation based on Global Findex database, 2021.

net programmes (NITI Aayog, 2021). To transfer the benefits and subsidies of various social welfare schemes in India, like LPG subsidy, MNREGA payments, old age pension, scholarships, etc., directly into the bank account of the beneficiary, the government has enforced Direct Benefit Transfer (DBT) on a large scale through the JAM Trinity model. This model involves the integration of the Jan Dhan Yojana, Aadhaar-enabled payment system, and mobile technologies that have led to a transformational change in digital profile and financial inclusion.

The underlying principle of flagship programmes such as the Pradhan Mantri Jhan Dhan Yojana (PMJDY), Ayushman Bharat (National Health Protection Scheme) and Pradhan Mantri MUDRA Yojana (PMMY) aligns with the spirit of SDGs and encourages a wholesome approach for development (Saha, 2019). PMJDY is the world's largest financial inclusion programme and one of the remarkable examples of inclusive development efforts (Sridhar, 2021). By leveraging PMJDY through Aadhaar-enabled services (biometric identity system) and Fintech technology, the total number of beneficiaries of PMJDY was 42.89 crore as of August 4, 2021 (PMJDY official website). Out of this, 23.76 crores were rural-urban female beneficiaries (ibid.). Pradhan Mantri MUDRA Yojana (PMMY) is another programme to bring financial support services to the bottom of the pyramid. In 2015, this programme was launched for providing loans of up to INR 10 lakh to non-cooperative and non-farm small and micro-enterprises. These three programmes would be helpful in achieving the underlying commitment towards 'leaving no one behind' in financial inclusion.

Financial Inclusion Indicators under SDG National Monitoring Framework in India

To monitor and evaluate SDGs, the UN has established 231 global indicators, out of which many indicators are not well-established, as their methodologies and availability of data are uncertain. In the case of India, the National Indicator framework by the Ministry of Statistics and Programme Implementation has 308 indicators, out of which some are directly and indirectly linked with FI. A snapshot of the process of the key targets and indicators in the last five years are listed in Table 4.

There is a direct indicator related to FI that has been finalized under the National Indicator Framework (NIF) 8.10, which is yet to be compiled. The two NIF indicators 8.10.3 and 8.10.4 capture the capacity of financial institutions in terms of infrastructure availability, and the number of banking outlets and ATMs, respectively. Table 4 summarizes the status of directly and indirectly linked targets and indicators of SDGs addressing FI in India. The total number of banking outlets in India per 1,00,000 population is 98.8 as of 2019-20.

Table 4. Selected Directly linked Targets and Indicators of SDGs addressing Financial Inclusion in India

Directly linked SDG Target	NIF 3.0 as of 31 March 2021	NIF 3.0 Latest Data
8.3 Promote development-oriented policies that support productive activities, decent job creation, entrepreneurship, creativity and innovation, and encourage the formalization and growth of micro-, small- and medium-sized enterprises, through **access to financial services**	8.3.3: Outstanding Credit to MSME, (in Rs. crore)	2015-16—12,16007.09 2018-19—15,10,650.54 2019-20—16,13,582.17
	8.3.4: Number of MSME units registered under the online Udyog Aadhaar registration	2016-17—23,73,195 2019-20—25,64,468
8.10: Strengthen the **capacity of domestic financial institutions to encourage and expand access to banking, insurance and financial services for all** **Global Indicators** 8.10.1 (a) Number of commercial bank branches per 100,000 adults and (b) number of automated teller machines (ATMs) per 100,000 adults	8.10.1: Indicator on financial inclusion	Under compilation
	8.10.2: Number of accounts (including deposit and credit accounts) of scheduled commercial banks per 1,000 population (similar to 1.4.5)	2015-16—1408 2019-20—1744
	8.10.3: Number of banking outlets per 1,00,000 population	2015-16—59.9 2019-20—98.8
	8.10.4: Automated Teller Machines (ATMs) per 1,00,000 population	2015-16—16.5 2019-20—17.5

(Continued)

9.3: Increase **the access of small-scale industrial and other enterprises**, particularly in developing countries, to **financial services**, including affordable credit, and their integration into value chains and markets **Global Indicators** 9.3.2 Proportion of small-scale industries with a loan or line of credit	9.3.2: Percentage of credit flow to MSME as a percentage of Total Adjusted Net Bank Credit	2015-16—18.18 2019-20—16.39
Indirectly Linked SDG Target		
1.3 Implement nationally appropriate social protection systems and measures for all, including floors, and, by 2030, achieve substantial coverage of the poor and the vulnerable	1.3.1: Percentage of households with any usual member covered by a health scheme or health insurance	2015-16—28.70
	1.3.4: Number of Self Help Groups (SHGs) provided bank credit linkage (in lakhs)	2015-16—18.32 2016-17—18.98 2017-18—22.61 2018-19—26.98 2019-20—31.46
2.3: By 2030, **double the agricultural productivity** and incomes of small scale food producers, in particular women, indigenous peoples, family farmers, pastoralists and fishers, including **through** secure and equal access to land, other productive resources and inputs, knowledge, **financial services,** markets and opportunities for value addition and non-farm employment	2.3.3 Ratio of institutional credit of agriculture to the agriculture output	2015-16—0.77 2016-17—0.54 2017-18—0.57

(Continued)

5.a: **Undertake reforms to give women equal rights to economic resources,** as well as access to ownership and control over land and other forms of property, **financial services,** inheritance and natural resources, in accordance with national laws	5.a.5: Exclusive women SHGs in Bank - linked SHGs, (in percentage)	2015-16—88.92 2016-17—90.41 2017-18—91.77 2018-19—87.66 2019-20—91.67
	5.a.6: Percentage of adults having an account at a formal financial institution	Indicator is under compilation
	5.a.7: Percentage of women having an account at a formal financial institution	Indicator is under compilation
Source: Author compilation based on MOSPI Sustainable Development Goals National Indicator Framework Progress Report 2021 and UN Global Indicators		

CONCLUSION

For the post-pandemic economic recovery, it is important to focus on expanding the entrepreneurial base of the country so that more jobs can be created for all, especially for women, girls, and vulnerable sections of the society. The looming effects of the mutating COVID-19 virus are causing many challenges to trade and businesses, and as a result, managing the flow of liquidity in the economy is becoming a major challenge for policy-makers. Thus, G20, being the largest cooperation forum, should aim to improve access to finance, which is one of the critical barriers to growth for the informal economy as well as women empowerment.

The average use of formal payment mode by developing countries is quite low in comparison to developed countries of the G20. For 2014 and 2017, only 28 per cent of developing countries used debit/credit cards to make purchases, while except for Russia and Saudi Arabia, other developed countries of the G20 used debit/credit cards in the range of 70–95 per cent in 2017 (See Table 3). Access to basic infrastructures such as ATMs per 100,000 adults in developing countries, particularly for India and South Africa, was lowest at 22 and 10 in 2017, respectively. After the COVID-19 pandemic, dependency on formal banking has significantly increased, but developing countries are still struggling with basic issues of access, equity, and quality of financial services.

For the post-pandemic recovery plan, the G20 members should adopt a composite development strategy to minimize exclusion and provide equal access and opportunities to all, particularly women and youth. The wider gap in financial inclusion, particularly among women, can be addressed through prioritizing inclusion and harnessing the potential of digital technologies for enhancing efficiency in the financial sector. The use of digital technologies and innovative business models can be a game-changer for SME financing and start-up funding.

It is recommended that the G20 should adopt a gender-sensitive approach to digital payment systems in order to reduce cost, and enhance credit and loans to promote financial inclusion, decent job creation and entrepreneurship in developing countries. Financial inclusion should lead to the formalization of the informal economy and the creation of more decent jobs. G20 leaders must ensure access to digital infrastructure for women, youth and SMEs in national plans, particularly for those countries with the most unbanked populations.

Low internet penetration in Africa and low broadband connection in rural areas in South Asia pose significant challenges for financial inclusion. The G20 should encourage investment in digital infrastructure, and strengthen the ecosystem of digital banking, e-commerce platforms for small producers and enhance the infrastructure for secure digital payment systems in less developed regions of Africa and South Asia.

Policy-makers should take appropriate risk-based regulatory approaches that would support responsible innovation in the financial sector. There should be robust, trustworthy, and comprehensive Fintech strategies for inclusion. Also, it is essential to ensure that participation in the digital economy is safe and secure from any financial frauds like money laundering, terror financing, and other illicit financial abuse. However, there is scope to strengthen this mechanism further and foster affordable financial services that respond to customers' needs in terms of both quality and range.

REFERENCES

ADB. 2019. "Strategy 2030 Operational Plan For Priority 1 Addressing Remaining Poverty And Reducing Inequalities, 2019–2024."

Aportela, Fernando. 1999. "Effects of financial access on savings by low-income people." December.

Banwo, A. O. 2020. "Financial Inclusion and Entrepreneurship as Drivers of Socially Inclusive Economic Growth: Lessons from China." *Jalingo Journal of Social and Management Sciences* 2 (4).

Demirgüç-Kunt, A., Klapper, L., Singer, D., and Ansar, S. 2022. The Global Findex Database 2021: Financial inclusion, digital payments, and resilience in the age of COVID-19.

FINACCESS. 2019. FinAccess Household Survey: Access, Usage, Quality and Impact. Central Bank of Kenya, KNBS, fsd Kenya.

G20. 2016. China Presidency Declaration. "G20 Action Plan on the 2030 Agenda for Sustainable Development." Summit Declaration China 2016.

G20. 2016. "G20 Leaders' Communique Hangzhou Summit." Hangzhou.

G20. 2020. "G20 Leaders' Communique." Saudi Arabia Riyadh Summit.

GPFI. 2016. "G20 Financial Inclusion Indicator."

GPFI. (October, 2020). "G20 2020 Financial Inclusion Action Plan". Global Partnership for Financial Inclusion.

Gurara, D., Klyuev, V., Mwase, N., and A. F. Presbitero, A. F. 2018. "Trends and challenges in infrastructure investment in developing countries." *International Development Policy | Revue internationale de politique de développement* 10.1.

IMF. 2017. "Chart of the week: Banking on women-A case for more." IMF Blog.

International Labour Organization. 2021. "ILO Monitor: COVID-19 and the World of Work. Updated estimates and analysis." 7th edition . International Labour Organization.

McKinnon, R. I. 1973. "On securing a common monetary policy in Europe." *PSL Quarterly Review* 26 (104).

NITI Aayog. 2021. "Reforms in Urban Planning Capacity in India-Final Report."

OECD and UNDP. 2019. "G20 contribution to the 2030 Agenda Progress and Way Forward." OECD and UNDP Publication.

UNSTATS. Statistics Division. Department of Economic and Social Affairs. United Nations. https://unstats.un.org/sdgs/indicators/indicators-list/.

Ratha, D. K., De, S., Kim, E. J., Plaza, S., Seshan, G. K., and N. D. Yameogo. 2020. *COVID-19 crisis through a migration lens. Migration and Development Brief,* 32.

RBI. 2008. *Financial Inclusion Chapter 7.* available at https://rbidocs.rbi.org.in/rdocs/Publications/PDFs/86734.pdf

RBI. 2017. *Report of the Household Finance Committee.* available at https://rbidocs.rbi.org.in/rdocs/PublicationReport/Pdfs/HFCRA28D0415E2144A009112DD314ECF5C07.PDF

Sachs, J., Schmidt-Traub, G., Kroll, C., Lafortune, G., Fuller, G., and F. Woelm. 2020. "Sustainable development report 2020. The Sustainable Development Goals and Covid-19." 1-99.

Siddik, M. N. A., and Kabiraj, S. 2020. "Digital finance for financial inclusion and inclusive growth." In *Digital Transformation in Business and Society* (pp. 155–168). Palgrave Macmillan, Cham.

Sridhar. G. Naga. 2021. Financial Inclusion. The Inclusivity Push: PMJDY adds 1.3 crore beneficiaries in H1 of FY22. *BusinessLine*. November 22. Available at https://www.thehindubusinessline.com/money-and-banking/pmjdy-adds-13-crore-beneficiaries-in-h1-of-fy22/article37613062.ece

Suri, T., and W. Jack. 2016. "The long-run poverty and gender impacts of mobile money." *Science* 354 (6317), 1288–1292.

Trivelli, C., Villanueva, C., Marincioni, M., Pels, J., Sachetti, F. C., Robino, C., Walbey, H., Martinez, L., and M. Magnelli. 2018. "Financial Inclusion for Women: A Way Forward." *Gender Economic Equity: An Imperative for the G20*, 88.

UN DESA, 2016. *Transforming our world: The 2030 agenda for sustainable development.*

UN Youth. 2015. "Office of Secretary General's Envoy on Youth, #YouthStats."

UNDP. 2014. "Mobilization of Financial Resources and Their Effective use for Sustainable Development. Special high-level meeting of ECOSOC with the World Bank, IMF, WTO and UNCTAD." New York, April 14-15.

United Nation 2017. *Financing for Development: Progress and Prospects 2017. Inter-agency Task Force on Financing for Development.*

United Nations. 2021. *MSMEs: Key to an inclusive and sustainable recovery.*

UNSGSA. 2020. *Annual report of the Secretary-General September 2020. Financial Inclusion: Beyond Access and Usage to Quality.*

UNSGSA. 2021. *High-Level Political Forum on Sustainable Development Report to the Secretary General, Progress towards the sustainable Development Goals.*

Währungsfonds, I. 2020. *World Economic Outlook, October 2020: a long and difficult ascent.*

World Bank. 2018. "Financial Inclusion Overview – Financial Inclusion is a key enabler to reducing poverty and boosting prosperity."

World Bank. 2020a. "COVID-19 To Plunge Global Economy Into Worst Recession Since World War II." June 8.

World Bank. 2020b. "COVID-19: Remittance Flows to Shrink 14 % by 2021. Press Release." October 29.

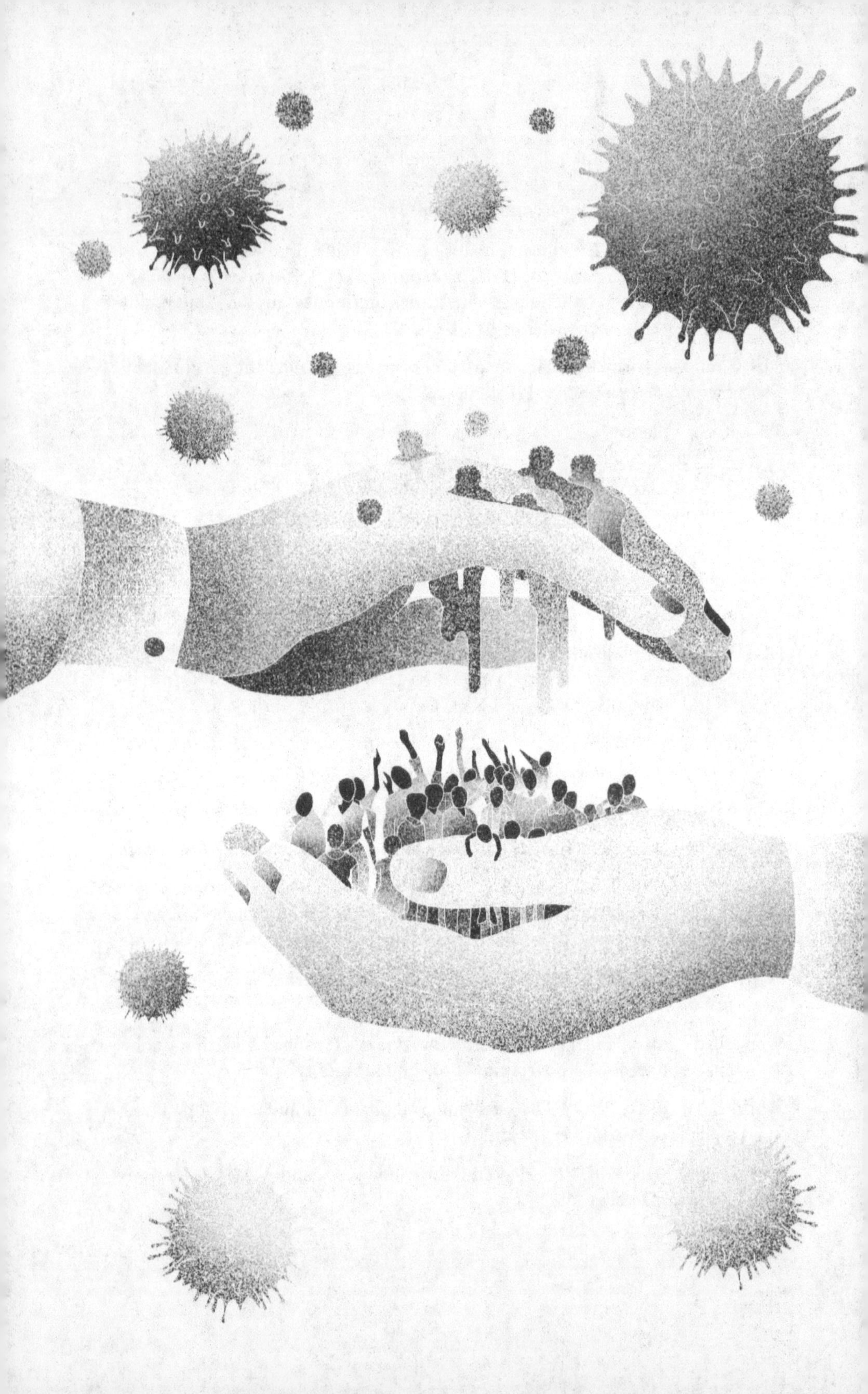

G20 and Social Security in Times
of Rising Inequalities

Aditi Anand and Anirban Bhattacharya

INTRODUCTION

G20 brings an opportunity for world leaders from major economies to come together to assess, deliberate and decide upon a way forward that promotes equitable developmental growth across the globe.

With digitalization, globalization, demographic transitions, and the changing nature of work, there has been an emerging need for reform to keep up with the evolving economic landscape. The G20 Ministerial Declaration of 2017, 'Towards an Inclusive Future: Shaping the World of Work,' committed to 'shaping the future of work by harnessing opportunities of structural change for new and better jobs and reducing risks through a focus on policies for skills development, effective social protection for all, and job quality' and identified the need to respond to 'gaps in social protection resulting in part from the rise in non-standard forms of employment[1] and the growing platform economy' (G20 Labour and Employment Ministers Meeting, 2017).

The COVID-19 pandemic forced the world to reckon with these gaps as those involved in non-standard forms of employment were forced to bear an unequal burden of the economic impact due to forced prolonged lockdown, subsequent losses in livelihood and limited or no access to social protection measures.

The 2020 Riyadh Summit Leaders' Declaration reiterated the support for 'comprehensive, robust, and adaptive social protection for all, including those in the informal economy' (Riyadh Summit, 2020), but critics observed that the declaration didn't attempt to go beyond general appeals of 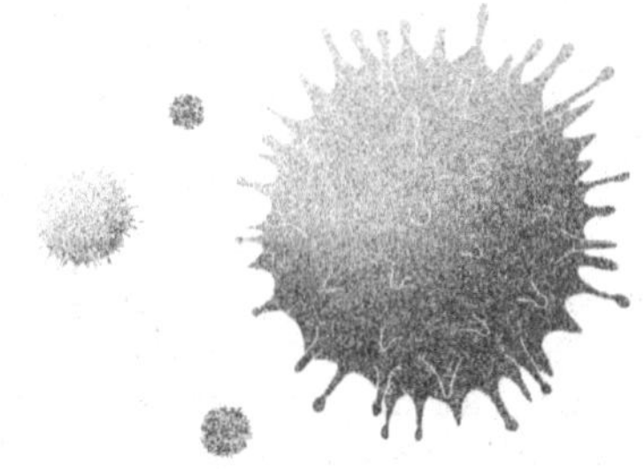

---

[1] As per International Labour Organization, 'non-standard forms of employment' include temporary employment; part-time and on-call work; temporary agency work and other multi-party employment relationships; as well as disguised employment and dependent self-employment including work from home. (https://www.ilo.org/global/topics/non-standard-employment/lang--en/index.htm)

global cooperation to offer any breakthrough announcements of support for developing countries (Kirton, 2020), where majority of the workforce is part of the informal economy.

Through the G20 Ministerial Declaration, 'G20 Policy Principles to ensure access to adequate social protection for all in a changing world of work' addressed the need to have social protection floors, especially recognizing the negative impact of the pandemic on vulnerable communities and informal economy (G20 Labour and Employment Ministers' Declaration, 2021). The policy principles also document how nations can strengthen social protection floors through engagement of different stakeholders but stops short of the G20's own role in facilitating this (ibid.).

Through its leaders, as per their own claim, G20 directly impacts 60 per cent of the global population and 80 per cent of the global GDP (McBride, Siripurapu and Berman, 2022). While representation from the global south within these numbers is disproportionately low, actions by the G20 have significant impacts in the region which is why it is important for the forum to come together to push for social protection and sustainable equitable growth globally.

Using the case of India, this paper attempts to showcase how the existing need for social protection has become urgent in the post-pandemic world.

COVID-19, G20 AND SOCIAL PROTECTION MEASURES

The pandemic served as a pressing reminder for the world about the need for closing coverage and adequacy gaps of social protection schemes. The G20 countries responded to the urgent need to expand, innovate and extend their social protection measures in varying degrees. This they did by deploying a range of means.

There was widespread use of sickness benefits, paid sick leave and extended special leaves in several countries. Several of the G20 countries substantially expanded or introduced new sick leave policies to respond to the crisis. South Korea, for instance used the 2015 Epidemic Act to extend paid sick leave to those hospitalized/quarantined while the US introduced two weeks of reimbursable mandatory sick pay for workers with symptoms. There were also attempts to expand the scope of such benefits like in the UK where gig workers were also brought under its purview, and in France and Australia where the self-employed were also counted in. In France paid special leave was extended to as long as schools and child care services stayed shut. Countries like France and Germany paid part salary and mostly the countries tried to take the burden off the employers by covering their contribution under social insurance (Saudi Arabia's G20 Presidency, 2020).

While in some instances there were explicit orders to ban dismissals and re-trenchments (Saudi Arabia's G20 Presidency, 2020) like in Argentina and Turkey, one crucial means used in many of the advanced G20 countries was job retention schemes to contain mass layoffs and protect incomes. Such schemes provide income security to workers who are at risk of losing their jobs or who are effectively unemployed. While some of the G20 economies (like Brazil, France, Germany Italy, Spain and Turkey) had pre-existing job retention schemes that could be speedily calibrated to deal with the pandemic, others like Australia and Canada introduced them in the face of the crisis. The countries with more preparedness in this regard were the ones that could avoid a surge in unemployment in the periods of lockdown.

In Germany, for example, a company could register short-time work if at least 10 per cent of its workers had their working hours cut by more than 10 per cent (ILO, 2020). This kept the workers on the payroll. Employers in Argentina, another member of the G20 from the global south, were eligible for a wage subsidy through the social security authority as long as they guaranteed that they would avoid retrenchment. Many of these retention schemes were administered and financed through the social security institutions of the concerned countries. Countries with robust social security institutions were able to intervene more effectively. Additional resources were allocated by several governments to support such interventions.

The other major arm in the hands of several countries was improving access to and coverage of unemployment benefits. While some of them extended such benefits, some even increased their levels. Such measures were aimed at providing much needed income support during the periods of lockdown. France (ILO, 2020), for instance, extended the duration of receipt of such assistance and relaxed the required criteria of qualification till the end of the lockdown to allow more to come under its purview. Considering workers beyond the pale of formal employment and those who are self employed get excluded, some countries like China and the US extended it to cover the self employed. Countries like Russia, Australia and others temporarily extended the benefit levels while Argentina and Italy took steps towards bringing the informal workers under its purview (Saudi Arabia's G20 Presidency, 2020).

Finally there were varying degrees of income support. Some involved cash transfers to targeted groups, while there were also instances of universal and unconditional basic income transfers. Particularly to ensure support for the informal workers that generally get excluded from social protection schemes, countries also adopted direct emergency cash transfer schemes. While some announced universal or unconditional cash transfers (or basic incomes) like Japan and South Korea, others like the US expanded their targeted measure to an extent that they covered nearly 90 per cent of the population (Saudi Arabia's G20 Presidency, 2020).

Apart from targeted (and inadequate) cash transfers and food grains, almost none of the measures described above were considered in India despite being far more vulnerable to the economic shock of the pandemic wherein the women and the other marginalized sections in the workforce were worst hit. One of the crucial factors behind this vulnerability of course is the fact that more than 90 per cent of the workforce in India are informal while in much of Europe and Americas, this proportion is under 20 per cent (International Labour Office, 2018). So, for instance, the March 2020 MHA order that issued guidelines for employers to pay their employees during the lockdown remained on paper for all practical purposes. 'The absence of any mechanisms for enforcement, monitoring or oversight meant that there was hardly any compliance with the order' said a study that found nearly 90 per cent of casual workers did not receive any wages during the period of the lockdown (SWAN, 2021).

With the overwhelming majority of the workers in India being outside the pale of social protection as workers, it was necessary that we find other means to support them. But apart from the Pradhan Mantri Garib Kalyan Yojana that was announced to provide additional food subsidies to the poor (extendable every six months), there were no substantive measures taken by the government. This showed in the measure of food intake as well as the dropouts in schools. The following section outlines the schemes that exist in the name of social security in India and their inadequacy is palpable even in normal circumstances, leave aside during a humanitarian crisis. An instance is of course the 200 rupees a month pension to the elderly. While there are some insurance-based schemes, but these are voluntary measures, and hence it is unlikely that the poorest and most vulnerable to exogenous shocks will be able to apply for these or even be aware of them. The tax based welfare boards do not provide pension, death and disability benefits, maternity benefits or any such key benefits and hence cannot be considered social protection measures. While there are a few targeted cash transfers, for example for maternity benefit and the PM KISAN that gives up to 500 rupees a month, the government refused to give basic income transfers of the kind witnessed even in better off countries and in fact derided such measures as 'helicopter money' that harms the economy.

While the world recognized the importance of social security in these trying times, India witnessed further dilution of labour laws. The G20 in fact recognized that the economic upswings in the aftermath of the viral waves are unlikely to undo the damage inflicted by the lockdowns and the economic recession because income losses suffered during such downturns become entrenched (G20 Labour and Employment Ministers' Declaration, 2021). As such it spoke of extending the temporary support mechanisms taken during the pandemic, but as a group it has not made any financial commitments so as to support in the endeavour.

It does however cite country-specific efforts that were able to extend social protection increasing their fiscal space through taxation. It is essential that developing economies fathom ways of expanding their fiscal space so as to be able to close the financing gaps that a robust social security network would entail. One such measure is taxing the super rich. We have seen several comparable countries taking steps towards it. For instance, in Argentina, about 80 per cent of the 12,000 odd millionaires whose assets exceed USD 2.1 million paid a one-off wealth tax raising more than USD 2.3 billion (AFP, 2021). The tax, called solidarity contribution, amounting to 0.5 per cent of GDP raised resources to pay for medical supplies and relief for small businesses battered by the pandemic in Argentina. In Bolivia tax collection from the Wealth Tax on the Super Rich Exceeded USD 32 million in 2021 from 203 millionaires with assets over USD 4.3 million. Bolivian President Luis Arce said that the new tax is part of the 'dismantling of neoliberalism to resume the Productive Community Social-Economic Model to get out of the crisis' (MercoPress, 2021). Even in Columbia a proposal has been made by the government to tax the rich that can raise more than USD 11.5 billion annually to fund anti-poverty efforts, free public university and other social welfare programmes (Janetsky, 2022). But none of that has been considered in India despite the fact that a minimal tax on the super rich could generate enough resources to ensure universal social and economic rights for all.

PRE-PANDEMIC EMPLOYMENT AND INCOME STATUS

Until 2019, India was being touted as the fastest growing large economy despite having an estimated 81 per cent (ILO, 2018) of its workforce employed in the informal sector. In the year leading up to the pandemic, the Indian economy had already started witnessing a significant slowdown (Kishore, 2020), putting most of the workforce at increasing risk of livelihood loss in the absence of robust social protection measures.

Trends in working age (taken as age 25 years and above[2]) and employment growth between 2011–12 and 2017–18 show that while the working age population grew by 115.5 million, the labour force grew only by 7.7 million and the workforce, in fact, shrank by 11.3 million. The rate of unemployment went up from 2.2 percent to 6.1 per cent in this period, with the number of unemployed increasing to 19 million (Nath and Basole, 2020).

---

[2] Not taken as the usual 15 years to exclude those for whom enrollment in education institutions could be a reason for withdrawal from the labour force

Amongst these, the rate of employment growth among rural women was found to be negative, indicating that the absolute fall in the aggregate levels was significantly driven by them (ibid.). Much of the decline in the number of female workers engaged in subsidiary activities was in the agricultural sector, followed by manufacturing and then construction (ibid.). Thus, it was observed that instead of enabling women to pursue productive jobs, the Indian economy was effectively pushing women out of the labour force.

The pre-pandemic figures of unemployment among the youth also reveal a grim picture—with 33 per cent of educated young males and 42 per cent of educated young females being found as unemployed (ibid.).

The labour force participation rate in India (for all ages) stood at 37.5 per cent in 2018–19, of which 52 per cent were self-employed and nearly a quarter were engaged as casual workers (Periodic Labour Force Survey, July 2018–June 2019, 2020). Further, over 68 per cent of those employed in the non-agricultural sector were engaged in informal employment. There was also a high degree of informalization in formal employment, with 70 per cent of regular wage/salaried (RWS) workers having no written job contract, 54 per cent not eligible for paid leave, and 52 per cent not eligible for any social security benefits (ibid.).

There is also a direct correlation in India between socially excluded communities and those in informal or non-standard forms of unemployment. These forms of employment are characterized by inadequate earnings, low productivity and difficult conditions of work that undermine workers' fundamental rights.

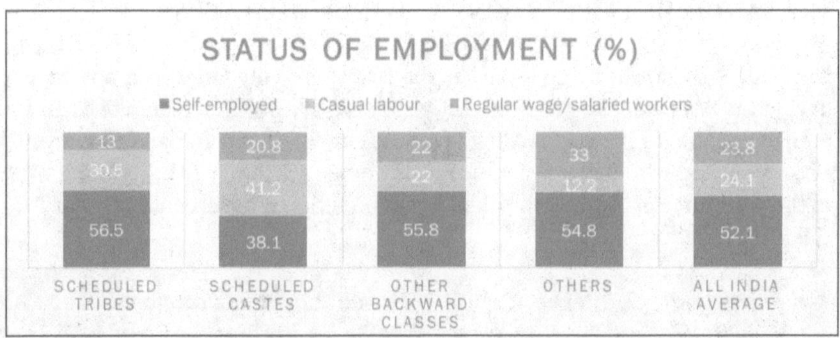

Figure 1.

Source: Periodic Labour Force Survey (PLFS), 2018-19

The vulnerable livelihood status of such communities is reflected in their overwhelming presence in informal sector (Figure 1) 87 per cent of Scheduled Tribes (ST), 79 per cent of Scheduled Castes (SC) and 78 per cent of Other Backward

Classes (OBC), are either casual workers or self-employed (ibid.). Estimates from 2016 document Muslims as the religious group to have the lowest labour force participation rate and only 27 per cent in RWS work (Employment and Unemployment Situation Among Major Religious Groups in India, 2016). In the context of these communities, 'self-employed' refers to small-scale farming, poultry, livestock, selling forest produce, street vendors and other similarly informal means which also retain them within an existence with no savings in most cases.

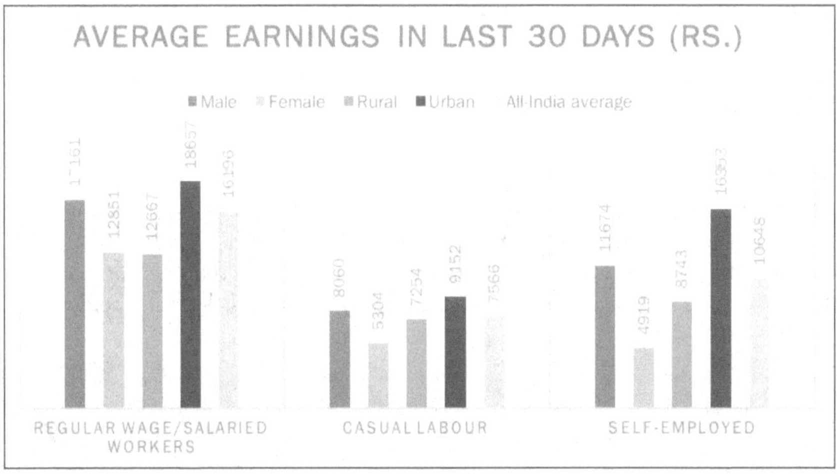

Figure 2.

Source: Periodic Labour Force Survey (PLFS) 2018-19

A stark disparity is visible (Figure 2) in the earnings of RWS workers vis-à-vis those who are self-employed or engaged as casual labour. However, even within these employment categories, there is a clear gender and rural/urban divide, with men and urban workers earning significantly higher than women and rural workers, respectively, employed in the same category.

UNEQUAL IMPACT OF THE PANDEMIC

At the start of 2020, when the reality of the COVID-19 pandemic was still emerging, and all nations started enforcing lockdowns, the coronavirus was frequently touted as the 'great equalizer'—referring that it impacts all equitably. It soon became clear though, that this could not be further from the truth. 

In India, the abrupt lockdown and its stringent guidelines that brought all economic activity to a halt resulted not only in large scale economic distress but also exasperated vulnerabilities of those subsisting on daily earnings without any savings, triggering unemployment, hunger, distress migration and untold hardship in its wake (Ray and Subramanian, 2020).

Sectors such as agriculture, manufacturing, construction, trade, hotels and restaurants, which collectively employ nearly 80 percent of India's workforce—85 per cent of those with secondary education and below—were the most vulnerable to the effects of the pandemic and lockdown (Kapoor, 2020). Also, since these sectors were unable to move work online, a widening inequality emerged in the labour market between those without stable employment or social protection and the hardest hit, and the small proportion of those with regular formal jobs and the ability to work remotely (ibid.).

While unemployment increased threefold to 23 per cent in April-May 2020 in comparison to the same time period in 2019 (Kapoor, 2020), the mass exodus of migrant workers amid strict lockdowns turned the health crisis into a humanitarian one, with hundreds dying due to reasons ranging from starvation, suicide, exhaustion, road and rail accidents, police brutality and denial of timely medical care.

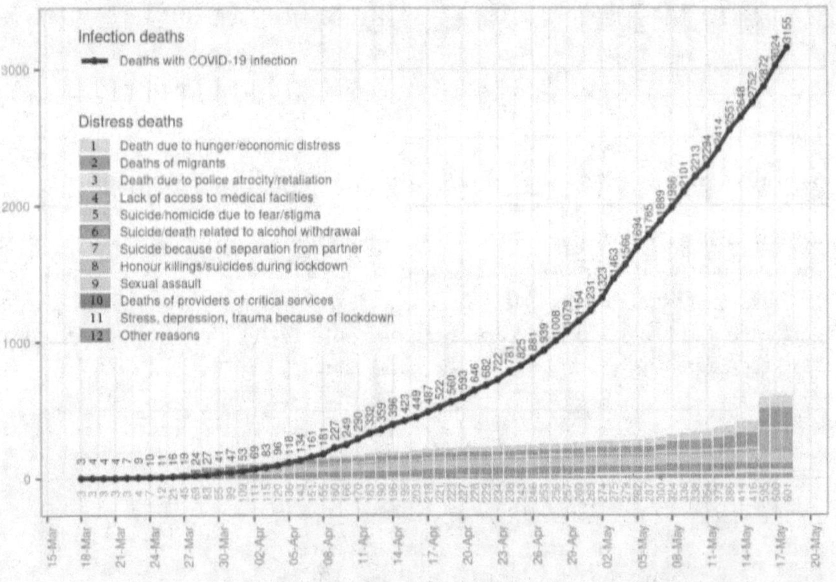

Source: http://coronapolicyimpact.org, last accessed on 27 May 2020

Figure 3. Deaths from COVID-19 and from distress related to containment policies (March 15 to May 18, 2020)

Source: Ghosh, "A critique of the Indian government's response to the COVID-19 pandemic," 2020.

While the immediate impact of the pandemic was harsher on urban India—with 48 per cent of the urban workforce having lost employment as compared to 39 per cent of the rural workforce—the recovery in urban areas has been sharper than that in rural areas, with 32 per cent of the urban workforce able to return to work after having lost employment compared to 25 per cent in rural areas (Basole et al., 2021). A significant increase was also observed in the poverty rate—with a 15 per cent increase in rural areas and nearly 20 per cent increase in urban areas (ibid.).

There is also an extremely visible gendered impact of the pandemic where, even after accounting for social, demographic, and labour market differences, women were found seven times more likely to lose employment during the lockdown relative to men and, upon having lost employment, eleven times more likely to not return to work post lockdown (ibid.).

Amid these, the wealth of billionaires in India increased by 35 per cent during the lockdown (The Inequality Virus, 2021). The increase in wealth of the top 11 billionaires during the pandemic was so high that it could sustain the costs of running India's health ministry or the rural employment guarantee programme for the next 10 years (ibid.).

SOCIAL PROTECTION ARCHITECTURE IN INDIA

In India, only an organized unit—primarily those establishments which are covered by the Factories Act, 1948, the Shops and Commercial Establishments Acts of State Governments, the Industrial Employment Standing Orders Act, 1946 etc.—is covered under the Employees' Provident Fund Organization and the Employee State Insurance Corporation. The vast majority of workers in the non-standard forms of employment and informal economy don't have access to these and have limited access to other social protection measures which directly accentuates the socio-economic crisis caused by the pandemic.

In the year since the pandemic started, nearly 66 per cent of respective respondents reported reduced consumption of food (The Wire Staff, 2020), 62 per cent households reported discontinuing children's school education (Save the Children-India, 2020), and monthly unemployment rates, as stated in the previous section, have soared high.

There has been a standing consciousness that access to social protection schemes and entitlements of food, education, health, and livelihood are the only means to break out of a vicious poverty cycle that impacts generations. While the government has initiated measures of social insurance and assistance since the pandemic, and already had such mechanisms in place before the crisis struck, the coverage and impact of these has been far from adequate.

Social Insurance Measures

National Social Assistance Programme (NSAP)

The NSAP began with a pension for the destitute elderly under the National Old Age Pension Scheme but was revised in 2008 to include all elderly below the poverty line (BPL). Covering the entire BPL population above 65-years-old, the non-contributory pension scheme aimed to extend financial assistance to the elderly poor having little or no regular means of subsistence.[3]

However, for the past 15 years, the amount of the pension has been fixed at a meagre Rs 200[4] per month—which has effectively resulted in erosion of the real value of this pension. Additionally, there is also criticism around the methodology used to identify the beneficiaries and the claim that it has resulted in significant errors of inclusion and exclusion among the estimated 28 million beneficiaries (Mehrotra, 2016).

Following the 2008 financial crisis and the fiscal stimulus put out by the central government, the scheme was expanded to support BPL widows above the age of 40 years with the same amount of Rs 200 per month (Government of India, 2014). At the same time, a pension of Rs 200 was also introduced for persons with disabilities of 80 per cent or above or multiple disabilities of 40 per cent each or higher belonging to the BPL category between the ages of 18 to 79 years (ibid.).

Even though these are pensions, these are not connected to a person's earlier work status as a worker in the informal sector. However, considering that all these pensions cater to the BPL population, the assumption is that the beneficiaries were, in fact, informal sector workers.

Public Insurance Programmes

Three sets of insurance programmes targeting the unorganized sectors and the economically vulnerable governed by the National Social Security Board have been running for over a decade:

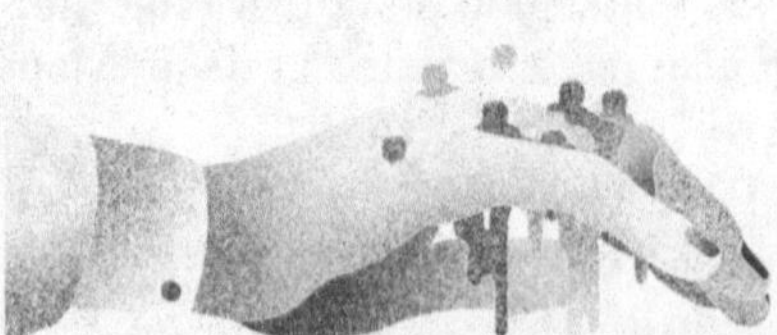

- Janashree Bima Yojana is a social insurance scheme started by the central government in 2000 to provide unorganized workers between the ages of 18–60 years from 24 approved occupation groups three defined covers in case of natural death, death or total disability due to accident and

---

[3] The beneficiary has not contributed any premium over his or her lifetime.
[4] 2.67 USD, as per exchange rate on Oct. 15, 2021

partial disability. The premium for these benefits is Rs 200 per beneficiary, of which 50 per cent is contributed by the central government from its Social Security Fund, and 50 per cent by the beneficiary/state government (Government of India).

■ Aam Aadmi Bima Yojana was introduced in 2009 to provide insurance cover to members of all rural landless households. The premium for this scheme is also Rs 200 and is borne by the central and state governments equally to provide payable covers in cases of natural and accidental death.

■ Life insurance components under the National Rural Livelihood Mission through the Self-Help Groups it promotes and those under the MGNREGA.

After the launch of Jan Dhan Yojana which aimed at increasing financial inclusion through the opening of zero balance accounts in public banks in 2015, three additional voluntary schemes of pension and insurance linked to it were launched for beneficiaries:

■ Atal Pension Yojana was launched for people between the ages of 18 to 40 years to begin contributing towards monthly pension payments which they can start receiving when they turn 60 years. The central government contributes 50 percent or Rs 1,000, whichever is lower, per annum for each beneficiary.

■ PM Suraksha Bima Yojana is an accident insurance for those between the ages of 18 to 70. It promises insurance worth Rs 2,00,000 in return for annual premiums worth only Rs 12 per annum.

■ PM Jeevan Jyoti Bima Yojana is a life insurance available for those between the ages of 18 to 50 years and promises insurance worth Rs 2,00,000 in return for annual premiums worth only Rs 330 per annum.

While all these schemes are aimed at workers of the informal sectors, under the budget allocations it is not clear how the funds are divided for these schemes (Ministry of Finance, GoI, 2022). Also, since these are voluntary measures, it is unlikely that the poorest and most vulnerable to exogenous shocks will be able to apply for these or even be aware of them.

To this point, it has been conjectured, that if these schemes were making the impacts they set out to, the central government wouldn't have moved to launch yet another voluntary pension scheme aimed at the unorganized sector, Pradhan Mantri Shram Yogi Maandhan, right before the 2019 elections (Mehrotra, 2020).

Welfare Funds for Specific Workers

The central and state governments provide tax-based and contributory welfare funds to support workers from specific industries, but these may still not count as measures of social protection.

Tax-based funds are created by the central government for six types of mines (mica, iron, manganese, chrome, limestone and dolomite), beedi workers, cinema workers, dock workers and construction workers. These funds are set up by acts of Parliament and rely on a tax levied on products or services provided, the revenue from which is earmarked for the use of workers belonging to that product/service group (Mehrotra, 2020).

These funds are used to cover costs for medical expenses, water supply, washing facilities, education and scholarship, housing, family planning and transportation for work, or to grant loan or subsidy to a state government for other welfare schemes for workers in that trade (ibid.). Since most of these funds don't provide pension, death and disability benefits, maternity benefits or any such key benefits they aren't considered social protection measures, and just welfare measures.

Contributory funds rely on the contributions made by employees and employers in the trade and have been set-up in several states of India, especially in the southern and western regions of the country. The coverage with these funds has also been limited amid difficulties in collecting contributions (ibid.).

Social Assistance Measures

India is characterized by narrowly based and fragmented social insurance mechanisms that leave most workers in the unorganized segment of enterprises uncovered. Additionally, such social assistance is mostly in kind, and not in cash.

Public Distribution System (PDS)

PDS is one of the longest running social assistance programmes in India, running in one form or another since the 1940s. It is focused on distributing subsidized fixed rations of cereal every month. The latest revamp in its system came with the National Food Security Act, 2013 (NFSA) which aimed to go beyond public distribution of ration and ensure the Right to Food for all.

Under the NFSA, PDS was linked with poverty lines and designed to cover 75 per cent of rural and 50 per cent of urban population to provide differential levels of food grains and protect against starvation. Currently, 237 million ration cards and 808 million beneficiaries are covered by it making it by far the largest safety net in the country (Government of India, 2022).

Despite its expanse though, NFSA continues to exclude several from its ambit because the mandated number of households continue to be as per the population levels of 2011. It is estimated that, accounting for the population increase in the past decade, 100 million people needing assistance are excluded from the food security net (Khera and Somanchi, 2020).

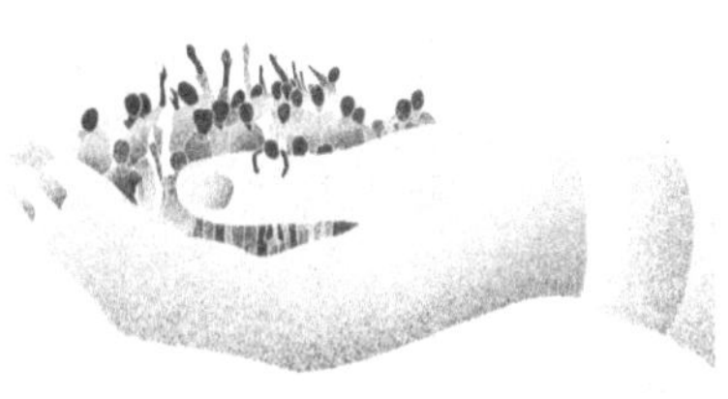

This exclusion is on top of the various challenges occurring in the revamped PDS due to which even those without ration cards are regularly excluded (ibid.). Disbursal of ration after biometric verification, which was implemented in order to deal with corruption, has proven to be one of the major reasons why daily wage labourers with ration cards can't get ration. This is because manual labour removes or alters their fingerprints which are mandatory for verification (ibid.).

Mahatma Gandhi National Rural Employment Guarantee Act (MGNREGA)

Alongside PDS, MGNREGA is the largest social assistance programme present in India. Legally binding the Government of India to provide work to those who demand it, the Act provides a guarantee of 100 days of employment in a financial year per household to adults willing to do public work-related manual work at a programme wage.

While MGNREGA is able to evade errors of exclusion and inclusion through its self-targeting design, the scheme still faces several challenges. These are unmet demands for work, wages lower than minimum wage, delayed or rejected payments, non-payment of unemployment wages if work isn't provided within 15 days, and more (Kapoor, 2018; Nandy, 2018; Nandy, 2019).

The national floor of the minimum wage was suggested to be Rs 375 by a government expert committee in 2019, but wages under MGNREGA have been set separately from state minimum wages (Nair, 2019). They will continue to be outside the purview of the statutory national minimum wage even under the new Code on Wages, 2020 (Mohanty, 2020). This also contributed to the minimum wage for MGNREGA workers under the COVID-19 relief package standing well below at Rs 202 (Seth, Ahmad and Viswanathan, 2020).

Cash-based Programs

There are no universal cash assistance programmes running in India; only a few conditional ones. There is a maternity benefit cash transfer that has been running since 2009, which was revamped and rechristened the *Pradhan Mantri Matritva Vandana Yojana* in 2017. This gives Rs 5,000 to pregnant and lactating women for the birth of their first child and it is disbursed in three installments.

Another scheme, which was initiated in 2019 and called the PM-KISAN, involves the disbursing of a cash transfer of Rs 6,000 to all landowner-cultivator farming families, regardless of how much land they own, in three installments. The design of the scheme includes multiple cash transfers for more than one landowner in joint families but excludes landless labour and tenant farmers from its ambit; those who would need the support of these cash transfers for sustenance just as much, if not more.

Other Welfare Assistance

The Government of India runs a few development programmes that offer social protection in kind. One such initiative is the Integrated Child Development Services Scheme which focuses on overall cognitive development of children through early age support for the child's nutritional, educational and vaccination needs.

The schemes for constructing housing (Pradhan Mantri Awas Yojana) and toilets (Swachh Bharat Mission) give conditional cash installments to beneficiaries upon construction. Another scheme supporting development is the Ujjwala scheme which aims to provide clean cooking fuel to poor households and replace unhealthy fuels such as firewood, cow dung, etc., through allotment of LPG cylinders and hotplate for the beneficiaries.

The overwhelming impression that this description gives is that social insurance has remained in its infancy in India, at least for the unorganized sector workers, and that social assistance is in the form of products or services.

Code of Social Security, 2020

This Code of Social Security rightly brings together the existing Employees Provident Fund Act of 1952, the Employees State Insurance Act of 1948, the Employees Compensation Act of 1923, the Maternity Benefit Act of 1961 and the Payment of Gratuity Act of 1972. Additionally, it repeals the Unorganised Workers (Social Security) Act of 2008, and two sectoral legislations—the Building and Other Construction Workers Welfare Cess Act, 1996 and the Cine-Workers Welfare Fund Act, 1981.

While most of these legislations cater to the social security needs of various worker groups, they are not all internally congruent (Bharadkar and Mathew, 2020). Therefore, assimilation and amalgamation of these acts into the consolidated code is by no means a simplification of the law. The code does nothing more than a cut and paste job of all existing social security laws retaining all their separate frameworks.

As discussed in previous sections, the existing social security schemes for unorganized sector workers provide them limited coverage and a very deficient social security net. This code, therefore, serves no useful purpose for workers or for labour administrators. It unnecessarily makes the social security framework for the unorganized sector complex and cluttered, and opens the door to the revisiting of all case laws since new definition clauses attract new meanings when re-enacted in a single code.

The code is a missed opportunity for policy makers to recognize that informal sector workers have multiple sources of income which are constantly and often involuntarily evolving and mobile lives that are tethered to availability of work. The code also doesn't address the social security needs of contractual workers and workers in an enterprise smaller than the threshold.

WHY THE G20 MUST INTERVENE

Social protection measures in the developed nations evolved alongside employment relations, and not after them. This was because of strong labour movements as well as the collective beliefs concerning the state's duty to take care of those who could not take care of themselves. As a result, in the post-colonial world, developed nations were able to embed systems for the care of their destitute and poor within their social fabric and governance (Government of India, 2007).

Despite low levels of income and a large informal economy, developing countries have made significant gains since decolonization, depicting the feasibility of promotional and protective social security setups. With coordinated global support, these have the potential to move towards social security systems that work for the current economies and don't exclude the majority of the workforce.

The G20 can come together to push for not just national action but also the facilitation of globally coordinated funds and actions. Global forces have transformed the nature of work with a dedicated move towards contractual jobs in the post-liberalized world. It is now imperative that they come together to globally push for reforms in social security for this influx of workforce into the informal economy.

Most of the G20 leaders come from economies that have had a social protection floor for years and are thus in a position to look at their history and identify good practices and challenges for developing nations. The G20 financial track could also assess pathways of financial support dedicated towards building social protection floors for the unorganized sector.

A global push to collect disaggregated data on vulnerable communities, including those in vulnerable occupations, will go a long way to aid and support sustainable development and inclusive growth in developing countries by providing a basis to form and assess policies. G20 declarations already include civil society as a stakeholder, but if they can also push for recognition of civil society data concerning communities,with guidelines that support evidence generation for policy action, governance would become more informed and inclusive.

REFERENCES

AFP. 2021. *AFIP says one-off Covid 'wealth tax' has brought in US$2.3 billion so far.* Buenos Aires Times. May 3.

Basole, A., Abraham, R., Lahoti, R., Kesar, S., Jha, M., Nath, P., Kapoor, R., Mandela, S. N., Shrivastava, A., Dasgupta, Z., Gupta, G., and R. Narayanan. 2021. *State of Working India 2021: One year of Covid-19.* Centre for Sustainable Employment, Azim Premji University.

Bharadkar, K., and B. Mathew. 2020. *Preliminary Notes on the Four Labour Codes* . Nirmana.

CBGA. 2021. "Budget in the Time of the Pandemic: An Analysis of Union Budget 2021-22." Centre for Budget and Governance Accountability, New Delhi.

Berkhout, E., Galasso, N., Lawson, M., Morales, P. A. R., Taneja, A., and Diego Alejo Vázquez Pimentel. 2021. *The Inequality Virus.* Oxfam International.

G20 Labour and Employment Ministers Meeting 2017. "Towards an Inclusive Future: Shaping the World of Work." Federal Ministry of Labour and Social Affairs. https://www.ilo.org/wcmsp5/groups/public/---dgreports/---dcomm/documents/meetingdocument/wcms_554414.pdf

G20 Labour and Employment Ministers' Declaration. 2021. *G20 Policy Principles to ensure access to adequate social protection for all in a changing world of work.* G20 Italia 2021, University of Toronto. Retrieved from G20 Toronto.

Ghosh J. 2020. "A critique of the Indian government's response to the COVID-19 pandemic." *J. Ind. Bus. Econ* 47(3), pp. 519–30. doi: 10.1007/s40812-020-00170-x. Epub 2020 Jul 11. PMCID: PMC7351648.

Government of India. 2007. *Social Security Report.* Ministry of Micro, Small And Medium Enterprises, Government of India. http://dcmsme.gov.in/Social%20security%20report.pdf.

Government of India. 2014. "National Social Assistance Programme (NSAP) Guidelines." Ministry of Rural Development. https://nsap.nic.in/nsap/aboutus.pdf.

Government of India. 2020. *Periodic Labour Force Survey, July 2018–June 2019.* Ministry of Statistics, Programme and Implementation, Government of India.

Government of India. 2022. *Notes on Demands for Grants, 2022-2023.* Ministry of Finance, Government of India.

Government of India. 2022. *https://dfpd.gov.in/pdscaeunfsa.htm.* May. Retrieved from NFSA Dashboard: https://nfsa.gov.in/public/nfsadashboard/publicrcdashboard.aspx.

Government of India. n.d. *Standard Operating Procedure (SOP) for Janashree Bima Yojana under Mahatma Gandhi Pravasi Suraksha Yojana.* Ministry of Overseas Indian Affairs, Government of India.

ILO. 2018. *Women and Men in the Informal Economy: A Statistical Picture (Third edition).* Geneva: International Labour Office.

ILO. 2020. *Unemployment protection in the COVID-19 crisis: Country responses and policy considerations.* ILO Brief, International Labour Organization.

—. n.d. *Non-standard forms of employment.* International Labour Organization. https://www.ilo.org/global/topics/non-standard-employment/lang--en/index.htm.

International Labour Office, Geneva. 2018. *Women and Men in the Informal Economy: A Statistical Picture (Third Edition).* International Labour Organization.

Janetsky, M. 2022. Colombia's leftwing government unveils tax-the-rich plan to tackle poverty. *The Guardian.* August 26. https://www.theguardian.com/world/2022/aug/26/colombia-tax-the-rich-plan-poverty-gustavo-petro.

Kapoor, M. 2018. 4 reasons why MGNREGA is not benefitting workers. *Business Today.* September 26. https://www.businesstoday.in/top-story/4reasons-why-mgnrega-is-not-benefitting-workers/ story/282891.html.

—. 2020. India's unemployment rate shoots to 23.5% in April: CMIE. *Business Today.* May 1. https://www.businesstoday.in/latest/economy-politics/story/india-unemployment-rate-april-cmie-highest-257055-2020-05-01.

Kapoor, R. 2020. "COVID -19 and the State of India's Labour Market. ICRIER Policy Series No. 18." June. http://icrier.org/pdf/Policy_Series_18.pdf

Khera, R., and Anmol Somanchi. 2020. *A review of the coverage of PDS.* Ideas for India. August 19. https://www.ideasforindia.in/topics/poverty-inequality/a-review-of-the-coverage-of-pds.html

Kirton, J. 2020. *A Small Short-Term Success at the G20's Riyadh Summit.* G20 Information Centre, University of Toronto. November 22. http://www.g20.utoronto.ca/analysis/201122-kirton-performance.html

Kishore, R. 2020. India's economy was facing worst-ever deceleration before Covid-19 hit. *Hindustan Times.* September 1. https://www.hindustantimes.com/business-news/india-s-economy-was-facing-worst-ever-deceleration-before-covid-19-hit/story-gOJfU86lJ64UPOjLBoypvN.html

McBride, James, Siripurapu, Anshu and Noah Berman. 2022. What Does the G20 Do? *Council on Foreign Relations.* December 15. https://www.cfr.org/backgrounder/what-does-g20-do

MercoPress. 2021. Wealth tax returns twice as much as expected in Bolivia. April 28. https://en.mercopress.com/2021/04/28/wealth-tax-returns-twice-as-much-as-expected-in-bolivia.

Mehrotra, S. 2016. *Seizing the Demographic Dividend. Policies to Achieve Inclusive Growth in India.* Cambridge University Press.

Mehrotra, S. 2020. *Building a Social Security Architecture for Informal Workers in India, Finally! Centre for Sustainable Employment. Retrieved from https://cse.azimpremjiuniversity.edu.in/wp-content/uploads/2020/07/Mehrotra_Social_Security_Code_Unorganised_Sector_July_2020.pdf.* Centre for Sustainable Employment, Azim Premji University.

Mohanty, P. 2020. Wage code leaves millions of workers out in cold. *Business Today.* September 29.

Nair, S. 2019. MGNREGA wages fall below minimum wage in 34 states, Union Territories. *The Indian Express.* April 2. https://indianexpress.com/article/india/mgnrega-wages-fall-below-minimum-wage-in-34-states-union-territories-5653792/

Nandy, D. 2018. MGNREGA is failing: 10 reasons why. *DownToEarth.* November. https://www.downtoearth.org/blog/economy/mgnrega-is-failing-10-reasonswhy-62035.

—. 2019. Underfunding, misleading claims: The story of MGNREGA in New India. *DownToEarth.* July 15. https://www.downtoearth.org.in/blog/economy/underfunding-misleading-claims-thestory-of-mgnrega-in-new-india-65627.

Nath, P., and Amit Basole. 2020. *Did Employment Rise or Fall in India between 2011 and 2017? Estimating Absolute Changes in the Workforce .* Centre for Sustainable Employment, Azim Premji University.

National Sample Survey Office. 2016. *Employment and Unemployment Situation Among Major Religious Groups in India.*

Ray, D., and S. Subramanian. 2020. "India's Lockdown: An Interim Report." *Indian Economic Review* 55: 31–79.

Riyadh Summit. 2020. *Leaders' Declaration*. Riyadh Summit, University of Toronto. http://www.g20.utoronto.ca/2020/2020-g20-leaders-declaration-1121.html.

Saudi Arabia's G20 Presidency 2020. 2020. *The impact of the COVID 19 pandemic on jobs and incomes in G20 economies*. ILO-OECD.

Save the Children-India. 2020. *Rights of Vulnerable Families and Children of India under COVID-19: Implications for effective response and mitigation strategies*. https://resourcecentre.savethechildren.net/pdf/rights_of_vulnerable_families_and_children_of_india_under_covid_240720f.pdf/.

Seth, A., Ahmad , S., and V. Viswanathan. 2020. *How has NREGA fared during lockdown?*. *idr*. November 19. https://idronline.org/nrega-performance-in-lockdown-social-protection-migrants/.

SWAN. 2021. "No Country for Workers." Stranded Workers Action Network.

The Wire Staff. 2020. *Hunger Index Among Poor in 11 States Continues to Be Dire Post-Lockdown: Survey*. *The Wire*. December 13. https://thewire.in/rights/hunger-watch-survey-lockdown.

FINANCE
ELIMINATE GENDER BASED VIOLENCE
EQUAL PAY + SAFETY AT WORK
REDUCE GENDER GAP
CLOSE DATA GAP
CAPACITY BUILDING
ENHANCE SOCIAL SECTOR BUDGET
EQUALITY
PEACE
SUSTAINABILITY
TRANSFORMATIVE FINANCING

Transformative Financing for Gender Equality and Gender Responsive Budgeting

Vibhuti Patel

INTRODUCTION

The main action agenda of transformative financing for gender equality is to ensure that gender needs are met in development planning, adequate funds are allocated for development to fulfil gender needs so that funds would benefit everyone equally and equitably. To transform gender commitments into financial commitments, affirmative actions and targeted efforts are often needed. Gender inclusive fiscal expansion by the G20 nation-states becomes an urgent necessity in the context of COVID-19-triggered health emergency. This emergency resulted in tremendous hardship and the loss of livelihoods for migrant workers, daily wage earners, and unorganized sector workers—including the self-employed women and men who were worst hit due to loss of wages with no money to pay house rent or buy daily necessities—and increased precarity due to hunger, malnutrition and infection. The lockdown and social isolation imposed by the coronavirus infection also forced women to bear the burden of unpaid care work, both, in terms of housework, home-schooling of children, and enhanced care burden of sick, children and elderly (Patel, 2020). Over the last 18 months, women's rights groups, community based non-government organisations, networks on right to food and right to shelter, citizens associations, self-help groups, and trade unions have been busy providing provisions for all necessary services (food, shelter, water, healthcare, information) for the marginalized and socially excluded poor people in the G20 nation-states. This is clearly not enough.

FORMATION OF GENDER EQUALITY FORUM

In July 2021, the civil society organizations from several G20 nation-states joined the recently formed the Generation Equality Forum (GEF) to demand fiscal expansion in the macroeconomic policies, for transformative financing aimed at gender equity and gender equality, proactive implementation of gender responsive budgets, and transparent and inclusive accountability processes. This was in response to the massive loss of livelihoods and human lives triggered by health emergencies as a result of the COVID-19 pandemic. In a statement by the 'Asia Pacific Sign-On Letter: accountability for the GEF commitments and civil society engagement' by intersectional feminist civil society (CS) organizations in the region of Asia and the Pacific, the efforts of the GEF have been appreciated, as its establishment in July 2021, brought gender audit and gender equality concerns centre stage. The forum has promised to raise USD 40 billion from government budgets, corporate houses, and global foundations towards the human development goal and towards achieving the targets and commitments of the GEF Action Coalition (2021).

The GEF unanimously decided to strive for collective action and global as well as local inter-generational dialogues for increased public and private investments in the areas of economic justice and human rights of the workers; reproductive health needs and rights of girls and women; environmental safety and climate justice; and addressing gender-based digital divide, promoting simple harvesting of technology and innovation for gender equality and ensuring gender inclusiveness in leadership of economic and political all decision making processes. The Generation Equality Action Coalitions (July 2021) also accepted that the GEF will strictly adhere to the human rights principles and adopt a data-driven, evidence-based consultative process that involves women's rights groups, community-based activists working for social solidarity during the pandemic, Government Organizations (GOs), Non-Government Organizations (NGOs), and employers' associations.

NEED FOR GENDER TRANSFORMATIVE FINANCING IN G20 COUNTRIES

During the pre and post pandemic periods, the GOs and NGOs of the G20 nation-states—Argentina, Australia, Brazil, Canada, China, France, Germany, India, Indonesia, Italy, Japan, the Republic of Korea, Mexico, Russia, Saudi Arabia, South Africa, Turkey, the United Kingdom, the United States, and the European Union—have been vociferous in the global discourses and campaigns on Gender Equality, with special focus on pay parity, safety at work-place, equal sharing of domestic work, and unpaid care and elimination of all forms of gender-based violence. Still, in the GEF, several G20 nation-states in Asia have not been prioritized, both at the level of engagement and in terms of allocation of financial resources. Asia is home to the world's largest population, with over 60 per cent of the world's youth. G20 nation-states of Asia, such as India, Indonesia, China, Japan, and the Republic of Korea are the most vulnerable to climate-related disasters which disproportionately affect women and marginalized groups. Almost 40 per cent of women in South-East Asia experience sexual and gender-based violence from intimate partners (UN Women,

2020). The GEF is envisioned as a space to position some of these issues with the governments and it is expected that the Paris Forum will provide funds and urgent action agenda to address these concerns. For this intersectional representation of the leadership from G20 Asian Countries as well as representation of socially excluded and marginalized groups like differently abled persons, sex workers, and trans people is a must (Anwar, Downs and Davidson, 2016).

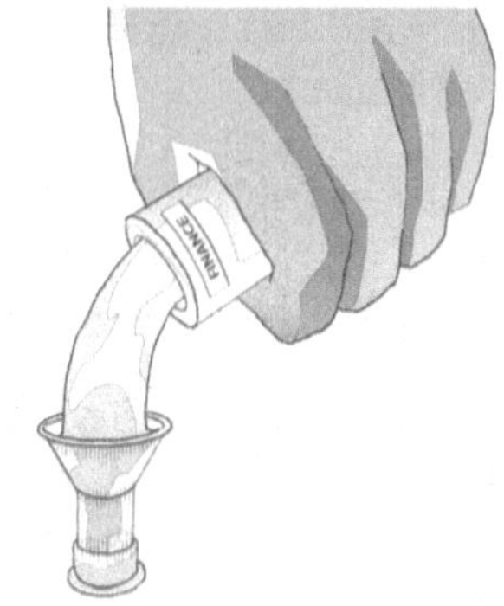

The feminist economists are demanding that the GEF make financial commitments to the Feminist Action and Climate Justice, to deal with massive loss of livelihoods and damage of asserts as a result of the climate and ecological emergency, as well as to advance the gender equality agenda across all regions and to precisely represent global Generation Equality realities (UN Women, 2021). They have averred that only by ensuring the participation of those who are interjectionally marginalized by ableism, heteronormativity, patriarchy, and colonial legacies and post-colonial inequities, we can achieve gender equality, and 'leaving no one behind' will be a reality in the coming future. Action Coalition (AC) principles of intersectionality, feminist leadership, and transformation for gender equality need transformative finances that promote women's economic empowerment; strengthened relationships between people, in the private and public domains, home and beyond; and more enabling of rules and practices, including socio-cultural norms.

For developing countries within the G20—like Argentina, Brazil, Mexico in Latin America, and India and Indonesia in the Asian region—financial exclusion is found to be the greatest barrier to economic empowerment and gender equality for women, trans people, ethnic and religious minorities, persons with disabilities, and elderly people below the poverty line. Over 90 per cent of them are in the informal sector that deprives them of social security, social protection, and labour legislations. A considerable proportion of poor women are self-employed and petty traders, and the piecemeal approach of the state and self-help groups to provide these women with low-end financial inclusion in terms of micro-finance has not improved their quality of life (ILO-OECD, 2020a).

GENDER IMPLICATIONS OF GLOBAL FINANCIAL CRISIS IN 2008

During the global economic crisis in 2008, women and girls from lower and middle income countries suffered the most in terms of deprivation of education, health and well-being, and employment; they also shouldered heavy burden of gender-based violence—in terms of domestic violence—and vulnerability to sexual abuse in the public domain (ILO, 2011). Similarly, with the downturn of economic activities triggered by the global pandemic, gendered vulnerabilities and marginalities have exponentially increased (Gifford and Zohra Khan, 2020). This backdrop had provided rationale for evidence-based feminist and gender-transformative macroeconomic policies. Such policies demand massive increase in social sector budgeting and simultaneously strike at the roots of socio-economic inequalities. To attain this action agenda, the nation-state needs to implement progressive labour laws by challenging gender norms of socially constructed factor-labour-product markets. Moreover, affirmative actions to reduce-reorganise-represent care work of women, preventive and punitive measures to combat gender-based violence in the domestic arena and at the workplace and area-specific gender responsive infrastructure as well as heavily subsidized public services are urgently required in G20 countries (ILO, 2020a).

According to Joy Anderson and Katherine Miles (2015), '[g]ender lens investing incorporates a gender analysis into a financial analysis in order to get to better decisions. This definition names a process standard. It focuses on an approach to investing that includes a broad set of potential outcomes.'

Seguino (2009) argues that the economic and financial crisis provides an opportunity to rethink the role of government in the economy. The author suggests:

> addressing the economic crisis requires among other interventions a direct focus on women's well-being. Women are likely to be targeted first for jobs layoffs, but have the fewest reserves with which to shield themselves and their children from the drop in income. Targeting public sector spending in activities that employ women benefits not only them but also their children. It is also an investment in long run growth. (Seguino, 2009)

MAJOR CHALLENGES FOR GENDER EQUALITY IN G20 COUNTRIES

G20 countries are clustered in five groups: Group 1 is consists of Australia, Canada, Saudi Arabia, United States; Group 2 includes India, Russia, South Africa, and Turkey; Group 3 is composed of the Latin American countries of Argentina, Brazil, and Mexico; Group 4 comprises three Western European countries—France, Germany, Italy, United Kingdom as well as the European Union; and Group 5 is constituted by China and the East Asian countries of Indonesia, Japan, and South Korea. In the G20 countries, there are five crucial areas in which the gender gap needs to be bridged: economic deprivation leading to feminization of poverty and work force participation, education, health, representation in decision-making bodies, and gender-based violence (Kulik, 2020).

Over the last two decades, among G20 countries, major gender sensitization efforts have resulted in acknowledgment that women are making crucial contributions to the economy through their paid, partially paid, and largely unpaid work. At the national level, the definition of 'work' has been rectified from time to time to increase the base of working women. Some steps have been undertaken at the international level to address this: International Labour Organization (ILO) held a convention in 1985 to revisit International Standard Classification of Occupation (ISCO) Efforts by the United Nations Food and Agricultural Organisation (FAO, 2018), which led to changes in the guidelines for the World Programme of Agricultural Censuses. UN Women has initiated a global debate with state and non-state actors on paid and unpaid work of women and consideration of women's work in the care economy.

ECONOMIC OPPORTUNITIES AND LIVELIHOODS OF WOMEN

In all five groups of G20 nation-states, due to shrinking economic opportunities after the 2008 world economic recession, more women are living in poverty in both developing and developed countries than men: women and girls represent 50 per cent of the number of people living in poor households in developing countries and 53 per cent in European countries (Chatham House, 2015).

As Figure 1 shows, the gender gaps are a challenge across countries at different levels of income: high income G20 countries, such as South Africa, Canada, France, Germany, UK, the EU, and Japan do not necessarily eliminate gaps. The political economy of these countries in terms of social policy, economic strategies, political decision-making and institutional contexts, and the gendered intersectionality of caste, race, class, and ethnicity determine women's economic opportunities. Whereas in the middle income countries of the Middle East and West Asia and the developing countries of Asia, Africa, and Latin America, the gender norms and cultural practices of male domination and female subordination are determined by religion, custom, tradition, and kinship networks.

GENDER GAP IN LABOUR FORCE PARTICIPATION IN G20 ECONOMIES

Among the G20 countries, Australia, Canada, China, France, Germany, Japan, Russia, USA, and the European Union have reported more than 65 per cent labour force participation of women and girls but the gender gap in employment of 10 percentage points is found. While Brazil, the Republic of Korea, and Argentina have nearly 60 per cent women's participation in the labour force and the gender gap in employment is 20 percentage points. Italy, Indonesia, and South Africa

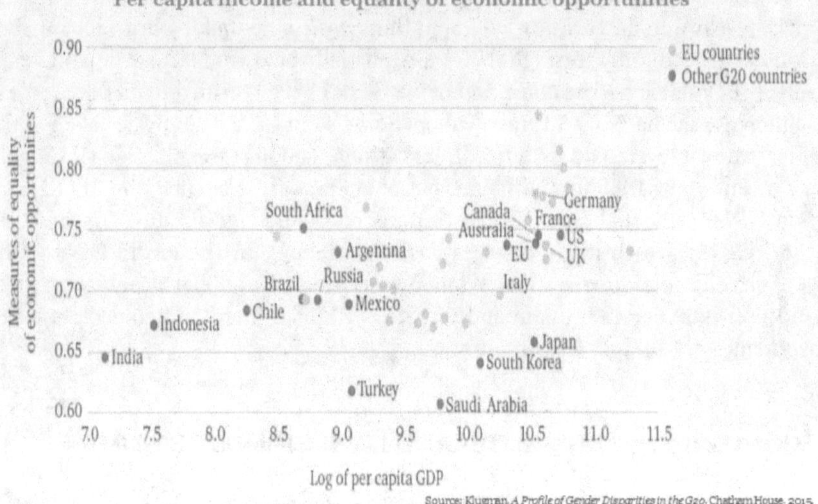

Figure 1. Per Capita income and equality of economic opportunities

Source: Klugman, *A Profile of Gender Disparities in the G20*, 2015.

have reported their labour force participation rate to be above 55 per cent; in the case of Italy and Indonesia the gender gap in employment is more than 10 per cent, while in South Africa, the gender gap is less than 10 per cent. Mexico has reported a 55 per cent labour force participation rate for women and a gender gap of 35 per cent. Turkey, with a 39 per cent labour force participation of women and a 39 per cent point gender gap is the 3rd last in the ranking. The lowest two nation-states in terms of labour force participation of women are India with 27 per cent and Saudi Arabia with 21 per cent. The former's gender gap in employment is 50 percentage points, while for the latter, the gender gap in employment is 58 percentage points. The gender gap in labour force participation is the largest in Saudi Arabia, India, and Turkey (Sorgner et al, 2020).

In the developing countries, most of the women are excluded from economic decision-making within their own households (UN, The World's Women, 2015), they also receive lower salaries than men, and work longer hours (ILO, 2019). Furthermore, they are often excluded from the labour market, do not have access to finance, and are denied property rights (ILO, 2021). Closing the gender gap, therefore, is not only a fundamental human right, but also smart economics

(Chatham House, 2015). At the G20 summit in Brisbane in 2014, the G20 leaders pledged to reduce the gap in labour force participation rates between men and women by 25 per cent by 2025 (G20 Information Centre, 2014). They need to come up with gender responsive budgeting and transformative financing for gender equality that will contribute to implementing the Sustainable Development Goals for the economic empowerment of women (UN Women, 2016).

Figure 3 reveals that 54 per cent of women in business face challenges with accessing credit from financial institutions.

The findings of the 2018 'Women, Business and the Law' report underscore the pervasiveness of legal and policy impediments affecting women by highlighting seven indicators across 189 economies. As reflected in Figure 1 below and corroborated by the report, 'over a third of the economies examined have at least one constraint on women's legal capacity as measured by accessing institutions. Similarly close to 40% of economies have at least one constraint on women's property rights as measured by the using property indicator' (Thomas et al., 2018).

For the nineteen G20 member countries (Figure 2), the average scores indicate the need to target reforms in laws, regulations, and policies, particularly in the areas of labour inclusion, access to credit, and protection from violence. Within this group, the average scores are consistent with the findings that higher income economies perform best across indicators.

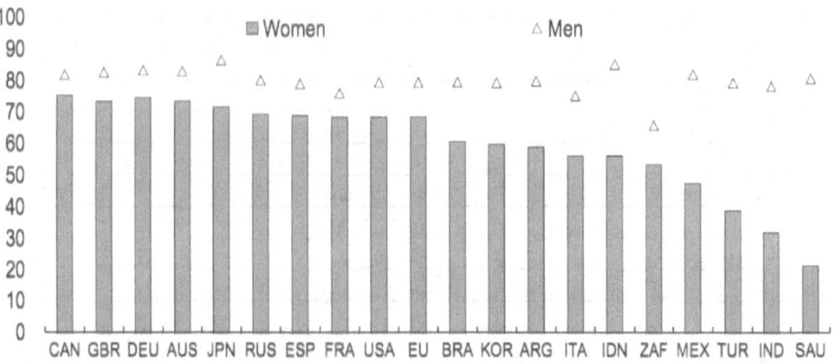

Figure 2. Percentage of the population aged 15–64 participating in the labour force, 2018

Source: OECD, "Enhancing equal access to opportunities for all in G20 countries", 2020.

Figure 3. G20 Member Countries: Women, Business and Law 2018 Indicators (Average Scores)

Source: Thomas et al., *Gender Mainstreaming: A Strategic Approach, Argentina: Think 20*, 2018.

THE POLITICS OF POLICIES AND PROGRAMMES

Several G20 member countries can potentially serve as models for systematically tackling the determinants of gender inequities by applying a gender lens to assess policies, align policies and programmes, and reform the relevant laws and regulations. The effective implementation of gender mainstreaming strategies requires political will, demonstrated actions at high levels of government, evidence-based policy formulations, target-oriented programmes and schemes, and efficient implementation at the ground level. Due to efforts of feminist economists, various non-governmental and civil society organizations and women elected representatives in the local self-government bodies, gender audit of earlier budgets and formulation of gender-sensitive budgets have started in all G20 nations. Some of the praiseworthy initiatives have been listed below.

The United Kingdom passed the Gender Pay Gap legislation that demands firms with 250 or more employees to report on gender-based pay differentials in 2017, implementation of which has had considerable impact in the direction of pay parity. This was made possible by a coordinated effort for visibility of working women in formal and informal sectors of the economy; they made visible statistics and indicators that enumerated systemic pay inequities, and identified structures and mechanisms that allowed gender pay gaps.

In 2016, the Canadian government instituted the Standing Committee on the Status of Women for stock-taking the implementation of the government's 1995 commitment to Gender-Based Analysis (GBA) as well as gender budget analysis. The committee concluded that 'despite the long history of work on the topic of

GBA+,[1] the federal government's commitment to the implementation of GBA+ is far from being fulfilled' (House of Commons, 2016). The Committee concluded that in 2009, only 29 of approximately 110 federal organizations committed to GBA+ through the 2009 Departmental Action Plan on Gender-based Analysis and identified political will as an important determinant of success in implementation. As a result, the Government of Canada had to announce a feminist agenda and set about systematically and strategically aligning politics, policies, and programs in support of funds for GBA (House of Commons, 2016).

Gender economists in Mexico worked hard to align politics, policies, and programs aimed at promoting gender equity by establishing the key elements of the framework for gender equality. As a result, in 2006, the government of Mexico adopted the General Law of Equality between Women and Men that aimed at gender mainstreaming in the Planning act as well as the Federal Budget and Fiscal Accountability Act. Under the National Programme for Equality and Non-Discrimination, from 2013 to 2018, Mexico ensured enhanced legal and political commitments to gender equality. The Organisation for Economic Co-operation and Development (OECD) report (2017), 'Building an Inclusive Mexico: Policies and Good Governance for Gender Equality', noted that Mexico has taken very important actions at the policy level to promote gender equality, including the establishment of 'the National System of Equality between Men and Women', headed, for the first time, by President Peña Nieto. The presence of the President showed renewed commitment to allow for the better integration of gender considerations into the policy cycle, in line with the original objective outlined in the National Development Plan 2013–2018. It also meant strong engagement to achieve better outcomes in the gender agenda and reaffirmed Mexico's commitment to the G20 gender target' (OECD, 2017). Yet, there are significant challenges regarding the implementation of the framework, as Mexico continues to lag significantly behind OECD members and countries in the Latin American region on issues such as work-force participation of women (as seen in Figure 2, 47 per cent in Mexico compared with Chile, Colombia, Peru, and Brazil at 60 per cent) and strategies to eliminate violence against women.

GENDER IMPACT ASSESSMENTS

The Gender Impact Assessment (GIA) is one of several evidence-based, policy-making tools that may be applied to facilitate the implementation of gender mainstreaming by systematically and objectively assessing the ex-ante impact of policies, laws, official rules, implementing regulations, and establishing a baseline

---

[1] GBA+ acknowledges that GBA goes beyond biological (sex) and socio-cultural (gender) differences. GBA+ considers many other identity factors, like race, ethnicity, religion, age and mental or physical disability.

and indicators against which subsequent implementation can be measured. The GIA is a useful ex-ante assessment of a proposed piece of legislation or policy from a gender perspective. Depending on the context and the nature of the policy being assessed, the GIA can be performed at different stages of the law-making or policy cycles.

The GIA implementation framework is put in place by several member states of the European Union (EU). Due to the efforts of women parliamentarians, Spain and Austria instituted the GIA in 2003 and 2013 respectively, as members of the EU. As of January 2021, the percentage of Members of the European Parliament who are women stands at 38.9 per cent (Shreeves and Boland, 2021).

One of the main findings of the European Institute for Gender Equality (EIGE, 2014) review of the GIA implementation case studies shows that for GIAs to effectively challenge gender blind policies, they must be performed early enough in the policy-making/legislative cycle to influence policy design and facilitate inputs by technical experts to substantively amend the proposed policy or legislation. Under these conditions, the evidence shows that ex-ante GIAs contribute to the quality and transparency of the law/policy-making process and improve the overall impact of new policies and regulations. In a similar vein, the evidence shows that ex-post policy and legislative evaluation undertaken from a gender perspective also contribute to increase accountability and quality governance.

Gender expertise is required to identify evidence of potential gender-blindness and the undesirable impacts of policies/laws on gender equality. In France, the High Gender Equality Council, an advisory body established by decree in 2013 and embedded into the law in 2017, has rapidly gained credit through its evaluation role, pointing out gaps to be filled in current legislation, acknowledging progress, supporting the government in implementing gender mainstreaming, and raising pending challenges to be addressed.

GENDER RESPONSIVE BUDGETING (GRB)

The budget represents the financial plan and hence is the most significant policy instrument of any government for establishing macro-economic stability, fiscal efficiency, strategic priority, and more importantly, for ensuring the equitable distribution of national resources. Gender Responsive Participatory Budgeting (GRB) is a means of integrating a gender dimension into all steps of the budget process. This includes participatory decision-making and transparent raising of financial resources and transparency in their expenditure. GRB is not a separate budget exclusively for gender concerns. It is about considering the different needs and priorities of both women, men, and sexual minorities without gender exclusivity. Gender Responsive Budgeting (GRB) ensures that budgets are gender-sensitive and not gender neutral, which means that they are geared towards establishing gender equality and are sensitive to intersectionality of gender with class, caste, race, religion, ethnicity, and geographical location. GRB consists of the use of tools to analyse the gender dimensions of budgets; adoption of procedures to ensure that the budget supports the achievement of gender equality; and implementation mechanisms for effective and efficient utilisation of allocated funds, functions, and functionaries. GRB focuses on equality, accountability, transparency, participatory process in policy-making and fulfilling the practical day-to-day survival-based gender needs as well as long term strategic gender needs that change the un-equal power balance. GRB is an important tool in the hands of the nation-state for affirmative action for Improvement of gender relations through reduction of the gender gap in the development process (Bureau for Gender Equality, 2005).

GRB strives to reduce the gender gap in the five vital areas of economy and society, namely economic participation, economic opportunity, political empowerment, educational attainment, health and well-being with special focus on the most marginalised and socially excluded, namely Dalit, tribal, disabled, minorities, HIV-positive women, and single women (Patel, 2002). It shares important principles with public governance for fiscal stimulus in the government expenditure at national and sub-national levels to bridge the gender gaps in vital areas of education, health, skill-building, employment, decision-making and prevention of gender-based violence. Gender budgeting has emerged as one of the critical pillars of efforts to advance gender equity in developed and developing economies (ILO-UN Women, 2021). The prerequisite for successful GRB is the identification of practical gender needs, taking into consideration, gender-based division of labour or women's subordinate position in the economy. They are a response to immediate perceived necessity, identified within a specific context. They are practical in nature and often are concerned with inadequacies in living conditions such as provision of fuel, water, healthcare, and employment, and strategic gender needs are different in different economic contexts and are determined by statutory provisions, affirmative action by the state, pro-active role of the employers to enhance women's position in the economy and social movements (Moser, 1993).

There is a broad range of experience and a lesson to be drawn from approaches to gender budgeting, starting with Australia in 1984, where the government was required to assess budgetary impacts on women and girls (Elson, 2006). The IMF survey (2016) of gender budgeting efforts—covering more than 80 countries—noted a range of outcomes, including: changes in fiscal policies (e.g., India and Mexico); improved accountability systems for public spending on gender-focused initiatives (e.g., Austria and Ecuador); the incorporation of relevant line ministries into gender budgeting processes and the institutionalization of tools such as gender budget statements, circulars, and spending reviews (e.g., Morocco, Philippines, and Timor-Leste); and the incorporation of gender budgeting at the level of sub-national entities. (e.g., in Bolivia and India) (Stotsky, 2016).

In response to the challenges of implementing policies and programs to advance gender equity, the Finance Ministers' Working Group on Gender Equity was convened during the 2015 World Bank Spring Meetings. A founding member of the Working Group, Ngozi Okonjo-Iweala (2016) opined that gender mainstreaming simply was not getting results fast enough, and proposed that finance ministers should leverage the budget more effectively to incentivize reform and achieve concrete impacts on gender equity. The assessment of the International Monetary Fund (IMF) Survey amplifies and substantiates this view with the assessment that gender budgeting efforts

> …seem to have led to meaningful fiscal policy changes only when they had the support of the political centre of fiscal decision-making … the leadership of the minister of finance has clearly been essential …. Parliamentarians and parliamentary committees are important supports to the executive branch and have sometimes been catalytic. (Stotsky, 2016, pp. 25–26)

> Gender budgeting efforts are intended to commit public budgeting to weighing the benefits and costs of policies that would promote gender equality and girls' and women's development, and then to taking action in response to this evaluation. The important point is not whether an initiative is labelled as gender budgeting but whether fiscal policies and administration are formulated with an eye to promoting gender equality and girls' and women's development. (Stotsky, 2016)

In this context, gender budgeting should be viewed not just as an essential tool for assuring implementation and impact, but also as critical for strengthening policy processes.

Mexico's experience with gender budgeting provides insights into the challenges of implementation despite political commitment. As noted in the 2017 OECD report, 'Mexico has been making progress in strengthening the integration of gender requirements through the Planning and the Federal Budget and Fiscal Accountability Acts, as well as the National Development Plan of Mexico, which … includes gender equality as a cross-cutting principle in support of Mexico's goal to 'unlock its full potential' (OECD, 2017). Despite the legal and procedural requirements for all government policies and budgets to be assessed in terms of their different impacts on men and women, and boys and girls, 'gender analysis is still missing from the mainstream budgetary process and women's initiatives are seen as "add-ons"' (OECD, 2017).

In 2017, the IMF Report, 'Women Are Key for Future Growth: Evidence from Canada', noted that if the 'gap of 7 percentage points between male and female labour force participation with high educational attainment were eliminated, the level of real GDP could be about 4 percent higher today' (Petersson et al., 2017). Canada's implementation of gender budgeting has received a new impetus with the feminist mandate of the current government and its efforts to increase economic growth. The 2017 Budget included a 'gender statement', said to be the first of its kind. The 2018 budget included a proposal for 'adopting a comprehensive and permanent approach to gender budgeting' (ILO-OECD, 2020b) and set out a 'gender results framework' with specific objectives and outcomes indicators covering education, economic participation, leadership and political participation, gender-based violence and poverty reduction. This rigorous approach to analysis and implementation provides a basis for assessing the gaps and increasing accountability for results (ILO-OECD, 2020b).

India offers a robust example of gender budgeting on the national and state level, with potential lessons on the complementarities, benefits, and challenges of gender budgeting within this framework. The IMF conducted an empirical analysis of gender budgeting at the state level in India, where 16 out of 29 states adopted and sustained gender budgeting efforts over a 15-year period, 'with varying degrees of intensity, complementing a central (or Union) government initiative' (Stotsky, 2016). The study concluded that 'gender equality, as measured by gender equality indices for enrolment in primary schools, improved significantly in gender budgeting states compared to states that did not put in place gender budgeting, ... [and] had an ambiguous influence on sector-level fiscal spending' (Stotsky, 2016).

On a regional level, within the European Union, several member states have developed and implemented gender budgeting. In Austria, Article 51 of the constitution establishes the principle of a gender-sensitive state budget, requiring each ministry to formulate gender-impact objectives for proposed budgetary measures. In Finland, national gender equality plans have been adopted starting in 2008, with specific requirements for each ministry's budget process. In Spain, the 2003 law demands gender integration and action in the State budgeting process, but the national level compliance was done only twice, in 2011 and 2017. However, at the regional government level, GRB implementation has been more successful, with Madrid and Valencia leading the way (Thomas et al., 2020).

Budgetary changes in the financial year 2006-07 in Australia came up with greater tax concessions to women pensioners, thereby raising the bar of women-friendly retirement income policy for senior citizens who are women (Sharp and Austen, 2006).

In 2005, over 100 developed and developing countries met in Paris to arrive at a consensus about global business practices. Donor and partner countries were persuaded in the Paris Declaration of Aid Effectiveness to make aid management and delivery gender responsive, and to ensure the monitoring experience of aid reforms from gender perspective and gathering evidence to influence and strengthen gender constituents (UNIFEM, 2009).

VISIBILITY OF GENDER IN STATISTICS AND INDICATORS

For the G20 nation-states, gender disaggregated data is important for robust and realistic analysis, advocacy of gender concerns, to ensure accountability in terms of translation of gender commitments into policies and programmes, and allocation of funds, functions, and functionaries to reduce gender gap and promote gender equity. There is an urgent need to go beyond the gender binary of men and women, and include developmental needs and demands of transgender persons in the discourse on gender responsive budgeting and transformative financing for gender equality. This can be in terms of their practical gender needs of livelihood, employment, education and skill, health and wellbeing. This also includes their strategic gender needs of participation in decision-making in the economics, social, and cultural matters of the community, electoral bodies, and governance structures. We cannot close the gender-gap without closing the data gap. In development planning and policy-making, data equality is a precondition for gender equality, because whatever is measured gets addressed by the state and non-state governance structures (Krishnaraj and Joy Deshmukh, 1993).

The visibility of gender in statistics and indicators is crucial for understanding the different demographic, socioeconomic, education, employment, skill, nutrition, and health-related realities in the lives of women/girls, men/boys, and transgender persons. Gender statistics comprise disaggregated data beyond the gender binary of male and female sex in matters concerning time use for paid and unpaid work, contribution to the care economy, intra-household inequalities, exposure to violence, mental and physical disability, access to natural and financial resources, income earning capacity, right to property-house-land-cattle and other entitlements as citizens. Without gender statistics, the nature of social exclusion gets invisibilized, and the developmental efforts fail to come up with socially inclusive measures for human development.

Gender data needs to be disaggregate in terms of sex and gender identity, age-wise break up of population, geographical location—urban, rural, and forest areas—migratory status, ethnicity, class—income and asset ownership—religion (only relevant for some indicators and countries), Marital status and number of children, employment status—formal and informal sector or unpaid family workers and unpaid care work (Lansky et al., 2017).

Gender indicators can refer to either 'quantitative' or 'qualitative' indicators based on sex-gender identity disaggregated statistical data (Imp-Act, 2005). 'Quantitative' gender indicators measure numerical changes over time expressed in terms of percentages and numbers, e.g., gross enrolment ratios and gross retention rate at primary, secondary, and higher education levels for male, female, and transgender students. While 'qualitative' gender indicators measure changes in lived experiences, decision-making power in family, community, and workplace politics, change in belief-systems—mindsets, norms, social practices, viewpoints, attitudes or perceptions that contribute to empowerment or in attitudes towards gender equality.

Over the last three decades, gender economists have made efforts to make the official agencies recognize women's multiple activities and contribution to a nation's economy, women's status and thereby, gender equality gets institutionalized and perpetuated. The situation leads to further exploitation and oppression in other spheres of life as well. Thus, women fall prey to a vicious circle where their labour is devalued, and thereby, they are pushed to the margins in all matters and spheres of development and empowerment, be it political processes, policy and legislations or any sphere of nation building. Hence broadening the definition of work to include occupational categories specific to women; economic activity to cover cultural, regional, and seasonal nature of work; and mechanisms to estimate women's unpaid work in terms of time and remuneration is important (Demetriades, 2007).

In India, since 1990, gender economists have been interrogating national systems of data collection such as the Census of India, National Sample Surveys,  and Time Use Surveys with regards to definition of work, workers, capturing women's work, migration, unpaid family work, unpaid care work, single women, widows, divorcees, deserted women. This constant questioning has resulted in partial elimination of conceptual and operational biases. Five rounds of National Family Health Surveys (NFHS) have provided comprehensive demographic data. Efforts of UNIFEM/UN Women, Food and Agriculture Organization (FAO), International Labour Organization (ILO), United Nations Development Programme

(UNDP) have provided both qualitative and quantitative indicators for women's contribution in the subsistence economy as well as the nature and extent of care work by using the Time Use method of data collection. Still, the data gap with regards to gender concerns in all sectors of the economy and all spheres of socio-cultural life is quite high (Mukherjee, 1996). The absence of data or inaccurate data due to the invisibility of women and transgender people in the socioeconomic concerns has hampered gender-responsive policy, the measurement of differential impact of unfolding reality, tracking of progress through affirmative action and the demanding of accountability from stakeholders (Patel, 2002).

With this perspective of generating gender-responsive, gender-sensitive, or just gender indicators to measure gender-related changes over time so that effective policies and programmes to reduce the gender gap can be formulated, feminist economists are continuing their dialogues with the official data-gathering bodies such as Census of India, National Sample Survey and The Social Statistics Division (SSD), Ministry of Statistics and Programme Implementation of Government of India, UN Women, and International Labour Organization, India Office.

In 2015, the European Institute of Gender Equality (EIGE) developed a regional Gender Equality Index, covering women's access to employment, money, knowledge, time use, power, and health. Drawing upon Eurostat, the EU statistical data collection system, the index provides a basis for identifying trends, establishing benchmarks, and measuring progress on gender equality. In addition, several EU member states have developed increasingly comprehensive systems to collect, process, and publish gender-disaggregated data (Morais, 2017). These systems include national annual statistics on men and women, legally binding obligations to collect sex-disaggregated data entrenched in general gender equality laws, data collection on specific topics, such as gender-based violence where collections have been fragmentary and lacking a unified definition due to the number of institutions involved in collecting the data. For this purpose, extensive surveys have been carried out on gender-based violence in G20 countries to reflect the multiple dimensions of this phenomena and inform policy-making that includes budgetary allocations for service providers such as hospitals, police, counsellors, helplines, shelter homes, childcare, and employment for survivor of gender-based violence (Vetten, Budlender and Schneider, 2005).

DISCOURSE ON TRANSFORMATIVE FINANCING FOR GENDER EQUALITY

Discourse on engendering micro-meso-macroeconomic policies of fiscal expansion to enhance social sector budgets, progressive taxation, investment in social protection floors, and an emphasis on women's economic rights have all gained momentum during the COVID-19 pandemic. Also witnessed during this period is a stronger focus on systemic issues to address reduction in the gender gap for enhancing equal access to opportunities for all in G20 countries. These triggered economic hardships, intersectional vulnerabilities of caste, race, ethnicity, religion, class, gender, and gender-based violence experienced by women, children, transgender persons, sex workers, persons with disabilities and elderly citizens. Financial accountability of the nation-states demands that G20 countries place people before profit to rebuild their economies ravaged by the pandemic-triggered lockdowns and the loss of lives due to three waves of COVID-19 infection over the last 18 months. The current health emergency triggered by the COVID-19 pandemic urgently demands translation of gender commitments into financial commitments for frontline workers, among whom 70 per cent are women who have been heroically providing their services as doctors, scientists, para-professionals, lab technicians, sanitary workers, poorly paid care workers and sanitary workers (PHM Health Systems Thematic Circle, 2021). G20 nation-states have legislations regarding domestic violence, rape, trafficking of children and women, child sexual abuse, but inadequate budgetary allocations makes implementation of these legislations half-hearted due to insufficient support services (ICRW, 2003). In India, since 2013, after the gang rape of a young physiotherapist in a moving bus in the capital city, Rs1000 crore has been allotted annually to combat gender violence and provide support to the victims/survivors of violence to rebuild their lives, but due to bureaucratic lethargy and lack of political will, year after year, the funds remain unutilised (Pandit, 2019).

RECOMMENDATIONS FOR ACTION

An overall vision and strategy for inclusive, gender-sensitive, and sustainable development is indispensable for framing policy reform with positive long-term goals. Efforts to integrate gender equality in public life should be anchored by a coherent national strategy and action plan instead of a piecemeal and ad hoc or reactive approach to addressing gender equity (Grantham, Stefov and Tiessen, 2019). A coherent, strategic approach is more likely to generate the support of key stakeholders, including the private sector. It would improve consistency across policies and foster policy certainty. These factors contribute to a more secure policy environment, making it more likely that political, public, and private resources will be invested in long-term initiatives such as gender mainstreaming. In addition, it must be recognized that the implementation of these recommendations will require not only resources but also capacity development.

All G20 nation-states must arrive at a consensus to provide time-bound and consistent ex-ante analyses of new policies, programmes, schemes, legislations, regulations, and procedures to limit biases that may disproportionately and negatively impact women. Ex-post impact assessments of targeted programmes, existing policies, laws, regulations, and procedures which have been embedded with systemic constraints to women's economic activity are a must, so that corrective measures can be taken to ensure gender equality. Hence, the twin approaches of gender mainstreaming as well as gender-specific, targeted interventions must be adopted.

For implementation of gender budgeting at national and sub-national levels, the ministries of finance must be the nodal ministry and must be made accountable for efficient implementation and gender-friendly fiscal decision-making. As articulated by the OECD, effective gender budgeting would

> …require that agencies mandated to verify the quality of proposed budgets, such as the Ministry of Finance and Credit, the Office of the President and the Parliament, would integrate the inclusion of gender impact assessments as a requirement within any stage of quality control. This commitment should show tangible results in terms of resource re-prioritization and re-allocation decisions across sectors, and ultimately result in better public spending, for the benefit of both men and women. (OECD, 2017)

Improving the collection and dissemination of gender-disaggregated data to support policy-making and implementation, identification of gender gaps, and reporting on progress in closing these gaps should be the top priority. The visibility of gender in statistics and indicators provides essential inputs for effective policy design, benchmarking and measuring progress on implementation, and accountability. Hence, the G20 nation-states must allocate human, infrastructural, and financial resources to close the data gaps on work participation in rural and urban areas, nature of feminization and de-feminization in the labour force, occupational diversification, poverty groups, child care services, persons with disabilities, and transgender persons.

The capacity building of government bodies, CSOs, NGOs, and elected representatives at local and national levels regarding gender-responsive budgeting and transformatory financing for gender equality, with focus on best practices, is strongly recommended by gender economists. G20 nations need to develop robust reporting and communication mechanisms to share gender concerns in budgetary matters, with stakeholders for analysis, policy design, impact assessments, monitoring and evaluation, and advocacy.

CONCLUSION

Global policies impact local economies. The Gender Equality Forum is a positive move in the direction of gender equality, and ensuring accountability for its gender commitments that are speedily entrusted to grassroots, local women's rights groups and community-based civil society organizations. They are addressing issues arising out of intersectional marginalities and problems of women in all

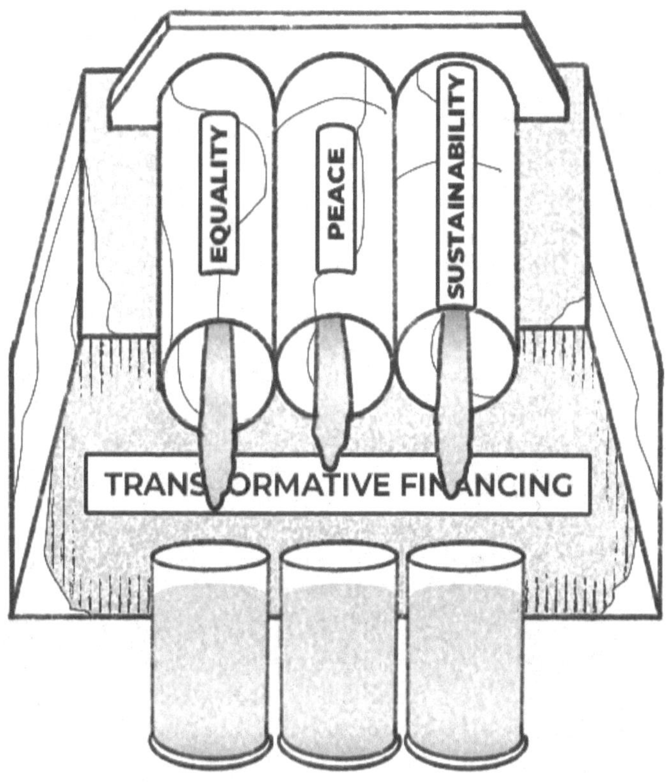

their diversity. This includes the urban poor, farmers, caste/ethnicity-based exclusion and discrimination, informal settlements, rural and maritime areas, sex workers, LGBTQI+, non-binary people and people living with disabilities, and internally displaced persons due to mega development projects or due to natural or man-made disasters from across the region. The G20 nation-states must make sufficient, sustainable, and flexible funding available to civil society, feminist-oriented, women-led, community and grass-roots, and youth-led organizations. They immediately need to establish a strong and effective accountability framework at regional, national, and global levels to monitor commitments made by all Action Coalition leaders and commitment-makers. The UN system needs to engage with intersectional feminists and civil society groups to advocate with governments, regional development institutions, and funders, to properly resource and implement a robust and inclusive accountability framework that evaluates transformative impact at the grassroots level. With collective efforts of GRB and transformative financing by G20 nation-states, the road map for realization of women's human rights for an equal, just, peaceful, and ecologically sustainable future can be carved out.

REFERENCES

Action Coalitions. 2021. *What are Action Coalitions?* Mexico: Generation Equality Forum. July. https://forum.generationequality.org/action-coalitions. Accessed on 27-7-2021.

Anderson, Joy and Katherine Miles. 2015. "The State of the Field of Gender Lens Investing A Review and a Road Map." Miles Criterion Institute. http://criterioninstitute.org/wp-content/uploads/2012/06/State-of-the-Field-of-Gender-Lens-Investing-11-24-2015.pdf. Accessed on 5-8-2021.

Anwar, Samina, Anna Downs and Euan Davidson. 2016. *How can PFM Reforms Contribute to Gender Equality Outcomes?*. UN Women and Department of International Development (DFID). https://gender-financing.unwomen.org/en/resources/h/o/w/how-can-pfm-reforms-contribute-to-gender-equality-outcomes. Accessed on 26-7-2021.

Bureau for Gender Equality. 2005. *Overview of Gender-responsive Budget Initiatives*. Geneva: International Labour Organisation. https://www.ilo.org/wcmsp5/groups/public/---dgreports/---gender/documents/publication/wcms_111403.pdf. Accessed on 20-8-2021.

Chatham House. 2015. Gender and Growth Initiative: Putting Gender Equality on the G20 Agenda. https://www.chathamhouse.org/about-us/our-departments/global-economy-and-finance-programme/gender-and-growth-initiative-putting. Accessed on 16-8-2021.

Demetriades, Justina. 2007. "Gender Indicators: What, Why and How?". BRIDGE's Gender and Indicators Cutting Edge Pack, Columbia. https://www.oecd.org/dac/gender-development/43041409.pdf. Accessed on 16-8-2021.

ESCAP. 2017. "Asia-Pacific Sustainable Development Goals Outlook." Environment and Development Division, United Nations Economic and Social Commission for Asia and the Pacific supported by ADB & UNDP, Bangkok. https://www.adb.org/sites/default/files/publication/232871/asia-pacific-sdgoutlook-2017.pdf. Accessed on 19-8-2021.

FAO. 2018. *Developing gender-sensitive value chains-Guidelines for practitioners*. Rome. http://www.fao.org/3/a-i6462e.pdf.

G20 Information Centre. 2014. 2014 Brisbane Summit, G20 Finance Ministers Meetings. November 16. http://www.g20.utoronto.ca/2014/2014-1116-communique.html. Accessed on 30-9-2022.

GEF. 2021. *Action Coalitions: A Global Acceleration Plan for Gender Equality*. Generation Equality Forum, Paris. https://forum.generationequality.org/sites/default/files/2021-03/AC_Acceleration%20Plan.Final%20Draft%20%28March%2030%29_EN.pdf. Accessed on 3-8-2021.

Gifford, Katherine and Zohra Khan. 2020. *Technical Brief - GRB in the context of COVID-19*. New York: UN Women. https://gender-financing.unwomen. org/en/resources/t/e/c/technical-brief---grb-in-the-context-of-covid-19. Accessed on 14-8-2021

Grantham, K., Stefov, D. and R. Tiessen. 2019. *A Feminist Approach to Women's Economic Empowerment*. Ottawa: Oxfam Canada. https://www.oxfam.ca/ wp-content/uploads/2019/01/a-feminist-approach-to-womens-economic-empowerment_FINAL.pdf. Accessed on 20-8-2021.

House of Commons. 2016. Implementing Gender-Based Analysis Plus (GBA+) in The Government Of Canada. https://www.ourcommons.ca/DocumentViewer/en/42-1/FEWO/report-4/page-66. Accessed on 19-8-2021

ICRW. 2003. *How to Make the Law Work? Budgetary Implications of Domestic Violence Policies in Latin America*. USA: International Centre for Research on Women. https://gender-financing.unwomen.org/en/resources/h/o/w/ how-to-make-the-law-work-budgetary-implications-of-domestic-violence-policies-in-latin-america. Accessed on 27-7-2021.

ILO. 2011. "Making the crisis recovery work for women!." International Labour Organization, Geneva. http://www.ilo.org/gender/Events/WCMS_151285/ lang--en/index.htm.

ILO. 2019. "Work-related gender gaps persist but solutions are clear." March 7. https://www.ilo.org/global/about-the-ilo/newsroom/news/WCMS_674816. Accessed on 30-9-2022.

ILO. 2021. Labour and Employment Ministers' Meeting. "Participation of women in the labour force." September 17. https://www.ilo.org/global/about-the-ilo/how-the-ilo-works/multilateral-system/brics/2021/WCMS_819798/ lang--en/index.htm. Accessed on 30-9-2022.

ILO-OECD. 2020a. "Enhancing equal access to opportunities for all in G20 countries OECD background note for the G20 Framework Working Group." https://www.oecd.org/economy/Enhancing-equal-access-to-opportunities-OECD-background-note-for-G20-Framework-Working-Group-july-2020.pdf. Accessed on 15-8-2021.

ILO-UN WOMEN. 2021. "How to Assess Fiscal Stimulus Packages from a Gender Equality Perspective?". https://www.ilo.org/wcmsp5/groups/public/---ed_emp/documents/publication/wcms_766991.pdf. Accessed on 7-8-2021.

ILO-OECD. 2020b. "Women at Work in G20 countries: Progress and Policy Action-Summary." p.1. https://www.ilo.org/wcmsp5/groups/public/---dgreports/--cabinet/documents/publication/wcms_713375.pdf. Accessed on 12-8-2021.

Imp-Act. 2005. "Choosing and Using Indicators for Effective Social Performance Management." *Imp-Act Practice Notes No. 5.* Brighton: IDS http://www.ids. ac.uk/impact/publications/practice_notes/PN5_Indicators.pdf.

Khan, Sarbuland, Ed. 2002. *Human Development, Health and Education: Dialogues at the Economic and Social Council.* New York: United Nations Economic and Social Council. https://www.un.org/en/ecosoc/docs/health&educ.pdf. Accessed on 22-8-2021.

Klugman. 2015. *A Profile of Gender Disparities in the G20.* Chatham House.

Krishnaraj Maithreyi, and Joy Deshmukh. 1993. *Gender in Economics: Theory and Practice.* Delhi: Ajanta Press.

Kulik, Julia. 2020. *G20 Performance on Gender Equality.* 14 April. https://www. g20-insights.org/policy_briefs/g20-performance-on-gender-equality/. Accessed on 17-8-2021.

Lansky, Mark, Ghosh, Jayati, Meda, Dominique, and Uma Rani. 2017. *Women, Gender, Work: Social Choices & Inequalities Vol. 2.* Geneva: International Labour Organisation. https://www.ilo.org/wcmsp5/groups/public/---dgreports/---dcomm/---publ/documents/publication/wcms_488475.pdf. Accessed on 17-8-2021.

Morais Maceira, H. 2017. "Economic Benefits of Gender Equality in the EU". *Intereconomics* 52, 178–183. https://doi.org/10.1007/s10272-017-0669-4. Accessed on 12-8-2021

Moser, Caroline. 1993. *Gender Planning and Development; Theory, Practice and Training.* UK: Routledge.

Mukherjee, M. 1996. "Towards Gender -Aware Data Systems- Indian Experience". *Economic and Political Weekly*, Vol. XXXI (43). October 26. WS 63-WS71.

Pandit, Ambika. 2019. Nearly 90% of Nirbhaya Fund lying unused: Govt data. *The Times of India.* December 8. https://timesofindia.indiatimes.com/india/nearly-90-of-nirbhaya-fund-lying-unused-govt-data/articleshow/72421059.cms. Accessed on 15-8-2021.

OECD. 2017. *Building an Inclusive Mexico: Policies and Good Governance for Gender Equality.* The Organisation for Economic Co-operation and Development. OECD Publishing.

OECD. 2020. "Enhancing equal access to opportunities for all in G20 countries".

Patel, Vibhuti. 1992. "Women and Structural Adjustment Programme in India". Development Studies Institute, UK: London School of Economics and Political Science.

Patel, Vibhuti. 2002. "GENDER BUDGET- A CASE STUDY OF INDIA." Department of Economics: Centre of Advanced Study in Economics, University of Mumbai. http://www.feministpolicyindia.org/documents/resources/Gender%20Budget-A%20Case%20Study%20of%20India%20Vibhuti%20Patel%202003%20(1).pdf. Accessed on 8-8-2021.

Patel, Vibhuti. 2020. "Gender Implications of COVID-19 Pandemic and Challenges for Community Interventions." https://keepingcount.wordpress.com/2020/06/22/aftermath-gender-challenges/. Accessed on 11-10-2021.

PHM Health Systems Thematic Circle. 2021. "A Political Economy Analysis of the Impact of Covid-19 Pandemic on Health Workers." USA: Making power and gender visible in the work of providing care Global Health Justice Partnership of the Yale Law and Public Health Schools. https://law.yale.edu/sites/default/files/area/center/ghjp/documents/phm_commentary_v2.pdf. Accessed on 15-8-2021.

Seguino, Stephanie. 2009. *The gender perspectives of the financial crisis*. USA: The United Nations. https://gender-financing.unwomen.org/en/resources/t/h/e/the-gender-perspectives-of-the-financial-crisis. Accessed on 27-7-2021.

Sharp, Rhonda and Siobhan Austen. 2006. "The Female-Friendliest Treasurer of them All???". https://www2.unwomen.org/-/media/files/un%20women/grb/resources/the%20female-friendliest%20treasurer%20of%20them%20all%20taxation%20in%20australia.pdf?vs=5323 Accessed on 15-8-2021.

Shreeves, Rosamund and Nessa Boland. 2021. "Women in politics in the EU State of play." European Parliament, Paris & Brussels: European Union. https://www.europarl.europa.eu/RegData/etudes/BRIE/2021/689345/EPRS_BRI(2021)689345_EN.pdf, Accessed on 18-8-2021.

Sorgner et al. 2020. *Achieving "25 by 25": Actions to make Women's Labour Inclusion a G20 Priority*. December 10. https://www.g20-insights.org/policy_briefs/gender-economic-equity-achieving-25-by-25-actions-to-make-womens-labour-inclusion-a-g20-priority/. Accessed on 30-9-2022.

Stotsky, Janet G. 2016. "Gender Budgeting: Fiscal Context and Current Outcomes." IMF Working Paper, WP/16/149. https://www.imf.org/external/pubs/ft/wp/2016/wp16149.pdf.

Thomas, Margo, Novion, Cesar Cordova, de Hann, Arjan, de Leon, Gimena, Maxime, Forest, and Sandhya S. Iyer. 2018. *Gender Mainstreaming: A Strategic Approach, Argentina: Think 20*. https://www.g20-insights.org/policy_briefs/gender-mainstreaming-a-strategic-approach/. Accessed on 18-8-2021.

United Nations. 2015. *The World's Women 2015: Trends and Statistics*. Department of Economic and Social Affairs. https://unstats.un.org/unsd/gender/downloads/worldswomen2015_report.pdf

United Nations. 2020. "A UN framework for the immediate socio-economic response to COVID-19." https://unsdg.un.org/sites/default/files/2020-04/UN-Framework-for-the-immediate-socio-economic-response-to-COVID-19.pdf. Accessed on 14-8-2021.

UN Women. 2016. *Gender-Responsive Budgeting: Analysis of Budget Programmes from Gender Perspective.* https://eca.unwomen.org/en/digital-library/publications/2016/05/gender-responsive-budgeting--analysis-of-budget-programmes-from-gender-perspective. Accessed on 30-9-2022

UN Women. 2021. "Action Coalitions Global Acceleration Plan." Generation Equality Forum, Mexico and Paris. https://forum.generationequality.org/sites/default/files/2021-06/UNW%20-%20GAP%20Report%20-%20EN.pdf.

UNHRC. 2013. *Realizing the Right to Development: Essays in Commemoration of 25 Years of the United Nations Declaration on the Right to Development.* New York and Geneva: UN Human Rights Office of the High Commissioner. https://ohchr.org/Documents/Publications/RightDevelopmentInteractive_EN.pdf. Accessed on 21-8-2021.

UNIFEM. 2009. *How Can Aid be Gender Responsive?* https://gender-financing.unwomen.org/en/resources/h/o/w/how-can-aid-be-gender-responsive-English. Accessed on 26-7-2021.

Vetten, Lisa, Budlender, Debbie, and Vera Schneider. 2005. "The Price of Protection: Costing the implementation of the Domestic Violence Act (no. 116 of 1998)." CSVR Gender Programme, Policy Brief No. 02. October. https://gender-financing.unwomen.org/en/resources/t/h/e/the-price-of-protection-costing-the-implementation-of-the-domestic-violence-act-in-south-africa. Accessed on 27-7-2021.

Exploring the Migration Policies and Dependency Patterns among G20 Nations: From Global Financial Crisis to Global COVID-19 Crisis

Elizabeth Edison

G20 attained prominence as a collective founded in the backdrop of the 1997 Asian financial crisis. Later on, the global financial crisis of 2008 brought our attention to the structural issues plaguing the global political economy. Attempts were made to study the multifarious impacts of the global financial crisis. Efforts were also put in to make the 'system' more resilient to future crises. Labour, the most crucial input in value creation, continues to experience adverse impacts of such efforts. This chapter seeks to look at the policies on migration espoused by the member countries. The responses of the nations to the humanitarian crisis of Syrian refugees and climate-induced migration are perused as referral points. The imminent challenge before the group takes the form of the coronavirus (COVID-19) pandemic which has taken millions of lives and has pushed the global economy into another financial crisis. Hence, the response of the group to the ongoing global pandemic shall be looked at. We point out the unequal power relations existing within this heterogeneous grouping. The conceptual framework provided by dependency theory is used in understanding the interdependence amongst G20 countries. The relations continue to remain pertinent and have evolved into collaborations which are bilateral and regional.

INTRODUCTION

The capitalist mode of production and development necessitates a zero sum approach to growth. This has been widely discussed by dependency theorists and a similar framework has been adopted to explore the changing nature of dependency in contemporary times. These nations have been dependent on one another for various resources, including labour. The nature of dependency among them has been looked into for an understanding of the contemporary culture of cooperation. Further, an attempt was made to look at how these dependency relations affected their responses to the global pandemic. This shall enable us to look at the prevalent power relations among the member nations and evaluate the relevance of the grouping. The essay shall rely primarily on secondary sources to understand the evolution of migration policies affecting the workers. The reports of ILO, United Nations and other international organizations have been perused for analysis. The responses of the nations to the raging pandemic were collated and analyzed to throw more light on the culture of cooperation prevalent among them. This shall also enable us to critically look at the relevance of the grouping amidst a global crisis, albeit in a different and more devastating manner.

MIGRATION AND GLOBALIZATION

Migration has always been a part of human civilization. People move around in search of better economic opportunities and standard of living. Migration theories postulate both 'push' and 'pull' factors which contribute to decisions on migration. The migrants often acquire the requisite skills and knowledge from the country of origin. The host country, in return, assures them better economic and social opportunities to lead secure lives (Parkins, 2010). Often the migrants follow their family members and ultimately decide to settle down in a different country and not return to their country of origin. Hence, it is said that people prefer to migrate to those countries where it remains easier for their relatives to migrate to as well (Khoo, 2003).

In 2015, there were 244 million international migrants, as per the International Migration Report of the United Nations. Among them, more than two-thirds lived in high income countries (Triandafyllidou, 2018). Most of the migrants intend to take up some work at the destination. The 'temporary movement of natural persons' is encompassed in Mode 4 of GATS. The General Agreement on Trade in Services (GATS) deals with international trade in goods and services and includes four modes of trade in services. Developing countries have demonstrated an enthusiasm in seeking greater Mode 4 liberalization owing to their 'comparative advantage in rendering services at lower wages' (Martin, 2006). However, the more developed countries are obviously quite skeptical of allowing such free flow of 'natural persons.'

There are consequences for both the host and the country of origin in this case. It is most often the case that the highly skilled workers are the ones desired at the destination in this Mode. The origin country, while sending highly skilled workers such as managers and professionals, is likely to lose by way of 'brain drain'. This may result in a vicious cycle in the country of origin. Since there exists ambiguity in how 'temporary' the movement is, greater expansion of the movement under Mode 4 could result in 'more professional migration, settlement, and fewer remittances and returns' (Martin, 2006). Yet, these are generally not seen as pressing concerns by countries such as India. This is owing to the better returns expected, the labour surplus prevailing in countries such as India and China and also an ageing workforce in countries such as Japan (Powell and Khan, 2013), which calls for more skilled workers from elsewhere.

Migration and globalization, hence, remain highly interwoven. Globalization as a complex phenomenon contributes to the manoeuvring of global production networks. The efforts to drive down costs have resulted in the creation of global value chains of production, which are spread across the Global North and Global South. Moreover, migrants themselves do not constitute a homogeneous category. Many can be entering the destination as job seekers while others may be migrating through 'family reunification schemes' (Khoo, 2003). Family networks  continue to play a key role in decisions on migration (Stark, 1991). Studies demonstrate how migrant workers form a key component of these global value chains, fulfilling the labour requirements at all nodes in the production network. Yet, trade and migration are deemed to be different flows. People perceive the flow of immigrants in a radically different manner. Owing to this, political leaders also become obliged to approach it differently (Goldstein and Venturini, 2016).

GLOBAL VALUE CHAINS AND G20 NATIONS: A RELATION OF DEPENDENCY

Gereffi and Fernandez-Stark (2016) define global value chains as 'the full range of activities that firms and workers perform to bring a product from its conception to end use and beyond.' The activities shall include research and development, production, marketing and promotion along with support rendered to the final customer. Most often these activities are divided across different firms, which are plausibly placed in different countries as well. Efforts are made to categorize activities into 'core' and 'non-core' activities. The core activities tend to generate more value and are expected to be 'performed better than other companies' in order to retain the firm's advantage in the market. The non-core activities can be outsourced as they are not extremely pertinent for a comparative advantage (Hernandez and Pedersen, 2017). Usually, G20 nations such as India, China, Indonesia, Brazil, Mexico, Argentina, South Africa and Turkey are countries where non-core activities are more prevalent.

Draper (2013) describes how an 'emerging factory China' is evolving amidst global production chains. China, which started as a 'sourcing hub' for the developed countries such as the USA, is climbing up the development ladder. Both India and China are touted as the 'Asian Drivers' with the potential to develop significant innovation capabilities in the near future. A surreal combination of innovative technologies and low-cost production offers much to a production chain (Altenburg, Schmitz and Stamm, 2008). Mexico remains a sourcing hub for the American corporations. In Southeast Asia, we see countries such as South

Korea emerging as major 'outward investors'. India remains crucial with respect to the services GVC, and Brazil with regards to the global agricultural value chain. China is involved 'selectively' in the production network. Without merely following the handbook of 'neo-liberal economics', China was able to evolve into the world's largest exporter. Further, China remains the central figure when it comes to manufacturing, especially in labour-intensive sectors (Draper, 2013).

Most often, one can find several labour-intensive sectors in the production chain. Here, ardent competition persists amongst the developing nations. The multi-national corporations outsource their production activities to countries that assure economical labour in terms of wages. The ability of these MNCs to keep a watch on labour standards throughout the value chain remains questionable. This 'modern slavery' continues to be promoted by corporations because it 'serves their needs' (Stringer and Michailova, 2018). Further, we are currently witnessing a globalizing world, a single global market and continuously emerging new production chains. This is concomitant with calls for 'convergence of international and national trade union agendas.' Hence, a newer challenge arises for labour, as conventionally, workers organize according to the national context and demands. While one cannot completely deny the presence of laws which advocate for the rights of workers, the limited unionization and collective representation render their implementation and enforcement insufficient (Schmidt, 2007).

The other concern is the adverse impacts on the local socio-economic milieu. Triandafyllidou (2018) elucidates how China, India and Brazil are emerging as major economies in the global system. Yet, the developing nations remain unfairly guided by rules and norms made and dominated by western players. The gulf between the developing and developed countries has increased, along with rising inequality within the nations. Another fallout of the integration process is the unsettling of 'local economies' of new industrial centres, during the process of prioritizing export-oriented production with little focus on domestic activity (ibid.). This process has culminated in creating a workforce which lives in extremely precarious conditions. Hence, Peterson (2010) asserts that 'precarious and informal work has become the structural feature of contemporary globalization'. Ensuring that a significant share of a country's workforce stays poor and vulnerable for the benefit of global capital to thrive underscores the priorities of twenty-first century capitalism.

G20 members such as the USA and the nations of the European Union represent the 'core' or 'metro' countries while the 'peripheral' or 'satellite' countries include Mexico, Indonesia, India and others. The mode of capitalist production created an all-encompassing system which necessitated the dependence of the peripheral nations in the international capitalist system. Such a dependency was crucial for the survival of the system. Hence, this dependency on core countries is the feature that remains common to all the countries in the periphery (Dos Santos,

1970). As a consequence, globalization is different for different members. The neoliberal agenda of completely opening up the markets for the rest of the world was to be put into action by the phenomenon of globalization. Some countries of the Global South have been able to make use of the benefits accruing from globalization. Yet, at the same time, some other countries found it as an 'imposition of the neoliberal structural adjustment programs' (Farny, 2016). In addition, this dependency is not just between the countries of the North and South. Rather, there exist unequal dependency relations among the countries in the South as well (Farny, 2016).

As Dos Santos (1970) argued, the development of the country in the periphery gets tied to the development and expansion of the core country, 'deepening and aggravating the problems of their peoples.' Here, development becomes a zero sum concept as one flourishes at the cost of other nations. The global financial crisis of 2008, touted as the worst economic crisis then, more clearly demonstrated the intricate loops and dependencies which existed among the developed and the developing world. It was a crisis created by the Global North, the ramifications of which were adverse even for the countries that played no part in its creation (Farny, 2016). As a result of the crisis, the formation of the G20 can be  viewed as a means to manoeuvre the new demands of the global order. Even though the effects of the crisis were not uniformly felt across the Global South, there exists a general consensus which seems wary of global alliances, and globalization in particular. To that end, several scholars call for regional blocks and associations, enabling cooperation at a smaller scale. A 'polycentric international structure' is the desired end, to which 'transnational South-South linkages are being formed' (Golub, 2013).

G20 AND THE REFUGEE CRISIS

At this juncture, we shall look at the migration policies of the grouping when the world witnessed one of the worst humanitarian crises. The conflicts in Syria began in 2011 and resulted in the displacement of people across the region. Ostrand (2015) cites the report of the United Nations High Commissioner for Refugees (UNHCR), which puts the approximate number of internally displaced people at 7.6 million. With over 3 million fleeing the country, the Syrian refugee crisis put enormous pressure on the countries in the immediate neighbourhood and also on the world at large. Turkey is the only G20 member country with physical borders with Syria and the crisis saw refugees settling down there, along with other neighbours such as Iran, Lebanon, Egypt and Jordan. Other member countries such as Sweden, Germany, UK and USA were more proactive in housing the refugees. Due to the availability of more resources within these countries however, it is often remarked that these well-off nations could have done more towards the resettlement of refugees in addition to helping them by way of financial assistance (ibid.).

It was during the Syrian refugee crisis that the G20 nations asserted how 'forced displacement constitutes a global concern.' The communiques from the summits of Antalya (2015) and Hangzhou (2016) called for concerted efforts to address this humanitarian crisis (Khasru, Mahmud, and Nahreen, 2017). There were inconsistencies in how the members approached this dire situation, however. While the principle of non-refoulement is widely accepted, no country is legally obliged to undertake refugees' resettlement (Ostrand, 2015). Unfortunately, the G20 countries in spite of possessing the wherewithal and financial resources needed to mitigate this crisis, have not risen to the demand. Their 'inefficient and bureaucratic fund mobilisation system' threatens the governance framework in its entirety. Further, scholars also argue that policy making with myopic considerations of only national interests at the cost of global, humanitarian ones shall culminate in heightened refugee victimization and bring in 'non-traditional security threats' in the future (Khasru, Mahmud and Nahreen, 2017). Interestingly, Turkey, despite hosting the highest number of Syrian refugees in the neighbourhood, did not see the refugees 'taking away' the jobs of the natives (Akgündüz, van den Berg and Hassink, 2015).

The perception of people in the host country towards the refugee population and migrant workers also vary. Goldstein and Venturini (2016) elucidate how the sentiment towards the refugee community in Germany and Sweden demonstrated more empathy at their plight. The migrant workers, however, enjoyed less favourable public perception, which was largely dependent on how the media portrayed the migrant workers as well. The rise of extremist political parties into power across the world is often pointed out as a direct fallout of the media giving ample air time to 'hate mongering' speeches, which are founded on xenophobic, antiminority, regressive principles. Herman and Chomsky (1988), in their seminal work on 'Manufacturing Consent', further elucidate how media propagandizes on behalf of the people with vested interests. This political might and economic power render any resistance against such connivance difficult to counter. Consequently, we see the largest share of refugees being housed in developing countries, which experience severe resource constraints. Since the political conflicts which culminate in these unfortunate events are global, it is only fair for the responsibility to be global as well. Hence, it becomes an international issue (Goldstein and Venturini, 2016).

Another crisis which looms overhead is that of 'climate refugees'. Climate-induced migrations are not uniform across the world and remain to be defined. At present the population displacements from this form of migration are at a smaller level, with people moving for a shorter duration. The concern shall become more pressing when we encounter irrevocable environmental damage as a dire consequence of climate change, necessitating permanent relocations of the populations. A range of 25 million to 1 billion environmental migrants are forecast to be alive for the year 2050 by the United Nations International Organization for Migration (Kraemer, 2017). The conventional understanding remains that the displaced people 'shall return' to their homes once the cause of displacement gets addressed. Unfortunately, in the case of 'climate-induced involuntary migration', the environment becomes inhospitable for them to return (Kraemer, 2017). This could also aggravate pre-existing tensions and result in more conflicts among countries. In that context, surviving the forces of nature as well as other conflicts (Sagar et al., 2017) shall be deemed necessary.

G20 nations, undoubtedly, remain highly vulnerable to this crisis. India, for instance, ought to prepare for the potential of receiving environmental refugees from neighbouring Bangladesh. A severe consequence of temperature increase arising from anthropogenic factors is the rapid melting of glaciers. This shall concomitantly cause a rise in the sea levels. The coastal zone covering about 30 per cent of the country renders the coastal population of Bangladesh the most vulnerable to this crisis. The 'fragile borders' between India and Bangladesh could enable them to enter the Indian subcontinent. There will undoubtedly be some socio-economic and political impacts of such a plausible scenario, understandably (Chowdhary, 2020). It is pertinent to point out how an impending crisis of such magnitude has not received proportional attention from the state. The plight of environmental refugees shall remain intrinsically tied to the political position adopted by the nations in the neighbourhood. So far, the issue of migrants from Bangladesh to India has only been studied 'tangentially as a political issue' (ibid.). Since India is conveniently not a party to any international refugee treaty, being oblivious to the plight of millions of people gets technically justified. Yet, what matters most during a humanitarian crisis is indeed the moral principles and actions one espouses. To that end, at least at the regional level, it is of paramount importance for India and neighbouring nations to explore possible ways to address the situation.

Most of the G20 nations themselves are susceptible to the vagaries of climate change. Indonesia remains vulnerable to even a moderate sea level rise and it has the potential to affect the nation's people, businesses and infrastructure. With over 60 per cent of the Indonesian population residing in low lying areas such as Jakarta and Surabaya, livelihoods and farming of the coastal populace are bound to be devastated (Measey, 2010). Flannigan, Stocks and Wotton (2000) point out how the incidences of forest fires are going to increase in the United States of America as an adverse consequence of climate change. The impacts of anthropogenic activities and climate change on the forest fire regime have consequences for migration patterns as well as species distribution. Recent years have witnessed a rise in forest fires raging across the Latin American countries as well. The European nations have also experienced higher temperatures and uncomfortable weather in the last couple of years.

By looking at the responses of the G20 nations to the refugee crises it becomes quite clear that there exists little unanimity among the member countries on these issues. Differences in their approaches to refugee groups and migrant workers demonstrate little empathy to their plight. Being oblivious to the concerns of a rising number of environmental refugees is apathetic when these countries should ideally be acting as responsible states, formulating policies to ameliorate the worries of the refugee community on humanitarian grounds. The unevenness within the group becomes conspicuous here. India and Indonesia, for instance, bear a greater brunt of climate change induced refugee flow as elucidated above. Hence, the richer and more developed countries should ideally pitch in their resources (Ostrand, 2015), if not on humanitarian grounds, definitely in the light of 'climate justice' which developing countries have been fervently pointing out. On the whole, the time is imminent for the grouping to seriously reckon with the reality of climate change and put into practice some of the tall assertions made during the summit of 2016 (Hangzhou) regarding climate change and taking the Paris Agreement into account in developmental trajectories.

G20 RESPONSE TO COVID-19 PANDEMIC

The magnitude of the loss brought about by the coronavirus pandemic has been beyond the expectations of most. The World Health Organization (WHO) claimed that around nine people were losing their lives to COVID-19 every minute during the pandemic. The multifarious spheres impacted as a consequence of this malaise demand to be looked into. Having started as a crisis in the health sector, the economy, infrastructure sector and polity were soon to be adversely affected. The initial efforts were in comprehending the possible fallout in terms of lives lost. Soon, concerted efforts became necessary to slow down the consequent economic crisis. Bektimur et al. (2020) suggest that the primary efforts were in complying with the International Health Regulations (IHR, 2005), along with information and data sharing among the countries. Health ministers of countries were to collaborate and work on mitigating the impacts of the COVID-19 pandemic. The authors also add that protecting lives and safeguarding jobs and incomes of the people were to be carried out in tandem. WHO and partners launched the Access to COVID-19 Tools (ACT) Accelerator partnership in order to speed up the development, production and equitable access to 'tests, treatments and vaccines' (WHO, 2020).

The concomitant effects of the COVID pandemic in the economic sphere is touted to be much worse than the fallout of the global financial crisis of 2008. Around 840 million workers of G20 nations are either poor or live just above the poverty line (ILO, 2014). The differential impacts of a pandemic on people of different classes remain conspicuous. ILO reports that more than 60 per cent of the workers in the world are in the informal economy. G20 nations like India have more than 90 per cent of its workers informally employed. It is about 61–70 per cent of the labour force in the case of Indonesia (Rothenberg et al., 2016) and about 47.1 per cent in Brazil (Romero, 2021). Due to variations in definitions, informal employment in the USA ranges from 3–40 per cent. Nevertheless, what remains pertinent is the precariousness of the informally employed. Being deprived of social security and social insurance, informal workers constitute the most economically vulnerable section of the population.

Luckhurst et al. (2020) demonstrate how the impacts of any crisis shall vary across the Global North and Global South, owing to its different contextual realities. Due to the pandemic, unemployment rates have soared and poverty levels have also been adversely impacted. In the USA, for example, in the month of April 2020, the employment rate dropped by over 8 percentage points as compared to the previous month and earnings in the same month fell by over 10 per cent (Han, Meyer and Sullivan, 2020). The situation remains even bleaker for a developing country like India where, Parvathamma (2020) estimates that over 120 million were rendered poor and around 40 million people were pushed to abject poverty. An unemployment rate of nearly 31 per cent was experienced in the urban areas in the country in April 2020. The impact of the pandemic was felt across various economic sectors such as exports, services, aviation, tourism, hospitality, construction, retail, etc. Luckhurst et al. (2020) also point out how the second quarter of the year 2020 saw the equivalent of around 305 million jobs being lost in work hours globally.

As a crisis with effects and consequences across all countries, the pandemic necessitated collective and collaborative efforts from the grouping. However, the initial response was to 'turn inward' (Atkinson, 2020). Most governments demonstrated a desire to 'act alone'. Around 80 countries banned or limited the export of equipment such as face masks, protective gears and gloves amidst the pandemic. This was to the detriment of import-dependent countries, putting them at a huge risk of shortage of medical supplies when the pandemic was raging across the continents (Kavuma, 2020). Interestingly, this inward-looking policy may not be viable because 'national barriers' in a highly 'interconnected' world makes it difficult for each nation to produce medical supplies which are vital in this fight. Baldwin and Evenett (2020) further argue how insular policies shall fail in fostering economic recovery. Moreover, it remains antithetical to the collaborative spirit which should ideally come about to defeat this 'threat to the human race'.

Further, in the European Union, most of the efforts to combat the coronavirus pandemic were promoted by government entities. Yet, Estonia, Sweden and Finland stood out as nations wherein civil society took greater initiative (Almeida, 2020). The perusal of open source and open data technologies aided in ensuring transparency of information. The countries of the EU contributed towards innovative solutions to combat the effects of the coronavirus pandemic. Initial efforts were made to 'trace' the contacts so that the spread of the virus could be minimized. To that end, several mobile applications were developed across countries. Gilbert, Degeling and Johnson (2019) argue how modern technology has 'revolutionised the accessibility, scope and speed of data collection and analysis.'

The USA also initiated similar travel restrictions at the beginning of the pandemic. Travellers from 'areas with known outbreaks' were restrained and warnings were given to avoid all 'non-essential travel'. Interestingly, a relaxation in the curbs led to a rapid spread of infection across the country and resulted in restrictions on gatherings and travels, yet again (Schucat, 2020). Okonkwo et al. (2021) point out how the effects of the pandemic across various communities were different. The virus had the 'greatest implications for the most vulnerable people.' Moreover, the pandemic is said to have exacerbated the health inequities which already define the American healthcare system. The position of incarcerated people became all the more precarious. The absence of tele-health facilities across the states furthered the plight of people with disabilities. Moreover, it remained unrealistic for the homeless to follow protocols of social distancing and hand sanitization (ibid.).

Japan adopted a 'cluster-based approach' in responding to the COVID-19 crisis. Calls for avoiding crowded, closed spaces were given to the public. A national state of emergency was also declared to curb the spread of infection. Perusal of 'mobile phone applications for contact tracing and close-contact management' became rampant (Oshitani, 2020). The containment efforts were largely successful, owing to the deployment of personnel for community engagement. Public health centres (PHC) took the lead in their response. The challenge of insufficient human resources was addressed by 'reemploying former PHC officers, and newly recruiting public health specialists from outside PHCs' (Imamura, Saito and Oshitani, 2021). Japan tried to ensure that only public health experts were put in charge of contact tracing and case investigations instead of outsourcing these tasks to people of other academic backgrounds. Japan's experience in dealing with 'outbreak investigations for Tuberculosis' helped in adopting 'enhanced retrospective contact tracing' (Imamura, Saito and Oshitani, 2021).

Some of the member countries demonstrated quite a different initial response to the then emerging pandemic. While most nations were trying to restrain people from other countries from visiting them, Indonesia tried to attract tourists who were intending on travelling to China, Korea and Japan as these nations had confirmed cases of coronavirus infections then. This promoted Indonesia as an alternate tourist destination, and thereby conformed to their 'economic developmentalist mindset', which was the priority (Almuttaqi, 2020). It was only much later that travel restrictions and lockdowns were imposed in such countries. The measures of 'testing, tracing, isolating and treatment' (Ashcroft, Lehtinen and Bonhoeffer, 2022). were all seen as inadequate in the case of Indonesia. Millions of dollars worth of loans were taken to fight the pandemic. A major fallout of the crisis was the pushing of several millions into poverty. The economic slowdown has pushed many non-poor people to abject poverty as well (Olivia, Gibson and Nasrudin, 2020). Years of efforts in ameliorating poverty were undone by the 'COVID-19 shocks'.

The immediate response of the Indian government towards the initial infections was to shut down the borders. The suspension of flights for more than two months ensured that the country remained in complete lockdown. The initial months saw a paucity of testing kits and insufficient surveillance measures. The health system was overwhelmed. The historically low expenditure on healthcare and infrastructure adversely affected the country's preparedness during and for the pandemic (Siddiqui et al., 2020). The economic sphere was devastated by the lockdown which brought life as one knew it to a standstill. The pandemic widened the already persistent gender gaps. The loss of livelihood and the threat of a deadly, unknown virus culminated in a 'crisis of mobility'. The lack of prior warning stranded millions of migrant workers on the roads (Rajan, Sivakumar and Srinivasan, 2020).

The economic impacts of the pandemic on women have been even more adverse. Many were forced out of the workforce in order to look after sick ones. Migrant workers, of whom women constitute a significant number, lost out on job opportunities. A major criticism levied against government interventions to mitigate poverty is that the 'transient poor' remained left out of such schemes (Olivia, Gibson and Nasrudin, 2020). Further, concerns about alleviating hunger levels as a result of lower food production remain. 'Nutrition shocks as a consequence of income shocks' could exacerbate child wasting, stunting and malnutrition. Equally worrisome is the possibility of lower immunization rates following the pandemic. With health centres focusing on COVID-19, immunization drives have taken a hit and a terrible fallout shall be the uptick of conventional diseases. Similarly, people with other acute diseases have remained home instead of visiting hospitals for special treatment, fearing infection (Barach et al., 2020).

Moreover, what can be observed as a common tool across countries in the fight against COVID-19 pandemic has been the use of tracking systems. The widespread use of contract tracing apps and surveillance measures have been criticized on several grounds. In addition to being a conspicuous violation of one's privacy, these applications are also bound to 'intensify the effects of discriminatory design and algorithmic oppression' (French et al., 2020). The authors argue how the 'corporate contact tracing systems' have been used to identify 'risk groups for targeted interventions'. This translates into furthered stigmatization. Undoubtedly, this leaves room for greater violence and discrimination (Davis, 2020) against some religious or marginalized communities. Racism, xenophobia and religious tensions have been augmented by the coronavirus pandemic. Minority groups such as LGBT people experience added concerns as a community whose behaviour is already criminalized and stigmatized (ibid.).

With respect to surveillance systems, when 'utility increases, privacy decreases' (Gilbert, Degeling and Johnson, 2019) and the key remains to maintain a balance between 'individual risk and community benefit'. Hence, French et al. (2020) elucidate that, in theory, 'public health should serve the public', and this should incorporate everybody. Moreover, the authors point to the possibility of 'de- centring the power of public health authorities' as a consequence of dependency on these systems. This happens when applications are run on smartphones which are individually owned, through telecommunication infrastructure and services that are privately operated. Thereby, these surveillance measures further run the risk of being exploited by corporate players to 'perfect their AI-enabled technologies' (ibid.).

In addition to such surveillance measures and consequent breach of privacy during the pandemic, there unfortunately was a disparity in the vaccination drives (Luckhurst et al., 2020). High-income countries were capable of administering nearly 100 times more vaccine doses per inhabitant than the low-income countries. This has rendered 'millions of healthcare workers and vulnerable populations unprotected in the world's poorest countries.' (WHO, 2021). This is in spite of the call of G20 grouping to develop tests, treatments and vaccines in addition to focusing on an equitable distribution of these across the nations (ibid.). The proposed coordination among the health ministers of these countries seemed to have been confined to mere press releases, lacking in concrete actions.

Further, we witnessed 'vaccine nationalism' wherein countries took measures to hoard vaccines and other WHO-approved drugs. Canada already possesses enough to vaccinate its population nine times over (as cited in Hassoun, 2021). Similarly, richer G20 nations like US, Australia, EU, Japan and UK are also capable of vaccinating their populace between 2 to 8 times. Further, Hassoun (2021) argues that vaccine nationalism is detrimental to the interests of the rich nations as well. This is due to the possibility of resurgence of the coronavirus when the other countries remain unable to vaccinate and protect its population from infection. The other more obvious argument against vaccine nationalism is that it is morally unethical for richer nations to keep vaccines to themselves when millions are deprived of even a dignified burial in the poorer parts of the world as a result of the pandemic (ibid.).

The efforts of the G20 nations towards the goal of improving public health management remain insufficient. Obstfeld and Posen (2020) argue how they have only rendered a 'lip service in preventing an escalation of economic aggression and in helping the world's poor.' An environment of distrust emerges from a zero sum approach to development. This further prevents any collective action during a time of crisis such as the present. While it is often lauded that G20 is 'lean and mean and not burdened by a maligned bureaucracy', they need some more 'institutional might' (Garrett, 2010). In fact, the G20 member countries do possess the wherewithal to respond to the aftermath of the pandemic. Any amount spent on the health sector at this juncture shall be small in comparison to the consequences of not 'defeating the disease'. This translates into a necessity to 'undertake large fiscal responses' (Obstfeld and Posen, 2020) so that global action earns the necessary results.

During the COVID-19 pandemic, the more powerful Western countries demonstrated a dependence on the emerging economies such as India and China for meeting their demands for masks, sanitizer, gloves and other medical equipment needed to fight the pandemic. Being locations of low-cost production, the manufacturing sector in these countries did gain momentum eventually in an otherwise bleak socio-economic scenario. Scholars call for 'concerted cooperation to enable the constrained countries to address the economic contraction brought about by the pandemic' (McKibbin and Vines, 2020). Since little effort was made to address the pandemic as a grouping, we can only analyze how the countries undertook bilateral cooperation arrangements.

The pattern of dependency amongst the G20 nations conventionally demonstrated a 'need-based' approach. Since Asian nations possessed the resources of labour, the countries of the Global North made use of the economic labour conditions present. In addition, during the COVID-19 crisis, some pre-existing dependent relations also came into the forefront with greater media scrutiny. For instance, active pharmaceutical ingredients (API) constitute a key ingredient in the making of any drug. Countries world over

are overwhelmingly dependent on China for this. India imported more than two-thirds of its API demand from China till last year. The USA imported 80 per cent of its API demand from just two countries—China and India (Varshney and Pandey, 2020). Amidst the blame game on 'the origin of the coronavirus', there remained an atmosphere of distrust and antagonism against China. This even translated into an 'informal boycott' of Chinese products in several countries including India (Tibrewala, 2020). Yet, the fact remains that global production and supply chains are woven in such a manner that it remains difficult for countries to press pause on their dependency on China.

CONCLUSION

There exists a need to look into the continuing power politics within the grouping (Garrett, 2010). This has been manifested in how the countries responded to different humanitarian crises, including the refugee crisis. Member nations have not demonstrated any keenness on jointly addressing the concerns of the refugee community. The efforts, hence, remain superficial and suboptimal, trying to adjust to the environment after a natural disaster strikes. The richer nations could also be seen doing 'too little' (Ostrand, 2015) while dealing with a humanitarian crisis, further questioning the relevance of such a grouping. On the ground, this necessitates concerted efforts at the regional and bilateral level from the more vulnerable members within the group. Similar situations could be observed in the case of the COVID-19 pandemic as well. Members with their 'inward looking' approach (Atkinson, 2020) failed to act collectively and this brought out their differences. Even in the midst of a global pandemic, member countries failed to prioritize global health, when they refused to work with a collaborative spirit. There was little effort to ameliorate the concerns of the world's poor (Obstfeld and Posen, 2020) as the member countries acted in isolation, promoting 'vaccine nationalism' and refusing to address the pandemic as a global crisis.

The G20 grouping does little to rejig the power relations between the Global North and Global South. The heterogeneous nature of the group ensures that most of its conventions intend on retaining the global status quo. As (Garrett, 2010) illustrates, the 'G2' (USA and China) in the G20 holds the major cards in the game of geopolitics. The world economy continues to be pulled into interactions between the USA and China (ibid.). This plausibly answers why the group has no permanent secretariat and continues to function as 'informally' as possible. As Draper (2013) argues, the grouping has to address the 'systemic challenges' arising from the varied trade policies espoused by these economies, which tend to place the developing countries amongst the G20 at a lesser footing. The elucidation of how the G20 countries participate in global value chains showcases the emerging cooperation and evolving dependency relations within the Global South.

The observations on G20 nations demonstrate that the member countries seldom go beyond their immediate national interests when required to address any issue. The inward-looking approach which suits the needs of the country has its shortcomings. We have continued to witness crafty manoeuvring when encountering them. The paucity of efforts was starkly visible during the COVID-19 pandemic, when in a matter of time, it became obvious that 'none is safe until everyone is safe'. Hence, the need of the hour becomes international cooperation among the 'most important economies' represented by the G20 group. The G20 grouping, which evolved as a response to the global financial crisis remains at the juncture of another global crisis. Hence, presently, this cooperation should take the form of a 'massive fiscal response', with the advanced countries taking the lead (McKibbin and Vines, 2020) to fight the pandemic. Concerted efforts and coordination remain key to ameliorate the fallout of the pandemic, in addition to demonstrating the relevance of the grouping which has been on a downward spiral.

REFERENCES

Akgündüz, Yusuf Emre, van den Berg, Marcel, and Wolter Hassink. 2015. "The Impact of Refugee Crises on Host Labor Markets: The Case of the Syrian Refugee Crisis in Turkey." February.

Almeida, F. 2021. "Innovative response initiatives in the European Union to mitigate the effects of COVID-19." *Journal of Enabling Technologies* 15 (1): 40–52.

Almuttaqi, A.I. 2020. "The Omnishambles of COVID-19 Response in Indonesia." *The Insights.* March 23.

Altenburg, T., Schmitz, H., and A. Stamm. 2008. "Breakthrough? China's and India's Transition from Production to Innovation." 36 (2): 325–344.

Ashcroft, P., Lehtinen, S. and S. Bonhoeffer. 2022. "Test-trace-isolate-quarantine (TTIQ) intervention strategies after symptomatic COVID-19 case identification." *PLoS One*, 11;17 (2). February. doi: 10.1371/journal.pone.0263597. PMID: 35148359; PMCID: PMC8836351.

Atkinson, C. 2020. "G20 leaders must answer to COVID-19." (Science, 368 (6487)), 111.

Baldwin, R., and S. J. Evenett. 2020. *COVID-19 and Trade Policy: Why Turning Inward Won't Work.*

Bektimur, Basak, Cebi, Merve, and Basak Kartal Bektimur. 2020. "Turkey: G20 Action Plan In Response To The Covid-19 Pandemic." *Mondaq.* https://www.mondaq.com/turkey/financing/926472/g20-action-plan-in-response-to-the-covid-19-pandemic.

Chowdhary, N. 2020. "Environmental Refugees: A Humanitarian Crisis in India and Bangladesh." In *Refugee Crises and Third-World Economies,* edited by S.K. Das and N Chowdhary, pp. 37–43. Bingley: Emerald Publishing Limited.

David, Sara L. M. 2020. "Contact tracing apps: Extra risks for women and marginalized groups." *Health and Human Rights Journal, Viewpoints Blog.* April 29.

Dos, Santos T. 1970. "The Structure of Dependence." *The American Economic Review* 60 (2): 231–236.

Farny, Elisabeth. 2016. Dependency Theory: A Useful Tool for Analyzing Global Inequalities Today? November 23. https://www.e-ir.info/2016/11/23/dependency-theory-a-useful-tool-for-analyzing-global-inequalities-today/ .

Flannigan, M.D, Stocks, B.J., and B. M. Wotton. 2000. "Climate change and forest fires. ." *The Science of the Total Environment* 262: 221–229.

French, M., Guta, A., Gagnon, M., Mykhalovskiy, E., Roberts, S. L., Goh, S., McClelland, A., and F. McKelvey. 2020. "Corporate contact tracing as a pandemic response." *Critical Public Health.*

Gilbert, G. L., Degeling, C., and J Johnson. 2019. "Communicable Disease Surveillance Ethics in the Age of Big Data and New Technology." *Asian Bioethics Review* 11: 173–187.

Goldstein, A., and A. Venturini. 2016. "International Migration Policies: Should They Be A New G20 Topic?" *China & World Economy* 24 (4): 93–110.

Golub, P. S. 2013. "From the New International Economic Order to the G20: how the 'global South' is restructuring world capitalism from within." *Third World Quarterly* 34 (6): 1000–1015.

Han, J., Meyer, B. D., and Sullivan J. X. 2020. "Income and Poverty in the COVID-19 Pandemic." NBER Working Paper No. 27729.

Hassoun, N. 2021. "Against vaccine nationalism." *Journal of Medical Ethics.*

Herman, E. S., and N. Chomsky. 1988. *Manufacturing consent: The political economy of the mass media.* New York: Pantheon Books.

Hernandez, V., and T. Pedersen. 2017. "Global value chain configuration: A review and research agenda." *Business Research Quarterly* 20 (2): 137–150 .

ILO, OECD and World Bank Group. 2014. "G20 labour markets: outlook, key challenges and policy responses."

Imamura, T., Saito, T. and H. Oshitani. 2021. "Roles of Public Health Centers and Cluster-Based Approach for COVID-19 Response in Japan." *Health Security* 19 (2): 229–231.

Kavuma, S. 2020. *Import Substitution as an Economic Response to the COVID-19 pandemic in Uganda.* https://www.acode-u.org/newsletter/content/Susan-Kavuma.html .

Khoo, Siew-Ean. 2003. "Sponsorship of relatives for migration and immigrant settlement intention ." *International Migration* 41 (5): 177–199.

Kraemer, R.A. 2017. "The G20 and Building Global Governance for "Climate Refugees"." Policy Brief No. 107.

Luckhurst, Jonathan, Ertl, Veronica, Fleurbaey, Marc, Grimalda, Gianluca, Kirton, John, Knight, Andy W., Reddy, K. Srikanth, Sidiropoulos, Elizabeth, and Margo Thomas. 2020. "Transversal G20 response to Covid-19: Global governance for economic, social, health, and environmental resilience."

Martin, Philip L. 2006. "GATS, Migration, and Labor Standards." International Institute for Labour Studies Geneva .

Measey, M. 2010. "Indonesia: A Vulnerable Country in the Face of Climate Change." *Global Majority E-Journal* 1 (1): 31–45.

Obstfeld, M., and A. S. Posen. 2020. "How the G20 Can Hasten Recovery from COVID-19." Peterson Institute for International Economics, April.

Okonkwo, N. E., Aguwa, U. T., Jang, M., Barré, I. A., Page, K. R., Sullivan, P. S., Beyrer, C., and S. Baral. 2021. "COVID-19 and the US response: accelerating health inequities." *BMJ Evidence-Based Medicine* 26 (4): 176–179.

Olivia, S., Gibson, J., and R. Nasrudin. 2020. "Indonesia in the Time of Covid-19, Bulletin of Indonesian Economic Studies." 56 (2): 143–174.

Oshitani, H. 2020. "Cluster-based approach to Coronavirus Disease 2019 (COVID-19) response in Japan—February–April 2020." *Japanese Journal of Infectious Diseases* 76 (3): 491–493.

Ostrand, N. 2015. "The Syrian Refugee Crisis: A Comparison of Responses by Germany, Sweden, the United Kingdom, and the United States ." *Journal on Migration and Human Security* 3 (3): 255–279.

Parkins, N.C. 2010. "Push and pull factors of migration." *American Review of Political Economy* 8 (2).

Parvathamma, G. L. 2020. "Unemployment dimensions of COVID-19 and Government response in India–An analytical study." *International Journal of Health and Economic Development* 6 (2): 28–35.

Peterson, V. S. 2010. "Informalization, Inequalities and Global Insecurities." *International Studies Review* 12 (2): 244–270.

Powell, J. L., and H. T. A. Khan. 2013. "Ageing and Globalisation-A Global Analysis. Journal of Globalisation Studies." 4 (1): 137–146.

Rajan, S.I., Sivakumar, P., and A. Srinivasan. 2020. "The COVID-19 Pandemic and Internal Labour Migration in India: A 'Crisis of Mobility'." *The Indian Journal of Labour Economics* 63: 1021–1039.

Romero, T. 2021. *Brazil: informal employment share 2011-2020* . https://www.statista.com/statistics/1232760/informal-employment-share-brazil/#statisticContainer .

Rothenberg, Alexander D. et al. 2016. "Rethinking Indonesia's Informal Sector." *World Development* 80 (C): 96–113.

Sagar, A. et al. 2017. *Building Global Governance for Climate Refugees.* G20 Insights.

Schmidt, V., ed. 2007. *Trade union responses to globalization: A review by the Global Union Research Network.* International Labour Office.

Siddiqui, Azizah F., Wiederkehr, Manuel, Rozanova, Liudmila, and Antoine Flahault. n.d. "Situation of India in the COVID-19 Pandemic: India's Initial Pandemic Experience." *International Journal of Environmental Research and Public Health 2020* 17 (23): 8994.

Stark, O. 1991. "The Migration of Labour." (Blackwell).

Stringer, C., and S. Michailova. 2018. "Why modern slavery thrives in multinational corporations' global value chains ." *Multinational Business Review* 26 (3): 194–206.

Tibrewala, P. 2020. "The impact of COVID19 on Consumer Behaviour on spending pattern with respect to Mobile Phones and the impact of Anti-Chinese Sentiment towards buying of foreign brands." *Psychology and Education* 57 (9): 6270–6273.

Triandafyllidou, Anna. 2018. "Globalisation and migration: an introduction," in Anna Triandafyllidou (ed.), *Handbook of Migration and Globalisation.* Cheltenham; Northampton: Edward Elgar Publishing. pp. 1-13. https://hdl.handle.net/1814/51884

United Nations. 2015. "International Migration Report." United Nations.

United Nations. 2020. " International Migration Report."

Varshney, V., and K. Pandey. 2020. COVID-19 and the big pharma mess. *DownToEarth.* https://www.downtoearth.org.in/news/health/covid-19-exposed-dependence-of-world-india-on-china-for-active-pharma-ingredients-71877 .

WHO. 2020. What is the ACT Accelerator?. https://www.who.int/initiatives/act-accelerator/about.

WHO. 2021. G20 leaders boost support of the Access to COVID-19 Tools (ACT) Accelerator but urgent and immediate action is needed to maintain momentum. https://www.who.int/news/item/21-05-2021-g20-leaders-boost-support-of-the-access-to-covid-19-tools-(act)-accelerator-but-urgent-and-immediate-action-is-needed-to-maintain-momentum.

The G20 Agriculture Policy, Food Systems and Global Supply Chains: The Answer to India's Food Security and Farmers' Livelihood Security?

Sagari R. Ramdas

> In a big win for farmers, India pushed for and was able to obtain a commitment from G20 nations on improving livelihoods for small and marginal farmers. The focus of the members will now be on the marginal farmers rather than just the prosperous ones. Livelihoods for small and marginal farmers were at the focus of our discussions and everybody has agreed that improving their livelihood is an important global effort that we all have to put in. (Gaurav, 2021)

Celebratory headlines in mainstream media, like the one above, hailed the Indian government's contributions and achievements at the October 2021 G20 summit in Rome. A flurry of G20 declarations emerged between June and October 2021, (G20 Italia 2021a; G20 Italia 2021b; G20 Italia 2021c), emphasizing the need to obtain food and nutrition security by enhancing increased access to finance via 'responsible investment', and 'promoting sustainable food systems via strengthening global, regional and local food value chains and international food trade' (G20 Italia 2021a, p. 6). According to the G20, this would 'make a major contribution to tackling the interlinked global challenges of climate change and biodiversity loss' (G20 Italia 2021a, p. 6.), benefit small and marginal farmers, and achieve zero hunger. The G20 governs 60 per cent of global population, 80 per cent of global economic output, 75 per cent of global exports, emits 80 per cent of global greenhouse gases (OECD, 2021), and contains 1/3rd the world's undernourished people (811 million) of whom the majority (208.6 million) are in India (FAO et al., 2021).

However, the Indian farmers' year-long protest (Express Web Desk, 2021)—demanding the withdrawal of three legislations in India, which would facilitate the corporate agribusiness capture of India's food and agriculture systems and their integration into corporate-controlled global supply chains—belied this hyperbole. Their resistance forced the Indian government to repeal the laws in November 2021 (The Times of India, 2021) and comes at a time when global capitalism is desperate to keep afloat, aggressively using all means including profiting from the pandemic and consolidating hegemonic control on food, which is life for every human being. The farmers movement visibilizes the fundamental internal contradiction in India: the interests of India's ruling classes are served by aligning with the G20 formation which, as pointed out by Walden Bello (Focus on the Global South, 2009), was floated by the original G7 ultra-elite rich boys' club of the Global North[1] to serve global capital. The bias of India's ruling classes is inherently opposed to the interests of India's vast majority of citizens.

At the G20 Agriculture Ministerial on September 17, 2021, which ironically coincided with the enactment of the now repealed controversial laws exactly a year earlier, India's Agriculture Minister, oblivious to the massive violence unleashed by his government against the farmers, brazenly gloated about India's various achievements and future intentions. This included, (i) its transformation from being a net food importer to a net food exporter, (ii) the country having achieved domestic food security, and (iii) emphasizing the Indian government's intentions to continue to harness cutting edge gene and digital technologies to increase productivity amidst depleting natural resources, which he stressed, were core to increasing farmers' incomes (The Economic Times, 2021), in addition to the total integration of India into global food and agriculture supply chains.

In early September 2021, I was driving through Maharashtra from Hyderabad, and witnessed tractor-loads of tomatoes literally being dumped along the side of the road, or left to rot on vines by farmers who found this cheaper than to harvest and process them for sales. Newspapers confirmed once more: A crash in tomato prices at the end of August throughout the country in all the major tomato-growing regions, including Maharashtra (The New Indian Express, 2021). Media reports attributed this to a supply glut of tomatoes due to good weather. However, disruptions in export supply chains were also blamed for the price slump (Biswas, 2021) including a stoppage in overland exports to Pakistan over the past 3 years (Bhosale, 2021).

A month later, in October, there was a massive rise in the prices of virtually all vegetables across large swathes of southern India (The New Indian Express, 2021), including the recently dumped tomatoes. In this case, it was pinned down to the enormous increase in fuel costs, which pushed up transportation costs (Biswas and Mungara, 2021). The price of chicken and eggs too, sky-rocketed, with poultry corporates citing increased transportation costs as the reason, since the majority of poultry feed (maize and soya) had to be shipped in from other states (ibid.). Most recently, in October 2021, onion prices rose steeply. A staple vegetable for India's majority Dalit-Bahujan-Adivasi and minority populace, the vegetable pretty much disappeared off their plate. Prices continued to be high, even after the government said it had released nearly half of its two lakh tonnes of onion buffer stocks to counter a shortage of onions in the market. The price rise was attributed to reduced production linked to heavy rains in October over parts of the country. The government, in its arrogant Brahminical style, reminiscent of

---

[1] Canada, France, Germany, Italy, Japan, United Kingdom, United States of America, and the European Union as a non-enumerated member.

December 2019 (Anandan, 2019) said it would not invoke provisions of the Essential Commodity Act to stop onion exports, as prices were not 'extraordinarily high' (Business Standard, 2021). All of this, once again, illustrates an utterly callous state, oblivious to a reality where Dalit-Bahujan-Adivasi-and other minority peoples predominantly earn their livelihood as workers in the informal/unorganized sector, which comprise 80–90 per cent of India's workforce. These pre-COVID pandemic 2018-19 estimates (Azim Premji University 2021, p. 44) have grown substantially amidst the pandemic, and have been accompanied by steep income losses (ibid., pp. 78–105) and mounting debts.

Finally, the government's blatant dishonesty about the marvels of India being a robust food and nutritional-secure food exporting nation were once again exposed by the data on malnourishment among children. Government data released by the Ministry of Women and Child Development in November 2021, stated that 3.3 million children in India are malnourished, of whom the majority (1.77 million) are severely malnourished (Business Today, 2021). This is nearly 91 per cent higher than last year. This data just adds weightage to the recent Global Hunger Index 2021 ranking India 101st of 116 countries, down from 94th position in 2020, which was rejected as being inaccurate by the Government of India (Sinha, 2021). The round 5 of the National Family Health Survey (NFHS-5) too reconfirmed an increase in child malnutrition indicators for stunting and under-weight levels of children under the age of five, and anaemia among women and children under five, between 2015–16 and 2019-2020 (Mathur, 2021; National Family Health Survey, 2021).This data very obviously contradicts the claims that higher production, coupled with exports and international trade, have addressed the problems of hunger and malnourishment. They have not addressed the livelihood concerns of small and marginal farmers either, who would otherwise not be out on the streets in protest.

As a food consumer, a member of an alliance organising for food sovereignty and social justice (Food Sovereignty Alliance, n.d.), a veterinary scientist who has studied the trajectory of India's dairy markets (one of the earliest markets to be deregulated in liberalized India), and a complete non-specialist on food and agriculture value chains, I interrogate the G20's food and agriculture proposals, as it concerns our collective futures. Will globally integrated agriculture and food supply chains from farm to fork and vice-versa solve the problems of hunger, climate change, biodiversity loss, small and marginal farmer livelihoods, gender disparities, jobs for youth, and result in 'prosperity for people and the planet?'[2] (G20 Italia, 2021d)

---

[2] Under the G20 Italian Presidency, the G20 focuses on these 3 pillars of action.

I begin by outlining key elements of the G20 proposal on Food Security, Nutrition and Food Systems, and deconstruct it through the lens of India's agriculture and food policy path using select commodities identified by the Indian government as key to 'doubling farmers' incomes and meeting food security' (GOI, 2017)). I conclude with what global capitalism hopes to gain by India's G20 presidency in 2023.

G20 PROPOSAL: GLOBAL FOOD TRADE AND INVESTMENTS TO BEEF UP THE VALUE CHAIN CORE TO FOOD AND NUTRITION SECURITY

Ever since the first G20 ministerial on agriculture in 2011 (G20 France, 2011; G20 Research Group, 2021) international trade which is 'stable, predictable, distortion free, and transparent and allows the unrestricted flow of food and agriculture commodities' (G20 France, 2011, p. 9) has been core to the G20 proposals on Food Security and Agriculture over the past decade. This coupled with public-private-partnership investments on a value chain approach has been deemed as a core mechanism to secure global food security and prevent food price volatility. It was argued in 2011 that securing higher investments in agriculture requires open and well-functioning markets, which would ensure increased agricultural production and productivity to meet growing demands. The investments along the value chain were for services (financial, agriculture education and extension), infrastructure and equipment (irrigation, harvest and post-harvest, agro-processing, transportation, roads, ports, cold chain, power, storage), research, information and communication technology, climate change mitigation and adaptation. They were also to improve market and value chain operators' cooperation, institutions such as cooperatives, and procurement from smallholders. There is also a very clear commitment to protect the interests of investors as evidenced by the following declaration: 'establish proper investment environments, including through improvement of law and regulations' (G20 France, 2011, p. 5).

In 2011, mention was also made of how international trade must operate within a well-functioning, open, and rules-based system of trade, which needed to be strengthened as per the regime of trade governance set by the WTO and its agreements (ibid., p. 10). They also fully endorsed the central role of the United Nations (UN), in particular, the Food and Agriculture Organisation (FAO) in the global governance architecture on food security. From 2016 onwards, after the UN adopted the Sustainable Development Goals 2030 Agenda in 2015, the G20 Agriculture Ministerial communiques began to include the importance of 'all types of food producers and the need for sustainable intensification of agriculture' (G20 China 2016, p. 6) 'to enable smallholders and family farmers particularly women and youth, to be integrated into food value chains' (ibid., p. 6). In support of this, there is specific emphasis placed on facilitating financial services and products—loans, credit, agriculture insurance schemes and risk management tools for smallholders, family farmers, women and youth. There is also an emphasis placed on revitalizing rural economies and harmonizing rural and urban development, catalyzing agriculture growth with industrialization and urbanization, and building rural infrastructure, all of which is projected to generate employment and income, forming the basis for inclusive rural transformation (ibid.c). This continues to be reiterated in every G20 Agricultural Ministerial thereafter, including the most recent one in 2021.

In short, nothing out of line with the capitalist market expansion/stabilization objectives of the original G7 countries (G7 Leaders Summit, 2021), which invited select developing countries to form the G20 to give legitimacy and endorse the project of shaping global frameworks directed towards advancing the march of capital through which developing countries would ostensibly 'benefit'. The entire framework is about obtaining consensus on the identification and freeing up of hurdles in accessing markets of value chains that characterize, in this case, agriculture and food systems which are serviced by the 'private' i.e, corporations, and facilitated by the public i.e, 'governments' or, in other words, the tax money of citizens. The structural conceptual underpinnings of 'rural development and rural economies' are drawn from the Global Donor Platform for Rural Development (Global Donor Platform for Rural Development, n.d.):

> …a process of comprehensive societal change whereby rural societies diversify their economies and reduce their reliance on agriculture; become dependent on distant places to trade and to acquire goods, services, and ideas…. (Berdegue et. al, 2014)

By 2021, under the Matera Declaration on Food Security, Nutrition and Food Systems (G20 Italia 2021c), the G20 countries acknowledge the deepening crisis of vast food insecurity across the globe which has been rising since 2014. They also acknowledge that the world is going to miss its target of achieving 'zero hunger' and ending malnutrition in all forms by 2030, as per the Sustainable Development Goals. They project that the number of hungry people across the globe would exceed 840 million by 2030, which are pre-pandemic figures. The pandemic has added, until now, another 161 million hungry people (FAO et al., 2021).

The mechanisms recommended to address this, evident in the above declaration, and the Agriculture Ministers declaration (G20 Italia 2021b) continue to be an intensification in capitalization of the food and agriculture value chains and building up of open and free global trade in goods and services related to agrifood trade as the means of fast-tracking efforts towards achieving food security via sustainable and resilient food systems. Key commitments in these recommendations outlined are:

(i)   Public policies and resources such as procurement and public development banks' funds are to be utilized to underwrite market failures and absorb/buffer any risks to private investment and blended finances, which, it is argued, is the way to attract the latter to invest in food value chains to shore up food security and nutrition and improve efficiency of the food value chains;

(ii)   This kind of private investment will be the primary modicum via which the productivity, capacity, managerial capital, accessibility to markets, incomes, and resilience of smallholders, family farmers, and fisherfolk will be enhanced;

(iii)   Private/blended investment is the crucial way for promoting innovation in technologies and practices for sustainable food systems;

(iv)   Integrating women and youth into agri-entrepreneurship across different levels of the food system and value chain;

(v)   Private sector will support public efforts to improve agri-food systems prioritizing digital transformation and innovation, with appropriate protection of intellectual property rights and data privacy consistent with national and international legal frameworks as well as the voluntary transfer of technologies on mutually agreed terms, for sustainable and resilient agriculture;

(vi)   An open, transparent, predictable, and non-discriminatory multilateral trading system, consistent with World Trade Organization (WTO) rules, to enhance market predictability and allow agri-food trade to flow, so as to contribute to food security and nutrition. International trade is crucial to ensure access to inputs, and goods and services to produce safe, nutritious, and affordable food. It is also relevant to guard against any unjustified, restrictive, and distortive measures that could lead to excessive food price volatility in international markets, and threaten the food security and nutrition of large proportions of the world population, especially the most vulnerable living in environments of low food security (G20 Italia 2021c, p. 4);

(vii)   Reiteration of the valuable role of family farmers, agriculture workers, migrant workers, smallholders, youth and women in rural areas, and the vital importance of their inclusion into agri-food value chains which will ensure them incomes, quality employment and business opportunities (G20 Italia 2021b, p. 2). This framework also forms the core mechanism towards transforming into sustainable food and agriculture systems, outlined and committed to by countries at the United Nations Food Systems Summit (UNFSS);

(viii)   Promoting sustainable and productive farming practices/technologies that are science-and-evidence-based, data-driven, conserve natural resources, soil health, and water, enable sustainable land management, reverse biodiversity loss, and contribute to climate change mitigation and adaptation (ibid., p. 4);

(ix)   In the context of (a) improving food safety and food security, (b) agriculture sustainability, and (c) enhancing agriculture productivity and food system resilience in the wake of climate change, investments in digital traceability down the agri-food value chain is a strong technological recommendation. Additionally, the technologies that should be explored and invested in include (a) disruptive technologies: Omics, (genomics, transcriptomics, proteomics, metabolomics), nanotechnology, and digital technology; (b) biotechnology: genetic engineering at one end, and what are termed as 'low-end' technologies, including artificial insemination, fermentation, and biofertilizers at the other; (c) gene editing, cisgenesis and GMO to create new plants resistant to disease, weather, and soil, and (d) codex, digital technologies: agrobots, precision agriculture, artificial intelligence, and block chain technology for traceability.

THE G20 PROPOSAL AND INDIA'S PLAN TO DOUBLE FARMERS' INCOME BY 2022

In 2018, the Organisation for Economic Cooperation and Development's (OECD) Committee for Agriculture, in a review of India's Agriculture Policy, flagged India as being one of the fastest growing G20 economies, 'reflecting an ambitious reforms agenda since 2014' (OECD/ICRIER 2018, p. 17). India's current right-wing Hindu Nationalist government was elected to power in 2014. In 2016, the government appointed an Inter-Ministerial Committee on Doubling Farmers Income (DFI) by 2022. The Committee released its report and recommendations in September 2018 after consulting with, amongst others, multilateral development and finance institutions (World Bank, World Food Program, International Fund for Agriculture Development, International Crops Research Institute for the Semi-Arid Tropics), philanthro-capitalists (Bill and Melinda Gates Foundation), and multinational corporations including those dealing with investment/wealth management (World Economic Forum, Deloitte, PhillipCapital, Ernst & Young, Elara Capital), all of them key protagonists in advancing global capitalist markets/systems under the pretext of development assistance. The World Economic Forum has elaborated on their partnership with India in seeding, piloting and conceptualizing this agriculture growth plan, ever since it launched its New Vision for Agriculture in 2009 (World Economic Forum, n.d.) (see box 1). This DFI plan features as India's contribution to a report by the G20 titled 'G20's Best Practices for Sustainable Agro-Food Sector' tabled at the 2019 G20's Agriculture Ministers Meeting in Japan (G20 Japan, 2019). The redefined DFI vision for Agriculture sets out that

> The mandate of Agriculture is to generate both food and raw material, to meet the requirement of modern society for feed, fibre, fuel and other in-

dustrial uses, and in a manner that is sustainable and with the aim to bring economic growth to farmers. (Government of India 2018a, p. 6)

The Doubling Farmers' Income (DFI) recognises agriculture as a value led enterprise empowering farmers with "improved market linkages" and enabling "self-sustainable models" as the basis for continued productivity-production and income growth for farmers. This builds the basic strategy direction for five primary concerns: optimal monetisation of farmers' produce, sustainability of production, improved efficiency of resource use, re-strengthening of extension and knowledge-based services and risk management. (ibid., p. 1)

Towards the capitalization of production and of all sources of farmers' incomes i.e., all-out capitalist agriculture growth, the following strategies were set out, apart from broad commitments by the state to deepen public-private interlinkages for capital formation:

i.   A demand-driven approach from the agriculture logistics system for post-production operations to aggregate produce, transportation, warehouse, and cold chains. Setting up farmer-producer organizations in all formats, to play an aggregator role for produce, where the farmers learn to integrate their production with the demands of the processing industry. Here, the primacy is for the farmers to play a supportive role to the industry, and thereby secure an assured income.

ii.   Establishing an Agriculture Value System (AVS) towards fixing the existing highly fragmented supply chains. This will enable integration of the supply chains and drive a market-led value system consisting of individual value chains at different levels, which collaborate and integrate into sector-wide supply chains. The AVS consists of input providers, farmers, transporters, warehousing, wholesalers, food and agro-processors and retailers. Developing hub and spoke systems at back-end and front-end to facilitate and promote the AVS.

iii. National agriculture market: The restructuring of existing markets into a new market architecture envisaged as a national digital platform of trade for better competition, better price realization, and enhanced transparency in trade. All levels of the market primary retail agriculture markets (PRAMs/GrAMs[3] numbering 22,000), primary wholesale agricultural markets (APMCs/APLMs[4]) and other markets numbering around 10,000), secondary and tertiary agricultural markets, are to be networked by online platforms where farmers and buyers trade commodities across the country with the vision of 'One Nation, One Market' (narendramodi.in, n.d.). This

---

[3] PRAMs: Primary Retail Agricultural Markets
GrAMs: Gramin Agricultural Markets
[4] APMCs/APLMs: Agricultural Produce & Livestock Market Committee

also integrates domestic markets with export markets by considering the latter as a targeted market activity and not just an add-on (see Figure 1).

iv. A marketing intelligence system to support demand-led decision making via forecasting for the demand and supply of agricultural produce and crop area estimation to aid price stabilization and risk management. Related to this is an agricultural risk assessment and management system that will provide forecasts on weather, management of drought, biotic stress including vertebrate pests, credit for farming operations, post-production finance to prevent distress sales, and crop and animal risk management through insurance.

v. Promoting sustainable agriculture/climate resilient farming that embraces everything from organic farming to biotechnology. Additionally, promoting continued employment of agro-chemical farming, where chemical usage will be moderated via soil health testing. Priority to agriculture mechanization, and hiring out such equipment.

vi. Enhancing production through higher productivity or achieving higher production out of less, thereby releasing land and water resources to diversify into higher value farming for enhanced income. Introducing market-based mechanisms of pricing/payment to regulate and manage agriculture inputs including water, power, seeds, and biofortification.

vii. Capacity building of farmers via agricultural extension, knowledge diffusion, and skill development.

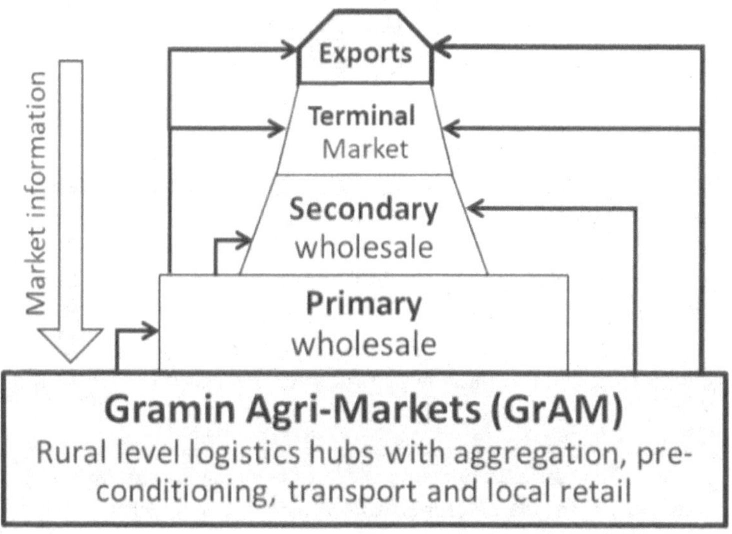

Refer Volume IV, chapter 5.

Figure 1: Proposed Restructuring of Agriculture Markets

Source: GoI, *Report of the Committee on Doubling Farmers Income*, 2018a.

viii. Research, development, and information and communication technology (ICT) designed to support the doubling of farmers' income strategy.

ix. Structural and governance reforms in agriculture such as building a database of farmers, farmer and produce mobilization, institutional mechanism for coordination, convergence, a digital monitoring dashboard at district, state and national levels for seamless and real-time monitoring of field delivery, utilizing Panchayati Raj Institutions, and farm income measurement as key delivery channels for transparent and inclusive development.

x. Tribal farming communities will be facilitated to capture higher value and non-farm incomes from non-timber forest produce (NTFP).

xi. An aggressive agricultural trade policy is recommended in order to raise agricultural exports to double the total volume of exports and achieve a target of USD 100 billion in value by 2022-23. Broad-base the basket of commodities beyond cereals and meat, which currently account for the bulk of exports. This requires investment in agri-logistics, infrastructure ports, and airports.

xii. Outside of the agriculture domain: A shift from farm to non-farm occupation, where off-farm and farm-linked activities, including secondary and tertiary sector activities, are opportunities to generate income.

Towards these structural reforms, the DFI proposed legal amendments which states should carry out, including (i) land lease laws to facilitate land pooling to enable 'productions of scale', (ii) contract farming laws as a means of risk protection for farmers against price volatility, and (iii) amendments to the states' Agriculture Produce and Livestock Marketing Acts to facilitate establishment of private markets and to encourage private sector investment.

AGRICULTURE EXPORTS AND INTEGRATION INTO GLOBAL SUPPLY CHAINS: KEY TO INDIA'S NEW AGENDA FOR DOUBLING FARMERS' INCOME AND ACHIEVING FOOD SECURITY

Evidently, this vision of agriculture is a massive shift away from India's agriculture policy formulated at the time of the nation's independence, which was about becoming food self-sufficient and ensuring food at affordable prices to the Indian people, whilst securing remunerative prices to producers and protecting their livelihoods. In the words of the DFI:

> Agriculture must undergo continuous transformation, to acquire the characteristics of an agri-enterprise, where farmers take to agriculture as a chosen option, and are able to earn their livelihood as entrepreneurs and simultaneously cater to the country's strategic requirements and global food and nutrition security. (Government of India 2018a, p. 16)

Considering itself to be 'food self-sufficient and a net exporter of food', India then positioned itself to cater to 'global food security' in light of the states' pronouncements that they were already meeting domestic food security demands (GOI, 2018a). In December 2018, within a couple of months of the DFI report, India announced its new Agriculture Export (AE) policy 2018 (Government of India, 2018b), which—unlike earlier, wherein exports only occurred as a surplus after meeting domestic demands—contained targets of agricultural exports to be met on priority, and would respond to the demands and preferences of an export market. The objectives in the AE policy summarized the scattered references to exports and supply chains in the DFI report. Some of the objectives were:

(i)   To diversify our export basket, destinations and boost high value and value added agricultural exports, including a focus on perishables

(ii)   To promote novel, indigenous, organic, ethnic, traditional and non-traditional agri- product exports

(iii)   To provide an institutional mechanism for pursuing market access, tackling barriers and dealing with sanitary and phytosanitary issues

(iv)   To strive to double India's share in world agri-exports by integrating with global value chains

(v)   To enable farmers to receive benefits of export opportunities in overseas markets (Government of India, 2018b)

In 2019, the XVth Finance Commission, constituted by the President of India, vide notification no. S.O. 3755(E) dated November 27, 2017, appointed a High-Level Expert Group (HLEG) on Agriculture Exports with the mandate to 'recommend measurable performance incentives for States to encourage agri-exports as well as to promote crops to enable high import substitution' (High Level Expert Group on Agriculture, 2020). The undeclared conflict of interests within the composition of the group is self-evident: The HLEG, apart from government members, was populated by corporate agribusiness representatives from Nestle India, UPL Limited, ITC and Olam Agro India Ltd, all of whom have direct corporate agribusiness profit interests from the suggested agri-export policies, and some of whom are members of the World Economic Forum's New Vision for Agriculture India Business Council, which 'serves as an informal, high-level leadership group to champion private sector collaboration and investment to drive sustainable agricultural growth in India' (World Economic Forum, n.d.) (see Box 1).

The HLEG submitted their report to the finance commission in July 2020, and, as critically analyzed by Ramdas and Charanya (2021),

> The mechanism elaborated in the report, details the massive structural changes envisioned for farming, resource-use, land control, public procurement and food. Increasing agriculture exports from USD 40 to 100 billion, is deemed a 'national imperative', to double farmers' incomes by 2022-23. This grand-plan, is by all accounts, not merely a 'national plan', but intrinsically part of a larger global agribusiness agenda. They cite global experience, in support of its blueprint for a 'single crop value chain cluster,'

Box 1.

The World Economic Forum defines its New Vision for Agriculture, launched in 2009, as a global initiative to strengthen food security, environmental sustainability and economic opportunity through a market-based, multi-stakeholder approach. In India, the NVA catalyzed and supported private partnership platforms in the states of Maharashtra in 2012, Karnataka in 2015 and Andhra Pradesh in 2016, in partnership with the state governments. The Andhra Pradesh partnership was launched under the leadership of the then Chief Minister Chandra Babu Naidu, to achieve double digit inclusive growth in the state identifying 25 growth areas covering agriculture, horticulture, animal husbandry and fisheries sectors. This program incorporates the much feted and celebrated by industry, UN and international farmer movements alike, Andhra Pradesh Zero Budget Natural Farming (ZBNF) agroecological program, referred to as Organic and Natural Farming in the AP NVA promo-document, and more recently renamed as the Andhra Pradesh Community Managed Natural Farming Program. This partnership enabled 16 Memorandum of Understandings (MOUs) and Letters of Intent (LOIs) with private sector (agribusiness) organizations committing approximately USD 72 million. As recently discussed by Ramdas (2021), this benign looking agroecological program is being financed through multistakeholder financial collaborations and capital market investments. The most recent being a GEF loan which secures USD 44 million as private blended finance from the Bank BN Paribas in the form of guarantees and equity funds. The project discusses how cutback in State agriculture subsidies on synthetic fertilisers, frees up the subsidies to service the loans from impact investors. In 2014 the NVA founded the NVA India Business Council consisting of global and national business leaders which identifies and develops new partnership opportunities at scale in India's agriculture sector. By 2016, they engaged with Government of India on developing the agriculture growth plan, specifically to evolve Agriculture Value System.

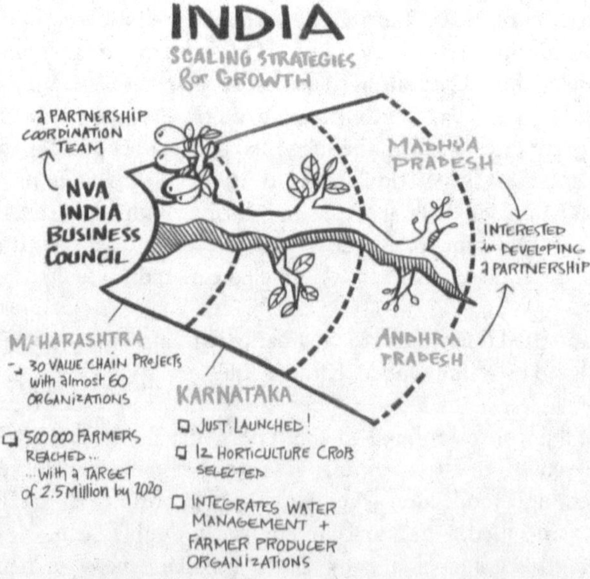

Source: WEF, New Vision for Agriculture (NVA) Initiative For India, 2007.

NVA India Business Council

In 2014, the NVA constituted the India Business Council to champion private sector collaboration and investment to drive sustainable agricultural growth in India. The Council serves as an action-oriented platform of global and national business leaders that will identify, develop and scale new opportunities for partnership and collaboration in India's agriculture sector. Members include:

UPL Ltd (*chair*)	DuPont	Novozymes South Asia Pvt Ltd
Adani Wilmar Group	IFC/2030WRG	PepsiCo India Holdings Pvt Ltd
Bayer CropScience Ltd	Jain Irrigation Systems Ltd	Rabobank International
Cargill India	Louis Dreyfus Company	State Bank of India
Dow Agrosciences	Monsanto Company	Swiss Re Services India Pvt Ltd
DSM India	MTR Foods Pvt Ltd/Orkla ASA	Wal-Mart India Pvt Ltd
		Yara Fertilizers

For more information, please contact Saswati Bora, Project Lead, Food Security and Agriculture Initiatives, World Economic Forum, at saswati.bora@weforum.org; or please visit: www.weforum.org/agriculture .

Source: WEF, *New Vision for Agriculture (NVA) Initiative For India,* 2007.

Apart from the fact that an overwhelming majority of these corporate business houses have been called out for their role in concentrating unbelievable hegemonic power along the agriculture value chain, which enabled them to shape global policies and markets (indeed, this formation being clear evidence of the latter), they have also, at some point or the other, been called out across the globe for human rights violations, labour violations, diease and health problems as a result of their products/ manufacturing sites, toxic environmental spills and pollution.

competitive within a state. They lobby for a network of producers, Farmer Producer Organisations (FPOs), agribusinesses, financiers, corporates, commodity boards, state and central governments, and country-level interventions in destination markets, to support a cluster chain. They seek to build vertical relationships, amongst input suppliers, processors, exporters and buyers and horizontal relationships between producers and facilitating organisations providing technology, training and research. What it outlines is how stakeholders have to join together across this value chain, to reduce the costs of doing business across all steps of production, processing, logistics, and markets to benefit agribusiness (and farmers as an afterthought). The role of FPOs is clarified too: It is to link the small and marginal farmers to *serve agribusiness*, via bulk procurement of inputs, aggregation of the produce, value addition and markets. These value chain clusters must be anchored by private sector players, and could spread across multiple states for reasons of 'economies of scales,' facilitated by government commodity boards for 'end-to-end' execution in the specific crop. The central government must play a role in pursuing policies that support '*ease of business, fast resolution of commercial disputes and any impediments to investments, export incentives, common infrastructure and required trade negotiations with destination markets.*' They also clearly state the need to minimize distortions in the markets to realise the competitiveness of the crops and illustrate this by emphasizing '*a pressing need for the state to restructure input subsidies as 'direct benefits transfers' to farmers, and restructure the government procurement at MSP into a Price Deficiency Payment Scheme.* (Ramdas and Charanya, 2021)

The XVth Finance Commission was tasked with laying out the distribution of net proceeds of taxes between the Union and the states, and also to review the design of fiscal principles for grants, particularly for performance-based incentives and support in various policy areas, both of which are constitutional instruments in the hands of the Commission for transfer of funds from the Union to the states (Government of India, 2020, p. 4). The Commission accepted the HLEG report in total, which forms the basis of finances to be awarded to the states as 'Incentives to carry out Agriculture Reforms, Self-Reliance, Export and Sustainability,' discussed under the Agriculture Sector and Rural Infrastructure Sections as part of performance-based incentives and grants (ibid., pp. 303–308).

Agriculture contributes 17.7 per cent of India's gross value added (GVA), absorbs 44 per cent of its workforce, and plays an important role in achieving the Sustainable Development Goals of 2030, including those that address hunger, nutrition, greenhouse gases, and environmental quality, states the Finance Commission (GOI, 2020). Keeping with the DFI, AE and HLEG recommendations, the commission argues that India, now surplus in several commodities, needs foreign markets to sell these products, so as to prevent a fall in farm prices. This requires radical restructuring of agriculture supply chains, logistics, markets, and infrastructure development as laid out in the HLEG report. Congratulating the Centre for having passed the now subsequently repealed legislations to deregulate and privatize agriculture markets, they propose fast-tracking the larger reforms agenda, with performance-based incentives of up to Rs 45,000 Crores, paid to States, subject to their operationalizing these reforms:

(i)   Land lease reforms: States should amend their land lease laws so as to facilitate short-term and long-term lease of agricultural land both for agricultural purpose as well as for agro-industry, and amend the logistics for agricultural trade and supply chains.

(ii)   Sustainable and efficient water use in agriculture: Replace subsidized power supply for agriculture with direct benefit transfers (DBTs), which they assume will force farmers to shift away from water-intensive crops, and encourage judicious use of water and the adoption of water-saving technologies. Grants will be made to states that augment and prevent a decline in their water table.

(iii)   Export promotion: 22 crop value-chains are recommended, including 2 for import substitution (oil and wood), which have the potential to double India's net exports in the medium-term. Seven so-called 'lighthouse must-win' value chains include rice, shrimps, buffaloes, spices, vegetables, fruits and mangoes, along with vegetable oils and wood as import substitution crops. Medicinal and aromatic plants and organic produce are marked as the other big money spinners. These agri-value chains must be supported holistically through a cluster approach, by addressing key enablers on both the supply side and demand side. This will increase farm productivity, improve quality, ensure regulatory compliance, enhance cost efficiency and boost competitiveness, while continuing with efforts to improve market access. The value chain clusters must be anchored by private sector value chain players to ensure market orientation through value added products. They project how the additional exports will result in the creation of seven to ten million jobs along the value chain, and higher farmer incomes. Hence, they recommend using growth in agricultural exports as a target indicator for awards for the export performance of a state.

(iv)   Contribution towards 'Atmanirbhar Bharat'—self-sufficient India: Import substitution for edible oil (60 per cent of which is imported) and wood (40 per cent of its non-fuel timber is imported). Increased production of oilseeds, pulses, and wood-based products as an indicator, to make India self-sufficient in these criteria (GOI, 2020).

What we have described thus far at the India level faithfully toes the line of the G20 proposals.

Despite a Supreme Court stay on operationalizing the laws (Rajagopal, 2021) throughout 2021, the government took decisions which continued to facilitate operationalizing various elements of this grand new reforms plan. In August 2021, the Prime Minister announced a National Mission on Edible Oils-Oil Palm to enhance land area for palm oil by an additional 6.5 lakh hectares by 2025-26 (Pandey, 2021). In September 2021, the government signed a slew of Memorandum of Understanding (MOUs) (Government of India, 2021c) with global/national big-tech companies (like Microsoft, Jio Platform, Amazon, to name a few), involving the adoption of Blockchain and other technologies to power a National AgriStack, or a digitalized database of all information on farmers and their farms, to facilitate digital traceability, climate precision farming, and so on. In October 2021, the government invited public comments on proposed amendments to the existing Forest (Conservation) Act, 1980 (Government of India, 2021d), to enable rapid de-reservation of forests. This was done in order to facilitate 'non-forest' purposes, which are defined as plantations of tea, coffee, spices, rubber, palms, oil-bearing plants, horticultural crops, or medicinal plants and any purpose other than reafforestation.

The ability of this government to set into motion and operationalize various second generation reforms thus far described, is rooted in historical political decisions made pre-1990, and subsequent first generation reforms undertaken during the 25 years of liberalized India post-1990, up to 2014. As recently analyzed by Ramdas (2021a), these include: unfinished agenda of land reforms (the root cause of 60–85 per cent Dalit landlessness); ecological, energy and sovereignty destructive Green Revolution chemical farming; slashed public financing of agriculture and food; and the entry of agribusiness corporate players down the value chain. Farmers responded by shifting from growing mixed diverse crop-animals to monocrop agriculture commodities, and have become net consumers of food from the market. Liberalized trade, resulting in volatile commodity prices, subsidized imports, and rising input capital costs controlled by agribusiness, has pushed farmers into massive debt and suicides. It has also reshaped India's agriculture map of 'One District One Product' clusters (Government of India , n.d.), (Figure 2) that are overwhelmingly exported out of their district (see Figures 3 and 4). Second generation reforms aim to deregulate and 'organize' the remaining 'fragmented' parts of the agriculture value chain, selectively integrating or displacing existing actors into corporate agribusiness controlled global supply chains (Figures 5 and 6).

WILL GLOBAL SUPPLY CHAINS SECURE THE FOOD, NUTRITION AND LIVELIHOOD NEEDS OF THE PEOPLE?

Dairy was amongst the first sectors in the country to be liberalized and deregulated as early as 1991, with key objectives being to spur growth, enhance milk production to make milk affordable to consumers and increase incomes for dairy farmers ensuring their prosperity. They were assured that negotiating with multiple dairy processors – both private and cooperative agribusinesses - would enhance their bargaining powers to set milk prices and ensure prosperity. Thirty years later, we are the global leaders of milk production, from a highly capitalised sector but which is characterised by high inequality in consumption. The top 5 percent of wealthy Indians consume 23 times of what the bottom 5 percent consume. India's growth trajectory has included exporting milk, and with the increased integration of dairy value chains with global markets, Indian dairy prices have been subject to the extreme global volatility of dairy markets. Each crash pushes out small and marginal farmers from production as they are not able to cover their costs of production and, once they are pushed out, they have had no means of being able to re-enter. Between 2000 and 2016, 5.25 million 1-2 cow/buffalo owning families left dairying as a livelihood. A deep structural shift at the production-end has occurred with small producers who comprised the majority pre-1991, but now comprise a mere 45% of the producer base, with the remaining being middle to middle-large farmers. Consolidation has occurred down the value chain, with fewer dairy processing corporations controlling larger volumes of the market, and a large number of small players, the so-called informal small traders, having been pushed out. The informal is today a mere 50 percent, and mergers and acquisitions of dairy processing companies between domestic and international ones continue. The next phase of dairy development is about export-led production, which promises more of the same, and a major objective is to formalise the remaining informal spaces and FPOs linked to dairy processors are the means by which this is expected to occur. (Ramdas, 2021b)

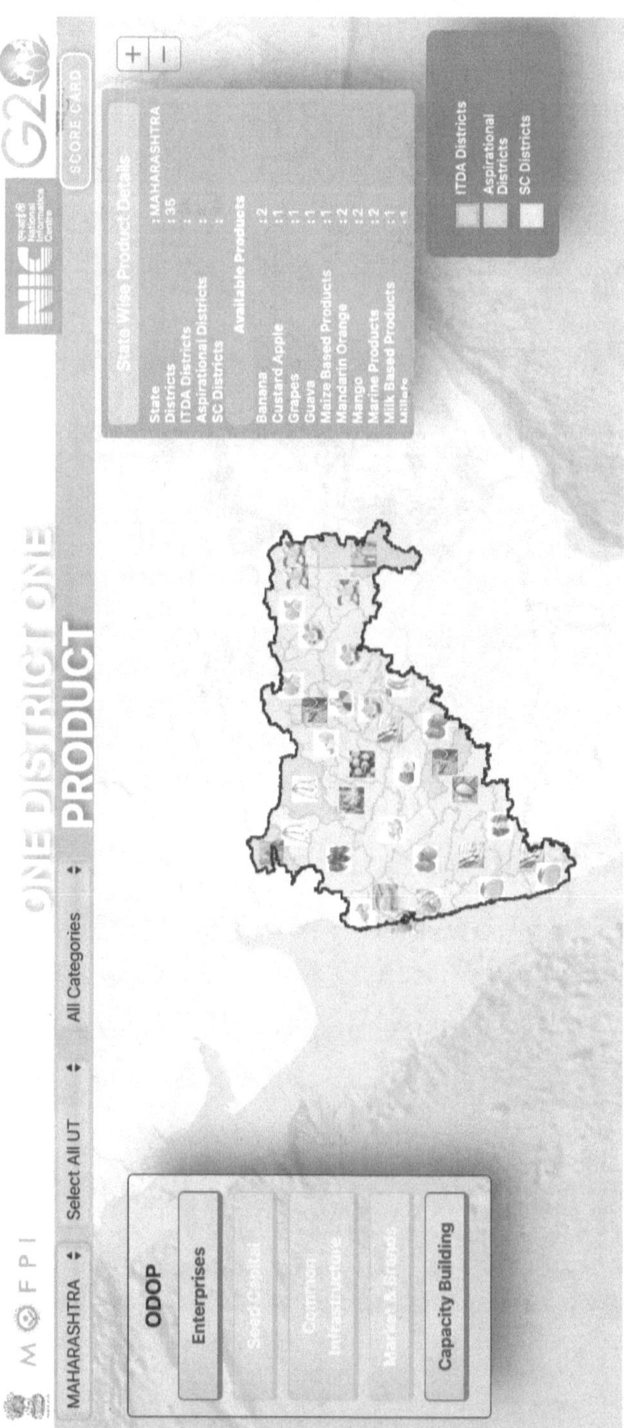

Figure 2.

Source: https://odop.mofpi.gov.in/odop/. Retrieved on September 3, 2021.

Tomato

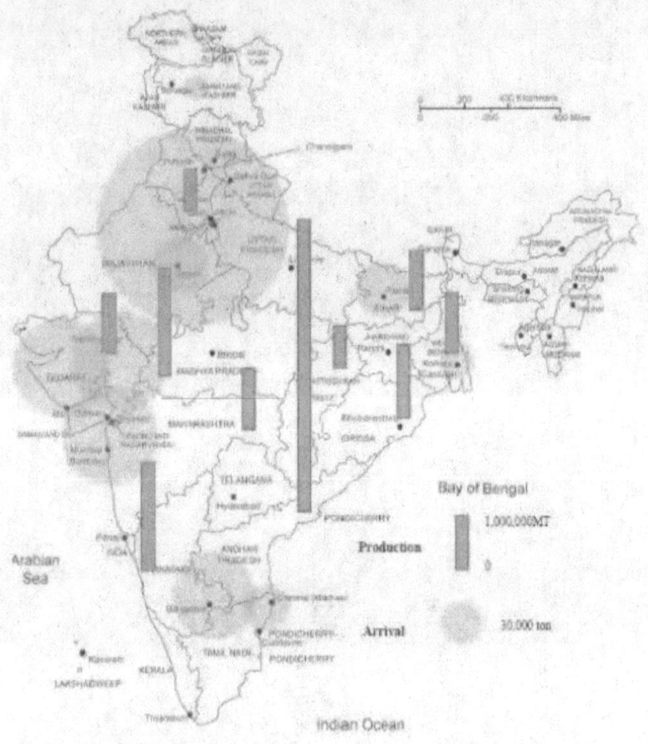

Source: Indian Horticulture Database 2013

Figure 3. Tomato: top sites of production and markets (2013)

Source: *Final Report for Data Collection and Confirmation Study for Agriculture Value Chains in the Republic of India,* 2015, p. 52.

Onion

Source: Indian Horticulture Database 2013

Figure 4. Onions : top sites of production and markets (2013)

Source: *Final Report for Data Collection and Confirmation Study for Agriculture Value Chains in the Republic of India*, 2015, p. 53.

Chilli value chain is characterized by consolidation for processors and exporters and millions of small Chilli farmers across India

~50-55% of total exports are whole Chillis

Simplified Chilli value chain		Input supplies	Chilli farming & production	Aggregation and logistics	Processing	Exporting (~5-10%) / Domestic end-markets
Activities		Licensing, Production & Distribution	Farming, drying, trade packaging of Chilli	Transport from farm to *Mandi*, storage, sorting, grading and supply to processors.	Crushing, grinding, cleaning, other value add processing	Marketing and exports foreign importers (in most cases processors are exporters)
Products		Seeds, fertilizers, pesticides	Dried and other cold stored	Sorted and graded Chilli	Crushed, grounded	Export packaged, processed and unprocessed
Key pain points throughout the value chain		Distribution of banned pesticides	Quality and variety not in line with global demand. Limited productivity and non-standard practices.	Contamination during handling. Low traceability to farm	Limited demand for Value added segment due to price competitiveness. Lack of Incentives for private sector investment in processing	Lower incentives for value added exports (2%) compared to basic (3%). (China gives 10% incentive). Increasing competition from other Chilli producing countries. Rejections because of SPS non-compliance
Consolidation level	Number of players	10's	1,000,000's	1000's	10's	100's
Key players in the industry		UPL, IFFCO, syngenta	~90-95% small and marginal farmers	Small traders, wholesalers, commission agents	AVT NATURAL, Synthite, NEDSPICE, JABS, Laxmi enterprises etc.	Olam Spices, plant lipids, ITC

1. ~3-5% margin in case of whole Chilli exports
2. < 5% of Chilli procurement is currently done through contract farming

Source: Expert interviews, Press Search

FIgure 5. The existing value chain

Source: High Level Expert Group on Agriculture, *Growing India's Agriculture exports through crop-specific, state-led plans, 2020.*

Chilli value chain is characterized by consolidation for processors and exporters and millions of small Chilli farmers across India

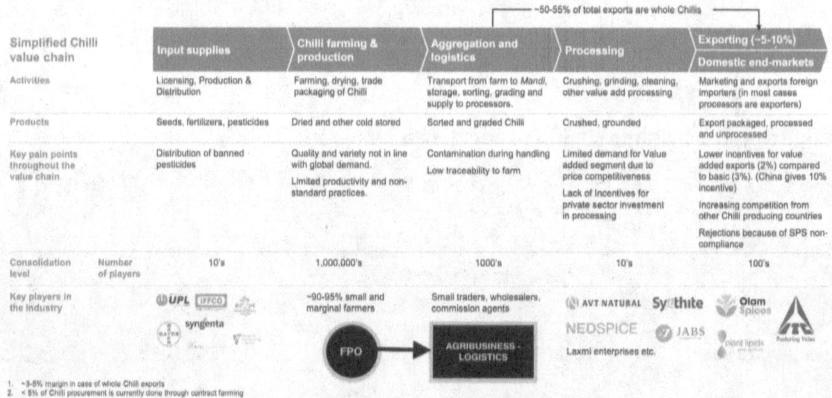

~50-55% of total exports are whole Chillis

Simplified Chilli value chain		Input supplies	Chilli farming & production	Aggregation and logistics	Processing	Exporting (~5-10%) / Domestic end-markets
Activities		Licensing, Production & Distribution	Farming, drying, trade packaging of Chilli	Transport from farm to *Mandi*, storage, sorting, grading and supply to processors.	Crushing, grinding, cleaning, other value add processing	Marketing and exports foreign importers (in most cases processors are exporters)
Products		Seeds, fertilizers, pesticides	Dried and other cold stored	Sorted and graded Chilli	Crushed, grounded	Export packaged, processed and unprocessed
Key pain points throughout the value chain		Distribution of banned pesticides	Quality and variety not in line with global demand. Limited productivity and non-standard practices.	Contamination during handling. Low traceability to farm	Limited demand for Value added segment due to price competitiveness. Lack of Incentives for private sector investment in processing	Lower incentives for value added exports (2%) compared to basic (3%). (China gives 10% incentive). Increasing competition from other Chilli producing countries. Rejections because of SPS non-compliance
Consolidation level	Number of players	10's	1,000,000's	1000's	10's	100's
Key players in the industry		UPL, IFFCO, syngenta	~90-95% small and marginal farmers	Small traders, wholesalers, commission agents	AVT NATURAL, Synthite, NEDSPICE, JABS, Laxmi enterprises etc.	Olam Spices, plant lipids, ITC

1. ~3-5% margin in case of whole Chilli exports
2. < 5% of Chilli procurement is currently done through contract farming

Source: Expert interviews, Press Search

Figure 6. 'Organising the Supply Chain': FPOs means a cog in the Corporate controlled Supply Chain

Source: Women Resist and Organise. pptx by S. R. Ramdas 2021.

The dairy experience demonstrates the flawed arguments of deregulated markets and exports as solutions to hunger, and raises big questions about leaving it to private, demand-driven mechanisms to address the crises of production and consumption. Dairying is undoubtedly a 'huge success' by the supply chain management yardsticks of the G20 and Government of India. Millions departing the livelihood is, for capitalist markets, a great indicator of the desired rural transformation shift from farm to non-farm occupation, regardless of the fact that a huge number of workers who were forced out have been unable to enter any alternate livelihood, save that of daily wage casual labour. Massive growth and exports have clearly been unable to correct inequality of consumption. Thus, as far as food, nutrition, and livelihood security goes, it has been a disaster, with benefits accrued by agribusiness corporations—cooperative and private.

The COVID-19 pandemic and accompanying lockdowns have only enhanced the extreme food and nutrition insecurity. Whilst the government may deny the reality of the worsening position on the Global Hunger Index (GHI), neither these figures nor any other recent figures capture the burden of additional hunger and malnutrition experienced by millions who have sunk into deep food insecurity during the past year and a half (Sinha, 2021). All investigations and studies have reported how the loss of employment has resulted in huge income falls, increased debts, and reductions in food consumption (Azim Premji University 2021, pp. 107–130).

However, through this grim pandemic period, the profits of corporate players (national and global)—be it Ambani (Chandra, 2021), Amazon (Rai, 2021), Adani (The Economic Times, 2021), or Amul (The Hindu Businessline, 2021)—have just skyrocketed.

The Rice, Beef, Palm Oil and Wood Lighthouse Clusters Conundrum

Rice

The past year was a 'record' for rice in several ways, as analyzed by Damodaran (2021): it was (i) the largest offtake of rice (93 mt) and wheat from the central pool governed by the Food Corporation of India, 50 per cent higher than the previous fiscal year. This was linked to the government's decision to increase distribution under provisions of India's' National Food Security Act, 2013, up to November 2021; (ii) it was the largest ever procurement of rice (55 mt), higher than the record of the previous year under Minimum Support Price (MSP), which was possibly a response by the government to the ongoing farmers' movement, in an attempt to counter the claim that the intentions of the Farm Laws is to stop MSP; (iii) despite the largest offtake, buffer stocks of rice in FCI crossed 100 mt for the first time, and (iv) the country recorded the largest rice exports totalling over 17.7mt, which the government said were sourced from the open markets, with a small quantity on humanitarian grounds sourced from the central pool. The exports were also aided by an all-time high in global rice prices (Damodaran, 2021).

With last year's highs, rice exports were projected to be as good this fiscal year too (Kasabe, 2021a). However, by August–September 2021, the industry reported that exports would only be 12 mt (Kasabe, 2021b), attributing the reduction to the massive clogs in global supply chains (high freight charges and other logistical bottlenecks), as also drops in global rice prices and volatility of markets. At the procurement end, the government in October 2021 instructed states to cap procurements and slow them down, citing huge stocks in the central pool (Mishra, 2021). States like Telangana, Andhra Pradesh, and Chattisgarh have been asked to stop procuring parboiled rice due to sufficient central pool stocks, which will reportedly last for 3–4 years. The Telangana state government, which encouraged farmers to cultivate rice in Kharif 2020, assuring them of complete procurement, then asked farmers to stop all paddy in Rabi 2021, as the state will not be able to procure rice because of the Centre's unwillingness to procure rice from Telangana (Pulipaka, 2021). Soon after Diwali, the government announced it would not be extending the additional free rations distributed under the Prime Minister Garib Kalyan Anna Yojana after November 30, as 'the economy has recovered' (Abraham, 2021). This decision was subsequently reversed by the government and extended upto March 2022 (The Hindu, 2021), which could well be a pre-assembly election decision with crucial states going to poll. In short, a complete reversal of last year. Whilst the organized farmers' movements in Punjab and Haryana were able to force procurements without pause, unorganized farmers, for instance in Telangana, have been unable to rally to force either state or Centre on the rice procurement question.

It is important to ask if these are signs of the government's intent to operationalize a patently G20-compliant global supply chain, market-based 'blueprint' for food security detailed by the HLEG (HLEG, 2021, pp. 64–67) and the OECD (OECD, 2018, 19), for rice.

Ramdas and Charanya (2021) exposed how the HLEG argues that local procurement and high rice MSP are the main blocks for export markets because of FCI's (Food Corporation of India) procurement beyond the buffer stock norms for food security, leading to diminishing of the surplus stocks meant for exports. This distorts the markets, thereby making Indian prices uncompetitive for exports. Their recommendation to increase exportable surplus is to alter FCI's procurement which, beyond buffer stock requirements, should be structured on a price-differential scheme. Wherein the difference between MSP and open market price gets credited into farmers' accounts as a direct benefit transfer so that the excess over buffer stock can be exported in the open markets at market prices. This reflects an irrevocably changed position of the current regime as compared to that of all previous governments, regarding agriculture, food, and rural livelihood security policies. Earlier governments prioritized effective tariff protection and subsidies to small producers, circumventing unfair competition from global agribusiness. However, today, the shared interest of domestic and global agribusiness with the state is reflected in India's reforms and finance plans of 2021–2026.

The OECD's recommendations are blunter on how food security should be met within a primarily export-oriented agriculture policy which is integrated into global supply chains:

- scale back the Public Distribution System (PDS) as incomes and the share of the middle class in the population rises;
- move gradually to targeted lump sum transfers (direct benefit transfers) or food stamp type mechanisms; and
- allow the private sector to play a role in managing remaining stocking operations.

As has happened increasingly across South East Asia, where 'food security' of the poorest is being met via the cheapest rice available in the market—which could be imported from Vietnam, Thailand, or India—it is evident how this is what the Indian state, too, is possibly pushing for. As pointed out earlier this year:

> Vietnam's 'miracle' transformation from a subsistence rice producing nation feeding its people, to being one of the top 3 rice exporting countries of the world today, is the 'shining' example highlighted by the HLEG, to

build food-security and incomes. However, this supposed 'success-story', as some of us at the Food Sovereignty Alliance discovered, is ruining small farmer livelihoods in South-East Asia. Small farmers in Indonesia, sell their organic home-grown nutritious rice and purchase cheaper priced chemically cultivated Vietnamese rice from the market to eat. Indonesian farmers frequently receive Vietnamese rice as part of their country's food security programme! Cheap rice from Vietnam, is making it non-viable for small farmers in Cambodia to grow their own rice, a vital source of food and livelihood security, and Vietnamese small peasants are indebted to global agribusiness companies, who control the entire value-chain 'end-to-end.' (Ramdas and Charanya, 2021)

It is this end-to-end control of the entire value chain by agribusiness that is being forced through in tune with the G20 proposals today. It is also clear that integration into global supply chains is no longer merely about importing food into India or exporting it out of India. A perusal of countries' pathways of transforming their food and agriculture systems, available on the United Nations Food Systems Summit (UNFSS) website (Food Systems Summit, 2021), which is strongly endorsed by the G20 (G20 Italia 2021c, 5), reveals the universal blueprint. It is about corporate agribusiness players (domestic-global entities in partnerships, as subsidiaries, via mergers and acquisitions), exercising their power to control and govern the global supply chain structure of food and agriculture, so as to source food anywhere in the world (based on factors such as price, supply chain movement, availability as a result of climatic or other disaster factors, etc.) and supply the same anywhere in the world.

For this, they require, and hence, will invest (with the intent to profit) in (i) foolproof agriculture value chains everywhere; (ii) re-localized production and processing hubs to integrate into these global value chains; (iii) digital traceability which will give them access to intimate data about farmers, their land, their production, and their every step down the value chain. This would allow them to have real time data on availability of commodities, prices, and logistics, in order to facilitate the movement of commodities and their delivery as quickly as possible to where they are needed, regardless of where they are produced. The global superstructure has to be put into place to make this work.

The role they see for multilateral finance institutions is to support investments—so, for instance, seed financing by the World Bank will provide assured signals for private investments. The role of the state is to remove all barriers to investment and stand guarantee to these private investors. This is where they demand international trade agreements by their governments to agree to legally binding mechanisms of 'investment protection and data protection.' The selective inclusion of Kirana shops by Amazon, Reliance, and Flipkart-Walmart into their supply chains. This is seen as a 'win-win' situation for the shop and the e-trade retail giants, resulting in gradual livelihood losses for small traders of the physical supply chains through which the Kirana shops have traditionally sourced their goods is also underway. The global governance role of food by the Food and Agriculture Organization (FAO) has been reduced to one of facilitating transformations of food systems to corporate controlled ones (Figure 7).

The United Nations Framework on Sustainability Standards (UNFSS) narrative includes empowering the thus far marginalized such as women , youth, and indigenous people through their integration into corporate-controlled value chains. However, in reality, this is part of the capitalist and, in the case of India, deeply Brahminical project, which profits from exploiting the alienated labour of Dalit-Bahujan-Adivasi women and youth. Their aggregation into Farmer Producer Organizations (FPOs) secures for the corporates easy access to products and a permanent market for capital and services. This translates into the financial enslavement of the most vulnerable, through permanent debt servicing, and

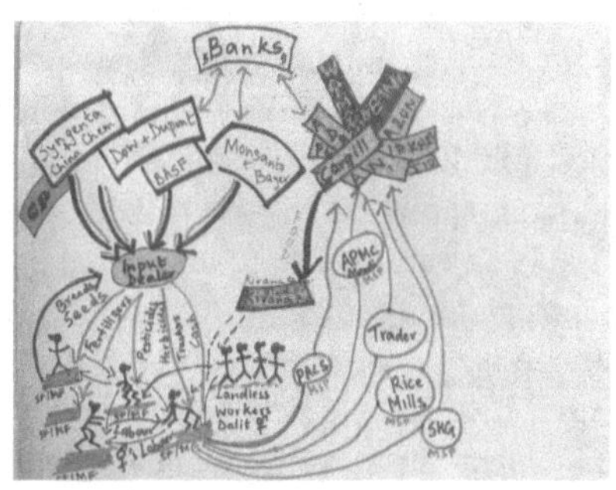
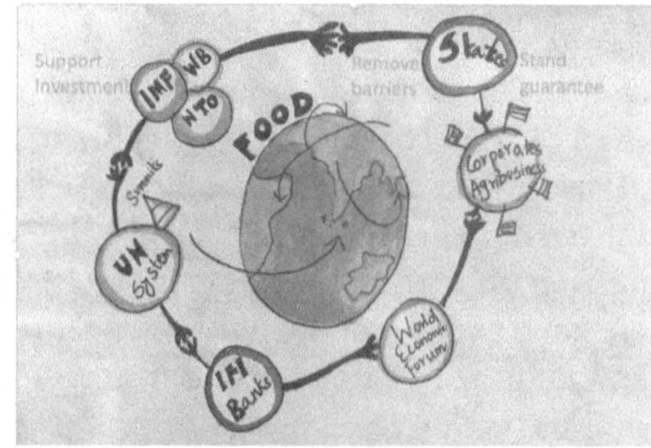

Figure 7 (i) and (ii).

Source: Presentation at Jan Sarokar Indian Counter Dialogue at the UN Food Systems Summit by S. R. Ramdas, 2021.

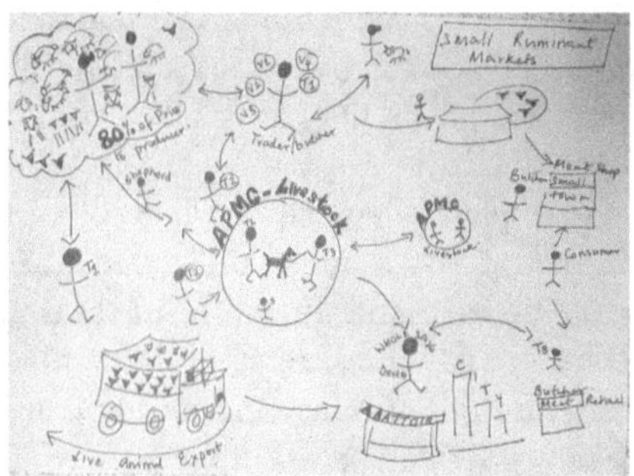
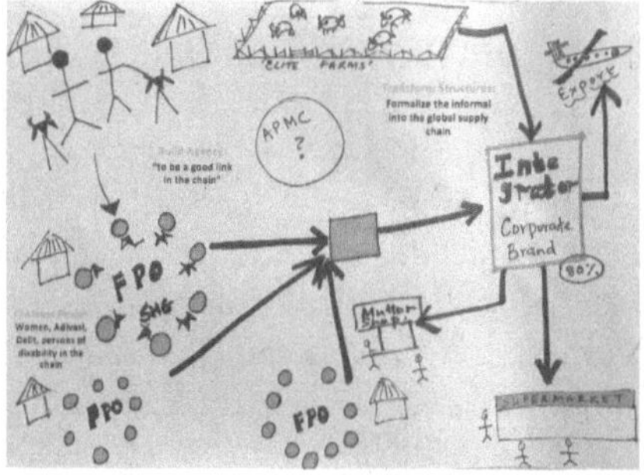

Figure 8 (i): Current Goat Markets; and 8 (ii): Goat Markets Corporate Take-Over: What they mean by empowerment

Source: Presentation at Jan Sarokar Indian Counter Dialogue at the UN Food Systems Summit by S .R. Ramdas, 2021.

finally, ensuring their total dependence on this system for food and livelihood (Ramdas 2021a, p. 5).

The framework also reflects the dangerous confluence of a 4000-year-old, yet to be annihilated, oppressive system of Brahminical patriarchy and capitalism, which gains collective power through its specific but interlinked forms of oppression. It does so by shaping the policies on food and livelihood security which are clearly deepening food insecurity and facilitating control of the value chains by capital.

Beef: The systematic criminalization of beef across the country is depriving every 13th Indian belonging to Dalit-Adivasi-minorities and Bahujan communities of vital nutrition and livelihoods. Yet, as one of the 'lighthouse' export value chains, it will now be taken off domestic food plates, and sourced and exported by eliminating millions of small traders and transporters down the value chain, who are mostly from Dalit and minority communities (Ramdas, 2021c).

Palm Oil: The geographies for expansion in the recently announced National Palm Oil Mission are the prime forests of North East India and the Andaman and Nicobar Islands, both of which are homelands and territories of indigenous peoples. Expendable as far as the Brahminic-capitalist state goes, the ecological devastation and massive health risks that palm oil plantations have wreaked onto the territories of indigenous peoples in Malaysia and Indonesia have completely been ignored whilst making these decisions. Indigenous people, whose territories are governed by special constitutional protections, have the right to free, prior and informed consent to accept or reject such investments based on complete information on the pros and cons of such plantation projects. They have a right to know the contents of the HLEG report which details (i) how palm oil is a water-guzzling crop requiring 300 litres of water per tree per day; (ii) how palm oil should be declared a plantation crop so as to attract private investment, which should co-finance oil palm on two million hectares of 'wastelands' and irrigated lands where paddy and sugarcane are cultivated in agro-climatically suitable zones; and (iii) how land lease norms should be relaxed, allowing leases for 30 years to facilitate private players to finally buy land from the farmers.

All of this points to a clear corporate land grab plan, where an obsolete colonial term 'wasteland' is used to describe common property resources utilized to graze animals, collect uncultivated foods, herbs, medicinal plants, fuel wood or shifting cultivation (Ramdas and Charanaya, 2021), all of which are integral to the food and nutritional security of indigenous communities. These stand deeply compromised now. In October 2021, the Telangana government asked the farmers to grow palm oil as a steady source of income in place of paddy, and set a target of 100 acres of palm oil plantations on farmers' lands in each of the 57 clusters in the state (The Hans India, 2021). FGV Holdings, a Malaysian company, committed to establishing palm oil processing units in the state, and the minister assured the company of large-scale cultivation across the state.

Wood: The governments' announcements to amend the Forest Rights Act so as to facilitate the entry of private sector to invest in forest plantations and access plantation funds to be sourced from Compensatory Afforestation Funds (CAMPA) (e-Green Watch, n.d.) and the Green India Mission (Government of India, n.d.) were scripted in the HLEG (Ramdas and Charanya, 2021). Once again, this points to yet another mechanism to resource grab forest lands that predominantly lie in the Schedule V and VI territories of Adivasi communities. This is garbed in arguments of how India can reduce its wood imports from USD 9.5 to USD 6.5 billion and increase forest cover by 1.5 per cent by 2025, via enhancing forest plantations (High Level Expert Group on Agriculture, 2020, pp. 211). Additionally, corporations will cleverly profit from market-based false solutions to the climate crisis—be it carbon offsets or carbon sinks.

The opportunities for timber plantations include (i) improving productivity of Forest Development Corporation land to be leased to industry (0.5 million ha), and (ii) 3 million ha of degraded forests under collaborative industry lease models, along the lines of Southeast Asian countries such as Malaysia. The states identified for this intervention include those with the largest Adivasi populations in Schedule V areas, such as Madhya Pradesh, Maharashtra, Orissa, Chhattisgarh, Andhra Pradesh, and Telangana. They also project how contract farming for industry-linked agro-forestry plantations can occur with land title owners, possibly with those who obtained titles under the Forest Rights Act, 2006.

They conveniently bypass other constitutional prerequisites such as Gram Sabha consent for any development, market or forest interventions in Schedule V areas, all of this undermining Adivasi rights and consolidating the power of corporations. The Prime Minister's commitments to achieve net zero emissions by 2050 by growing millions of trees is linked to this process of undermining Adivasi rights and constitutional protections. Furthermore, we need to flag here how these forest titles are lands where adivasis have traditionally cultivated diverse food crops, including millets, pulses, and oilseeds, and are rich sources of wild uncultivated foods, key for household and community food and nutritional security. Thus, each time such projects with objectives to grow trees on forest farming lands of adivasis are conceptualized, the Adivasis' basic food plates are under threat. Ironically, the government has lobbied with the FAO to declare 2022 as the year of millets. Whilst championing the health wonders of millets, it carries out projects and plans that are capitalizing millets as monocropped commodities, ensuring their domestic and international exports for consumption by elites, pricing them out of reach of the Adivasi/Dalit producers themselves.

At the producers' end: The ecological vulnerabilities of cultivating a mere 1 or 2 primary crops, coupled with the economic vulnerabilities of extreme volatility of prices as the commodities become increasingly integrated into global markets, are a far cry from livelihood/farmer security. Another classic example of such happenings this year is that of cotton, where India is the global leader after China in exports, and farmers are seeing all time high procurement prices in the open market (Ghodekar, 2021). The reasons for this have been attributed to (i) huge demand internationally and domestically from textile industries for cotton bales as production was ramped up post-COVID in garment factories, (ii) additional huge demand from China, (iii) an overall decline in production area, (iv) lower production and yields this year, and (v) the slowdown and jamming up of global supply chains in shipping. This came as a windfall for farmers in those regions where climate disruptions destroyed part of the crop/reduced yields. However, this will certainly not be the case next year. Meanwhile, in light of this year's boom, there will be a rush to cultivate cotton next season, and with volatile prices, the outcome could very well be the reverse of that of 2021.

When it comes to food security: For the entire gamut of informal and unorganized working class—be it agriculture workers, small producers, small traders, small processors, vendors, shopkeepers, and the vast numbers of unemployed and underemployed—whose numbers just went up, we flag two issues:

Food rights activists and academics have consistently argued that the buffer stock, which is misleadingly termed as 'surplus', should be distributed through a universal PDS (Sinha, 2020). They reiterate (i) the criticality of universalising the PDS, more so in the current COVID-19 context, due to massive increases in destroyed livelihoods, unemployment (Misra, 2021), and hunger, and (ii) suggest the need to enhance these 'buffer stock' values, along with (iii) diversifying and decentralizing the procurement of food to meet the basic caloric and protein nutritional needs of people. This is very doable with the National Food Security Act (NFSA), 2013, as it encourages decentralized and localized procurement.

The arguments that DBT and a demand-led agriculture-food supply chain system will serve the food needs more effectively is a deeply flawed argument on several accounts. Regardless of how globally integrated the supply chains of a commodity (from milk to maize) are, there continues to be extreme volatility of prices, which is controlled by corporations for their profits. The huge crises in the global supply chains linked to shipping and transportation of goods around the world which, according to analysts, was in the making even prior to the COVID-19 pandemic lockdowns (Broadman, 2021) and will possibly not be resolved in the near future, implies continuing volatility in prices of all essential foods. Mere cash in the bank does not translate into the ability to convert that cash into food, as that critical essential food may well be priced sky high, placing it beyond the purchasing power of those populations who are entitled to subsidized food under India's NFSA, 2013.

Furthermore, with the overall situation of India—marked by highest levels of inequality, resource alienation, rising unemployment, livelihood loss, systematic reduction in allocation of budgets to essential welfare measures, including work under National Rural Employment Guarantee Scheme (NREGS) and public distribution system, privatised education, health, power, and rising costs of fuel, overlaid with entrenched Brahminical patriarchy—there is no guarantee that the money will be used for food or reach the bellies of the most undernourished and anaemic children and women from Dalit, Bahujan, Adivasi, and other minority communities. In short, the global supply chain arguments are never going to be able to address the deepening crises of hunger and chronic nutritional deficiencies, either with or without techno-fixes like biofortification of foods, genomics, and genetic manipulations announced by the agriculture minister as being India's solutions to food security.

IN CONCLUSION

India's taking on the G20 presidency mantle in 2023 coincides with the run up to India's national elections in 2024. The current regime, if elected back to power, will push for the above macro-framework, which can best be described as a 'win-win' situation for the ruling class-castes nationally and globally, and complete destruction for the struggling oppressed majority people of India. In the 'I pat your back and you pat mine' scenario, the interest of the G7 capitalist nation to sustain capitalism—which is in deep crisis—is deeply tied to the market and investment opportunities and geo-political interests they currently see in India. This imperialist interest of the global north will take precedence over calling out the current Indian regime for its human rights violations, and their violent attempts to make India into a monolith Hindu nation, structured on the oppressive ideology of Brahminism. Countering this is embedded in the large-scale massive project of liberation from the entwined oppressive structures of caste, patriarchy and capital (Ramdas, 2021a). It involves sharpening radical collective actions to dismantle the state-backed, corporate-controlled agri-food system down the value chain, and revision actions to reorganize and re-localize food farming systems built on the principles of food sovereignty and social justice.

REFERENCES

Abraham, Bobins. 2021. No more free rations for 80 Cr Indians after November 30, as Economy has recovered, says Govt. *India Times*. November 6. https://www.indiatimes.com/news/india/no-more-free-ration-for-80-cr-indians-after-november-30-under-pmkgay-553474.html.

Anandan, Sujata. 2019. Onion, poor man's staple is worth more than its weight in gold Madame Minister!. *National Herald*. 08 December. https://www.nationalheraldindia.com/opinion/onion-poor-mans-staple-is-worth-more-than-its-weight-in-gold-madame-minister.

Azim Premji University. 2021. "State of Working India 2021: One year of Covid-19." Centre for Sustainable Employment, Azim Premji University.

Berdegué, Julio A., Tomás Rosada Rosada, and Anthony J. Bebbington. 2014. "The Rural Transformation." In *International Development: Ideas, Experience, and Prospects*, edited by Bruce et al Currie-Alder. Oxford Academic .

Bhosale, Jayashree. 2021. Tomato prices crash to Rs 3/kg, farmers demand support measures. *Economic Times*. August 26. https://m.economictimes.com/news/economy/agriculture/tomato-prices-crash-to-rs-3/kg-farmers-demand-support-measures/articleshow/85658427.cms .

Biswas, P. 2021. Maharashtra: Tomato prices crash across state, farmers blame bumper crop and blocked export routes. *The Indian Express*. August 27. https://indianexpress.com/article/cities/pune/maharashtra-tomato-prices-crash-across-state-farmers-blame-bumper-crop-7472206/.

Biswas, Preeti, and Sunil Mungara. 2021. Veggies and meat get drearer as fuel prices continue to spiral. *The Times of India*. October 26. https://timesofindia.indiatimes.com/city/hyderabad/veggies-meat-get-dearer-asfuel-prices-continue-to-spiral/articleshow/87265776.cms.

Broadman, Harry G. 2021. Global Supply Chains' Crisis Is Much Bigger Than The Pandemic; The Transformation They're Undergoing Is The Cure. *Forbes*. September 30. https://www.forbes.com/sites/harrybroadman/2021/09/30/global-supply-chains-crisis-is-much-bigger-than-the-pandemic-the-transformation-theyre-undergoing-is-the-cure/?sh=27e115f57f80.

Business Standard. 2021. Onion prices not 'extraordinarily high'; no case for banning exports: Govt. *Business Standard*. October 22. https://www.business-standard.com/article/current-affairs/onion-prices-not-extraordinarily-high-no-case-for-banning-exports-govt-121102201292_1.html.

Business Today. 2021. More than 33 lakh children in India malnourished, 17.7 lakh of them severely malnourished: Govt data. *Business Today*. November 7.   https://www.businesstoday.in/latest/trends/story/more-than-33-lakh-children-in-india-malnourished-177-lakh-of-them-severely-malnourished-govt-data-311528-2021-11-07.

Chandra, Jagriti. 2021. India billionaires increased their wealth by 35% during the lockdown, Says OXFAM report. *The Hindu*. January 25. https://www.thehindu.com/news/national/oxfam-study-shows-rich-got-richer-during-pandemic/article33655044.ece.

Damodaran, Harish. 2021. *How 'food' has become the real social safety net in pandemic.* Centre for Policy Research. 11 June. https://cprindia.org/news/9841.

e-Green Watch. n.d. *Integrated e-Governance Portal for Automation, Streamlining & Effective Management of Processeslated to Plantation & Other Forestry Works under all Schemes.* http://164.100.195.16.

Desk, Express Web. 2021. Farmers end year long protest: A timeline of how it unfolded. *The Indian Express.* December 9. https://indianexpress.com/article/india/one-year-of-farm-laws-timeline-7511961/ .

FAO, IFAD, UNICEF, WFP, WHO. 2021. *The State of Food Security and Nutrition in the World 2021. Transforming food systems for food security, improved nutrition and affordable healthy diets for all.* Rome: FAO.

Final Report for Data Collection and Confirmation Study for Agriculture Value Chains in the Republic of India. 2015. Japan International Cooperation Agency (JICA), pp. 52–53.

Focus on the Global South. 2009. The G 20, Global Capital, and the Conjuncture: An Interview with Walden Bello. *Focus on the Global South.* December 3. https://focusweb.org/the-g-20-global-capital-and-the-conjuncture-an-interview-with-walden-bello/.

Food Sovereignty Alliance. n.d. *About Food Sovereignty Alliance.* https://foodsovereigntyalliance.wordpress.com/about/.

Food Systems Summit Dialogues. 2021. *Member State Dialogue Convenors and Pathways.* https://summitdialogues.org/overview/member-state-food-systems-summit-dialogues/convenors/ .

Gaurav, Kunal. 2021. India achieves key successes at G20, shapes language of climate action. *Hindustan Times.* November 1. https://www.hindustantimes.com/india-news/india-achieves-key-successes-at-g20-shapes-language-of-actions-required-101635690349645.html.

Ghodekar, Rutika. 2021. October records historically high cotton prices in India. *Mintec.* November 2. https://www.mintecglobal.com/top-stories/october-records-historically-high-cotton-prices-in-india.

IISD. 2021. *G7 Leaders Summit 2021.* IISD. 11-13 June. Accessed December 26, 2021. https://sdg.iisd.org/events/g7-leaders-summit-2021/.

G20 China. 2016. "Agriculture Ministers Meeting Communique." G20 China.

G20 France. 2011. "Ministerial Declaration Action Plan on Food Price Volatility and Agriculture ." G20 France, Paris.

G20 Italia. 2021a. "G20 Rome Leaders Declaration." G20 Italia.

G20 Italia. 2021b. "G20 Agriculture Ministers Communique." G20 Italia.

G20 Italia. 2021c. "Matera Declaration." G20 Italia.

G20 Italia. 2021d.http://www.g20italy.org/italian-g20-presidency/priorities.html.

G20 Japan. 2019. "G20 Best Practices for Sustainable Agro-Food Sector." G20 Japan.

G20 Research Group. 2021. "G20 Meetings of Agriculture Ministers." G20 Research Group.

Global Donor Platform for Rural Development. n.d. *Challenges and Opportunities of Rural Transformation.* Global Donor Platform for Rural Development. https://www.donorplatform.org/challenges-and-opportunities-of-rural-transformation.html .

Government of India. 2018a. "Report of the Committee on Doubling Farmers Income Vol XIV. "Comprehensive Policy Recommendations." Ministry of Agriculture and Farmers Welfare. New Delhi.

Government of India. 2018a. "Report of the Committee on Doubling Farmers Income Vol V, Chapter 5. Ministry of Agriculture and Farmers Welfare. New Delhi .

Government of India. 2018b. "Agriculture Export Policy." Ministry of Commerce and Industry, Department of Commerce, Governmernt of India.

Government of India. 2019. Agriculture Census Division, Ministry of Agriculture and Farmers Welfare, Department of Agriculture, Cooperation and Farmers Welfare, Agriculture Census of India 2015-16.

Government of India. 2020. *Finance Commission in Covid Times Report for 2021-26 Volume-I Main Report.* XV Finance Commission.

Government of India. 2021c. *MOUs on developing Proof of Concepts on Farmer's Database.* Department of Agriculture & Farmers Welfare. https://agricoop.nic.in/en/farmingagreement.

Government of India. 2021d. "Consultation Paper on Proposed amendments in the Forest (Conservation) Act, 1980." New Delhi : Ministry of Environment, Forest and Climate Change., October.

Government of India. n.d.-a. *One District One Product.* Ministry of Food Processing Industries. https://odop.mofpi.gov.in/odop/.

Government of India n.d. -b. *Climate Change Knowledge Portal Details of Mission.* Ministry of Environment, Forest and Climate Change.

Government of India. n.d. *Climate Change Knowledge Portal Details of Mission.* Ministry of Environment Forest and Climate Change. https://cckpindia.nic.in/details-of-missions/.

High Level Expert Group on Agriculture. 2020. *Growing India's Agriculture exports through crop-specific, state-led plans.* Submission to the XV Finance Commission.

Kamdar, Bansari, and Shreyasee Das. 2021. No title, No money – Women grow 80% of India's food, but new arm laws unlikely to help them. *The Print*. March 13. https://theprint.in/opinion/no-title-no-money-women-grow-80-of-indias-food-but-new-farm-laws-unlikely-to-help-them/620961/.

Kasabe, Nanda. 2021. India set to clock record rice exports in current year too. *Financial express*. June 30. https://www.financialexpress.com/economy/india-set-to-clock-record-rice-exports-in-current-year-too/2280941/.

Kasabe, Nanda. 2021b. Rice exports from India to take a hit this year. *Financial Express*. August 18. https://www.financialexpress.com/market/commodities/rice-exports-from-india-to-take-a-hit-this-year/2312671/.

Mathur, Barkha. 2021. National Family Health Survey (NFHS-5): Child Mortality Rate and Vaccination Improve But Concerns Around Malnutrition And Anaemia Remain. *NDTV*. January 1. https://swachhindia.ndtv.com/national-family-health-survey-nfhs-5-child-mortality-rate-and-vaccination-improve-but-concerns-around-malnutrition-and-anaemia-remain-54864/.

Mishra, Prabhudatta. 2021. Kharif Season 2021: As FCI stock pile up, entre prunes paddy purchases at MSP. *Financial Express*. October 4. https://www.financialexpress.com/economy/kharif-season-2021-as-fci-stocks-pile-up-centre-prunes-paddy-purchases-at-msp/2342947/.

Misra, Udit. 2021. ExplainSpeaking: Why rising unemployment, not GDP growth, is the biggest challenge for India. *The Indian Express*. April 24. https://indianexpress.com/article/explained/explainspeaking-why-rising-unemployment-not-gdp-growth-is-the-biggest-challenge-before-india-7198941/.

narendramodi.in. n.d. "One Nation, One Market." Accessed at https://www.narendramodi.in/mobile/one-nation-one-market.

National Family Health Survey (NFHS-5). 2021.

OECD/ICRIER. 2018. *Agricultural Policies in India*. OECD Food and Agricultural Reviews, Paris : OECD Publishing.

OECD/ICRIER. 2018. *Agricultural Policies in India*. OECD Food and Agricultural Reviews, Paris: OECD Publishing.

OECD. 2021. G20 economies are pricing more carbon emissions but stronger globally more coherent policy action is needed to meet climate goals, says OECD. October 27. https://www.oecd.org/tax/g20-economies-are-pricing-more-carbon-emissions-but-stronger-globally-more-coherent-policy-action-is-needed-to-meet-climate-goals-says-oecd.htm.

Pandey, Samyak. 2021. To make India 'atmanirbhar' on palm oil, Modi govt approves separate National Missions. *The Print*. August 18. https://theprint.

in/india/to-make-india-atmanirbhar-on-palm-oil-modi-govt-approves-separate-national-mission/717963/.

Pulipaka, Balu. 2021. CM KCR warns farmers not to sow paddy , refuses to reduce VAT on petrol, diesel. *Deccan Chronicle*. November 7. https://www.deccanchronicle.com/nation/politics/071121/cm-kcr-warns-farmers-not-to-sow-paddy-refuses-to-reduce-state-vat-on.html.

Presentation at Jan Sarokar Indian Counter Dialogue at the UN Food Systems Summit by Ramdas, S. R. 2021.

Rai, Saritha. 2021. Amazon reveals scorching growth in India as Flipkart fight deepens. *Business Standard*. April 8. https://www.business-standard.com/article/companies/amazon-reveals-scorching-growth-in-india-as-flipkart-fight-deepens-121040801089_1.html.

Rajgopal, Krishnadas. 2021. Farmers Protest: Supreme Court stays implementation of controversial farm laws. *The Hindu*. January 12. https://www.the-hindu.com/news/national/sc-suspends-implementation-of-three-farm-laws/article33557081.ece.

Ramdas, Sagari R., and Charanya R. 2021. The New Farm Laws May Facilitate a Shift in India's Agricultural Export Policy. *The Wire*. https://thewire.in/agriculture/the-new-farm-laws-may-facilitate-a-shift-in-indias-agricultural-export-policy.

Ramdas, Sagari R. 2021c. Economic Rationale of Slaughter and Beef Ban in Karnataka. *The Leaflet*. https://www.theleaflet.in/economic-rationale-of-slaughter-and-beef-ban-in-karnataka/.

Ramdas, Sagari R. 2021b. India's Deregulated Dairy Sector Signposts The Future of our Food. *The Indian Forum*.

Ramdas, Sagari R. 2021a. "Towards Food Sovereignty: Dismantling the Capitalist Brahminic-Patriarchal Food Farming Regime." *Development*, 276-281.

Sharma, Niharika. 2021. Indias mom-and-pop stores have proved yet again why the Amazons of the world need them. *Quartz India*. June 11. Accessed September 7. https://qz.com/india/1994922/why-amazon-and-reliance-need-indias-humble-kirana-stores/.

Sinha, Dipa. 2021. A reminder that India still trails in the hunger fight. *The Hindu*. October 26. https://www.thehindu.com/opinion/op-ed/a-reminder-that-india-still-trails-in-the-hunger-fight/article37168319.ece.

Sinha, Dipa. 2020. Grain aplenty and the crises of hunger: on universal Public Distribution System. *The Hindu*. June 30. https://www.thehindu.com/opinion/op-ed/grain-aplenty-and-the-crisis-of-hunger/article31948530.ece.

The Economic Times. 2021. India adds 40 billionaires in pandemic year; Adani, Ambani see rise in wealth: Report. *The Economic Times.* March 2. https://economictimes.indiatimes.com/news/company/corporate-trends/india-adds-40-billionaires-in-pandemic-year-adani-ambani-see-rise-in-wealth-report/articleshow/81289912.cms.

The Economic Times. 2021. Higher investment required in agri R&D: India says at G20 agri meet. *The Economic Times.* September 18. https://economictimes.indiatimes.com/news/economy/agriculture/higher-investment-required-in-agri-rd-india-says-at-g20-agri-meet/articleshow/86320069.cms?utm_source=contentofinterest&utm_medium=text&utm_campaign=cppst.

The Hans India. 2021. Sircilla: KTR stresses on palm oil cultivation. *The Hans India.* September 21. https://www.thehansindia.com/telangana/sircilla-ktr-stresses-on-palm-oil-cultivation-707405.

The Hindu. 2021. Centre's free food grain scheme on till March. *The Hindu.* November 24. https://www.thehindu.com/news/national/govt-extends-5-kg-free-foodgrains-scheme-till-march-2022/article37660568.ece.

The Hindu Businessline. 2021. Amul turnover grown 2% amidst Covid-19 challenges. July 20. https://www.thehindubusinessline.com/companies/amul-turnover-grows-2-amidst-covid-19-challenges/article35423185.ece.

The New Indian Express. 2021a. Tomato prices crash to Rs 4/kg amid supply glut in most growing states. August 30. https://www.newindianexpress.com/business/2021/aug/30/tomato-prices-crash-to-rs-4kg-amid-supply-glut-in-most-growing-states-2351870.html.

The New Indian express. 2021b. Kitchen staple prices soar across South Indian States. October 20. https://www.newindianexpress.com/states/kerala/2021/oct/20/kitchen-staple-prices-soar-across-south-indian-states-2373362.html.

The Times of India. 2021. Parliament passes bill to repeal three farm laws. November 29. https://timesofindia.indiatimes.com/india/lok-sabha-passes-bill-to-repeal-three-farm-laws/articleshow/87976235.cms.

Women Resist and Organise. pptx by S. R. Ramdas. 2021. Presented at IAFFE 2021 Closing Plenary Feminist Resistance. https://www.youtube.com/watch?v=--Xe0VlbNl0

World Economic Forum. 2007. *New Vision for Agriculture (NVA) Initiative For India.*

World Economic Forum. n.d. *The World Economic Forum's New Vision for Agriculture (NVA) Initiative in India.* Accessed December 26, 2021. https://weforum.ent.box.com/v/FSA-India-Background. http://environmentclearance.nic.in/writereaddata/OMs-2004-2021/263_OM_02_10_2021.pdf

Climate Crisis and G20 Emissions Reductions: The Critical Connection

Soumya Dutta

BACKGROUND

The world is facing some unprecedented ecological crises, chief among which are the looming climate catastrophe and species extinction. Both these and several other crises are mostly driven by the 'development pathways' of the post-industrial revolution society, but dominated majorly by the massive extraction of energy and materials, their sharply increased use and dumping the resulting waste into nature-commons by the G20 group of countries. The climate crisis is driven majorly by the emissions of Greenhouse Gases (GHGs), chiefly carbon dioxide, as a result of burning of humongous amounts of fossil fuels (coal, oils derived from petroleum and natural gas)—both in the present and historical times from around 1800 onwards. With CO_2 emissions reaching about 38 billion tons in 2019, the G20 countries presently emit roughly 80 per cent of global GHGs (Ritchie et al., 2020). From the late twentieth century scene of the worlds' largest economies comprising mostly early industrialized European and American countries, the G20 has spread far in the geographic sense (map of G20—Figure 1 from G20 Germany), to every permanently inhabited continent.

Though the climate-threatening GHG emissions dipped globally in 2020 because of the sharp global economic slowdown due to the COVID-19 pandemic (the significant downward dip visible in Figure 2), emissions have started rising again as of 2021. This rise can also be attributed to the increased funding for fossil fuels provided by G20 countries, as part of their 'economic recovery' process.

A list of G20 member countries (in alphabetical order):
1. Argentina
2. Australia
3. Brazil
4. Canada
5. China
6. European Union (not a single country, but a Union)
7. France
8. Germany

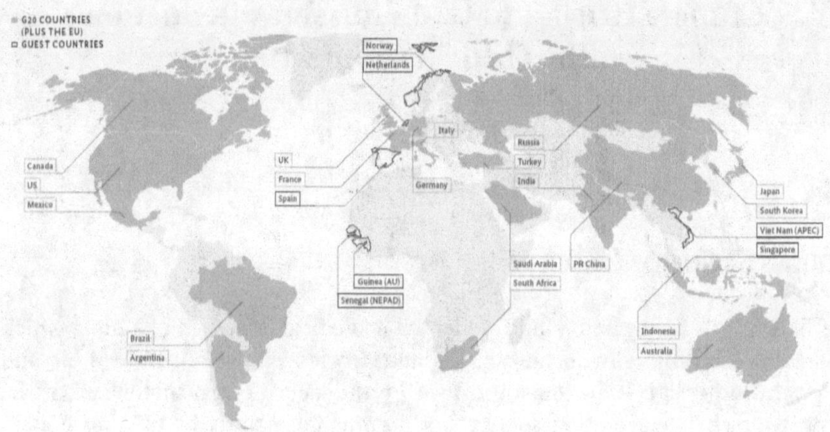

Figure 1. *Map of G20 countries* (dark grey) *locations.*

Source: G20 Germany, "G20 - a meeting at the highest level", n.d.

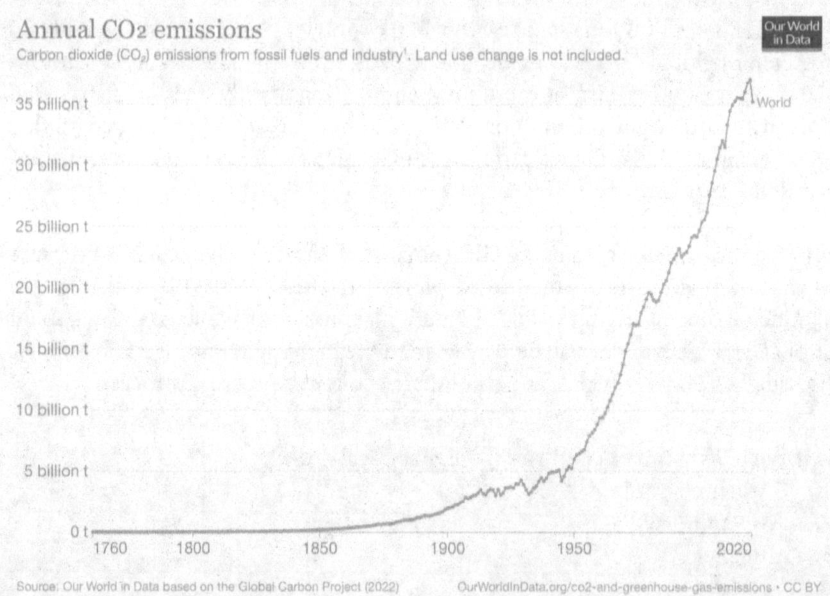

Figure 2. *Global Annual CO2 emissions 1760-2020.*

Source: Ritchie et al., *Annual CO₂ Emissions*, In "CO₂ and Greenhouse Gas Emissions", 2020.

9.   Italy
10.   India
11.   Indonesia
12.   Japan
13.   Mexico
14.   Republic of Korea
15.   Russia
16.   Saudi Arabia
17.   South Africa
18.   Turkey
19.   United Kingdom
20.   United States

The 2019 population of G20 countries of about 4.6 billion (China and India account for over half of this) represents about 60 per cent of the world population. They account for close to 90 per cent of the world GDP, and about 75–80 per cent of world trade. They also contain about 60 per cent of all agricultural land in the world, and are involved in over 80 per cent of trade in agriculture (European Commission, n.d.). Both, the high GDPs and the high percentage of global trade are driven by huge amounts of fossil energy consumption. The chart from International Energy Agency given below shows the percentage of total energy consumed from different sources: fossil fuels is represented by using black for coal, grey for oil, and white for natural gas, with Saudi Arabia, Australia, Canada, and USA leading the per capita energy consumption at the top of the heap (International Energy Agency, 2021). The emission figures (Figure 3) also clearly reflect this massive dependence on fossil fuels.

It is now abundantly clear that this massive fossil fuel burning (along with cement production, deforestation, and land use change) is the primary contributor of the looming climate crisis, and must be sharply brought down in the coming decades. It must be brought to zero before 2050, according to the IPCC SR1.5, released in 2018 (IPCC, 2018), if the biological systems on the earth are to have a reasonable chance of surviving, and human civilization is to continue without imminent collapse.

This essay will briefly examine the role of G20 Carbon Dioxide emissions—both historical and current—in supporting and financing fossil fuels even after the Paris Climate Agreement. It will examine whether the G20 countries are compliant to the 1.5°C or even 2°C temperature rise commitment (as agreed and ratified during and after the Paris summit), and think about what needs to be done to get there.

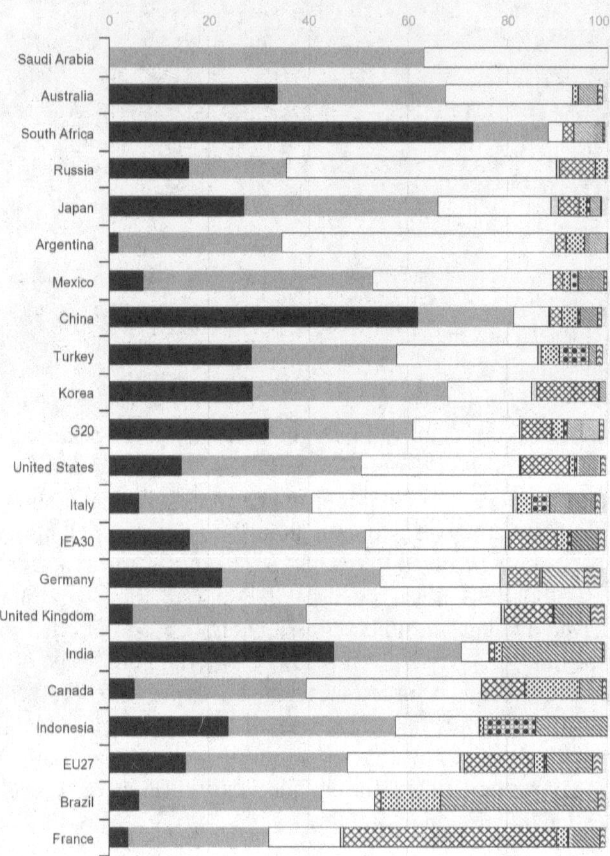

Figure 3. *G20 Primary energy by source /type.*

Source: IEA, "Total energy supply by source, G20 countries, 2019", 2021.
Note: IEA30 represents the member countries of the IEA and is shown for reference. EU27 represents the member states of the European Union and is a member of the G20.

G20 RESPONSIBILITY FOR CREATING 'ANTHROPOGENIC CLIMATE CHANGE' - CURRENT AND CUMULATIVE EMISSIONS

Currently, China, USA, and India are the three biggest annual emitters of Greenhouse Gases, with China being almost twice as big an emitter as the second biggest USA, and India a distant third (if the European Union is taken as a unit, it becomes the third biggest emitter). But the 'anthropogenic' or human society's contribution to global temperature rise (and resultant climate change) is a result of the total accumulated concentration of GHGs in the atmosphere. This has resulted from total cumulative CO_2 emissions (and other GHGs, the balance of what is emitted and what is 'absorbed' or sequestered by natural systems) from

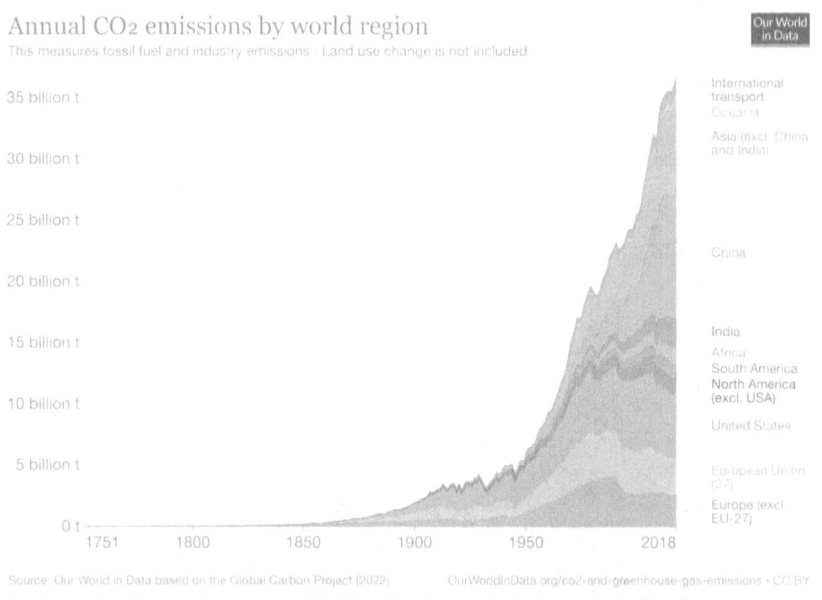

Figure 4. *Total Annual CO$_2$ emissions by region.*

Source: Ritchie et al., *Annual total CO₂ emissions, by world region*, In "CO₂ and Greenhouse Gas Emissions," 2020.

Note: This measures CO₂ emissions from fossil fuels and cement production only – land use change is not included. 'Statistical differences' (included in the GCP dataset) are not included here.

around 1800 CE (generally accepted baseline for historical GHG measurements), not present day emissions only. This 'anthropogenic contribution' is a derivative of the cumulative CO$_2$ emissions from the beginning of the 'Industrial revolution'. With that perspective, if one takes a look at the cumulative or historical emissions, starting from what is considered a baseline to measure temperature rise against—the year 1800—the Industrialized world, or the OECD (Organisation for Economic Cooperation and Development) members of the G20, stand out. With just over 4 per cent of the world population today, the USA has contributed to 25 per cent of global cumulative emissions from 1750 to 2011. Similarly, the EU countries together, with about 5.7 per cent of the world population today, are responsible for about 29 per cent of cumulative emissions. India, on the other hand, with about 17.7 per cent of the world's population today, is responsible for less than 3 per cent of cumulative emissions.

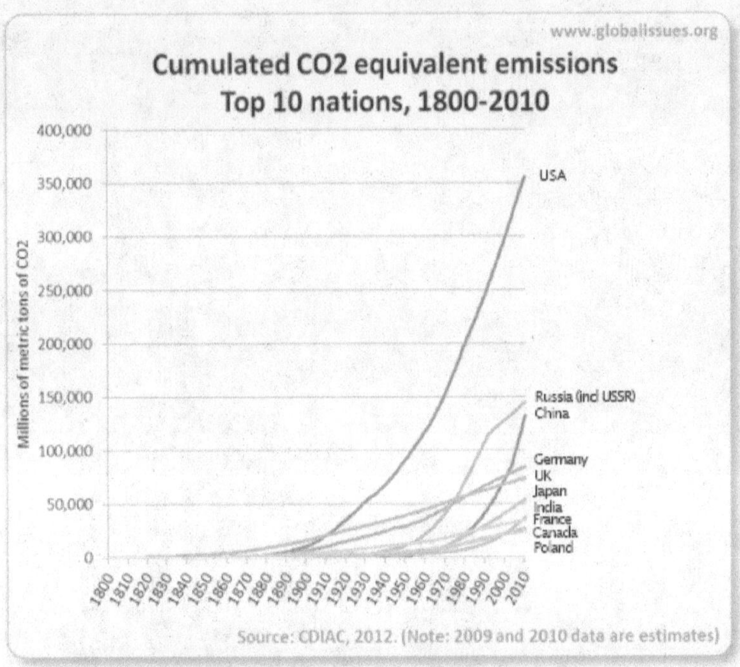

Figure 5. *Cumulative CO₂ emissions of top 10 emitters.*

Source: Boden, Maryland and Andres, Global, Regional, and National Fossil-Fuel CO2 Emissions, 2011.

These figures will, of course, change somewhat, if increased emissions from bigger non-G20 developing countries in the decade of 2011–2020 are taken into account, but the overall picture remains the same: the G20 group is still emitting about 80 per cent of climate-changing GHGs. As the G20 includes the big economies of non-OECD countries, like China, India, Indonesia, Brazil, Russia, Mexico, South Africa, etc., it is still the overwhelming contributor to climate-changing GHGs, both in current terms and in the historic context (cumulative emissions since 1850). This is due to the fact that bigger developing G20 countries are increasing their emissions faster than any other economies, and are likely to contribute a larger share of the future GHG emissions, in comparison to the OECD-G20 countries.

There is a reason why the years 1800 and 1990 are taken as references globally. The impacts of the Industrial revolution started becoming 'visible' in many senses, from around the time of the early 1800s. The large-scale instrumented measurements of different weather parameters, particularly temperature, relative humidity, rainfall, etc., were also available from around 1850–1860 onwards, help-

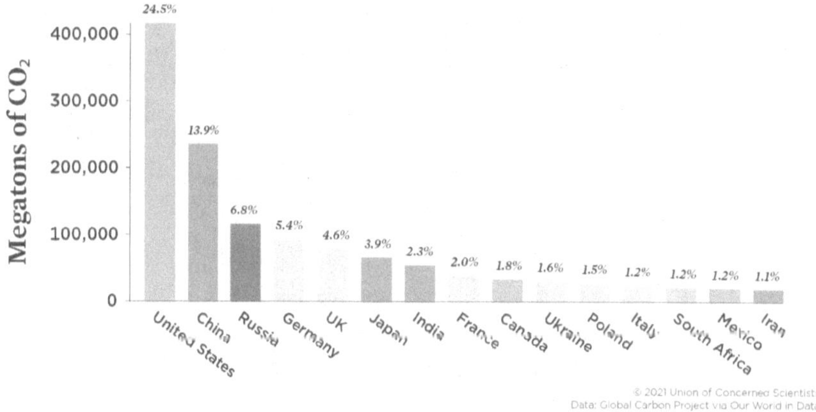

Figure 6. *Top 20 countries by cumulative CO₂ emissions 1750–2020.*

Source: 2021 Union of Concerned Scientists; Data Global Carbon Project via Our World In Data.

ing scientists to determine long-term changes in these parameters. On the other hand, from the early 1990s onwards, global awareness and coordinated climate actions in the United Nations Framework Convention on Climate Change (UN-FCCC), and other forums, like the Intergovernmental Panel on Climate Change started on a large scale (with sadly, very little positive impact for many years, it now seems). The IPCC was established in 1988, and the Earth Summit, held in 1992, established the three environmental global compacts: UNFCCC , UN-CBD (UN Convention on Biological Diversity), and UNCCD (UN Convention on Combating Desertification). Additionally, in the first global agreement to cut CO$_2$ emissions (though on a limited scale)—the Kyoto Protocol—it was agreed the 1990 emission figures would be used as the baseline, from which future emission reductions would be calculated. It's unfortunate that due to pressure from the US, this baseline was later changed later to the figures from 2005, as this higher baseline suited the US interest better, as its emissions peaked around 2005–07.

It's also no coincidence that the OECD countries in G20 started getting richer after the industrial revolution. From the later part of the twentieth century, this was largely powered by the increasing extraction and exploitation of fossil fuel resources, by the exploitation of the agricultural, climatic, rural-industrial, and human resources of the colonised countries before that—massive sugarcane farms in colonised countries, slave trade, textiles from Asia are just some examples. And this massively increased fossil fuel extraction and burning that they started (and continue to do today) is exactly the cause of the civilisation-threatening climate change.

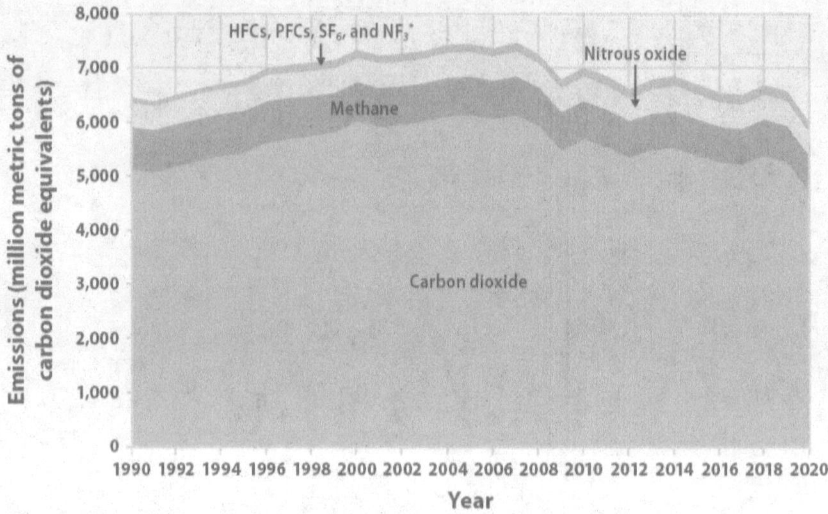

Figure 7. *U.S. Greenhouse Gas Emissions by Gas, 1990–2020*

Source: EPA, *U.S. Greenhouse Gas Emissions by Gas, 1990–2020*, "Climate Change Indicators: U.S. Greenhouse Gas Emissions", 2022.

Before proceeding further, let's classify the two types of G20 countries. The first category is that of the OECD countries, which are mostly responsible for the historical global consumption and emissions of fossil fuels and climate change, till the beginning of the twenty-first century. The second category of G20 countries belong to the non-OECD large economy countries, where the economic growth, consumption levels and CO_2 (and other GHG and pollutant) emissions started rising significantly and continued to do so from towards the end of the twentieth century. The G20 or Group of Twenty countries is a group of the 20 largest economies (or 19 countries with the largest economies plus the European Union), and was founded in 1999. By including the non-OECDcountries in this, the global decision-making powers were somewhat realigned, to provide representation to some of the earlier colonised and exploited countries, which are now growing to become major economic powers. 'The G20 is composed of most of the world's largest economies, including both industrialized and developing nations, and accounts for around 90% of gross world product (GWP), 75–80% of international trade, two-thirds of the global population, and roughly half the world's land area' (G20 Foundation, n.d.). This includes countries like China, India, Brazil, Russia, Saudi Arabia, South Africa, etc., from the non-OECD group of countries with large economies, in addition to the larger OECD economies.

LAST DECADE, POST PARIS AGREEMENT EMISSIONS AND INADEQUATE CLIMATE ACTIONS BY G20

Let's now turn from the historic emissions and responsibilities for the last 200 odd years of Industrial Revolution to the last decade and the post-Paris Agreement phase. This responsibility of cumulative emissions was enshrined in the principle of 'Common But Differentiated Responsibilities with Respective Capacities' of CBDR-RC, signifying the dominant economic history that the early industrialized countries grew their economies massively by extracting and burning a hugely disproportionate share of total use of fossil fuels and other natural resources. This has also resulted in the much higher per capita incomes of these countries as well as larger per capita share in creating the climate crisis), up to the last decade and also in the post Paris Agreement phase. Let's go about this with the caveat that though they are now part of the 20 largest economies, countries like India, Indonesia, etc., are still very much developing countries, and their per capita energy consumption, incomes, GHG emissions, are still low in comparison to global averages, even more so compared to developed economies. Countries like Brazil, South Africa, etc., have started consuming and emitting at scales (in per capita terms) which are approaching the European standards (China has already reached that level of consumption and emissions), but their 'developmental pathways' have left a large part of their population way behind, at medium to low-medium incomes, and at high risk for intensifying climate change impacts, with low resilience to cope. There is a significant difference in the per capita incomes of the developing countries and the developed countries within the G20, but developing countries like China not only reach the latter's levels of per capita emissions but also exceed their levels in many other pollutants. So, although we will stick to the treatment of G20 as a group in this short analysis, it is somewhat problematic.

The charts of G20 countries' energy sources (like Figure 3 from IEA above) reveal that most of their energy still comes overwhelmingly from fossil fuels. As evident from their continuing massive GHG emissions, the G20 countries (as many other smaller economies/countries) do not seem to have taken the dire warnings by the IPCC, the World Meteorological Organization, and many global research bodies about the urgent need to drastically cut down GHG emissions seriously enough. As a result, the Earth continues to heat up relentlessly, and the last decade has seen eight out of the top ten warmest years ever recorded on instruments. This is a direct result of continually rising GHG emissions, even after the Paris Climate Agreement was signed in 2015 (Storrow, 2018).

This insufficient action has not only led to a large gap in desired mitigation—reduction of GHG emissions to achieve the Paris Agreement goals of limiting global average annual temperature rise from pre-industrial average to well below 2°C, and the provision of best efforts to limit this to 1.5°C—but in fact, has increased the 'emissions gap' by the G20 countries, as shown in the figure below from Cli-

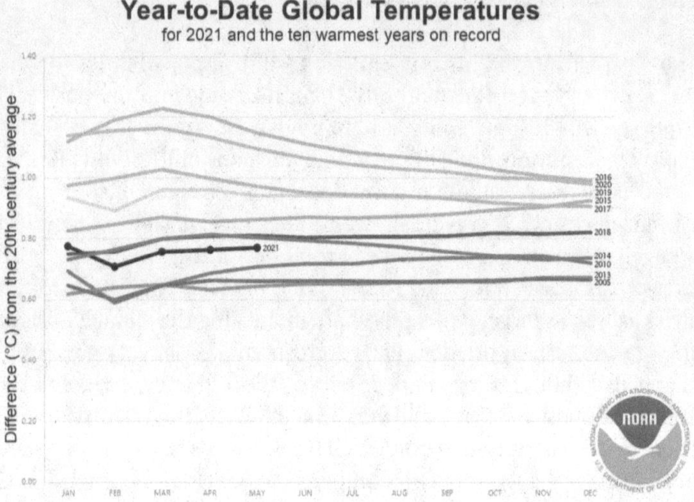

Figure 8. *Ten warmest years on instrumented records.*

Source: NOAA NCEI, "Monthly Global Climate Report for Annual 2019", 2020.

Note: 'This graphic compares the year-to-date temperature anomalies for 2021 (black line) to what were ultimately the ten warmest years on record: 2016 (1st), 2020 (2nd), 2019 (3rd), 2015 (4th), 2017 (5th), 2018 (6th), 2014 (7th), 2010 (8th), 2013 (9th), and 2005 (10th).'

mate Transparency (Climate Transparency, n.d.). Despite their 2015 PA pledges, it is clear that the G20 countries have not done anywhere close to what is actually required, as part of their mitigation efforts. Furthermore, it is clear that their Nationally Determined Contributions (NDCs)—all countries first submitted their plans to reduce GHG emissions at the PA, then revised/upgraded targets were submitted just before and in the CoP-26 at Glasgow—are falling way short of the minimum required emissions reduction (emissions gap figures below, from Climate Transparency). One can notice that the G20 GHG Emissions Gap is a huge 16–17 Gigatons, above the required 'fair share' of 20 Gt by that year. Please note that these figures are exclusive of LULUCF (Land Use and land Use Change and Forestry).

DOUBLE SPEAK AND DECEPTION AS CLIMATE ACTIONS BY G20 LEADERS

Looking at all the above data, it is clear that the G20 countries, as a group, are pledging to do something, while their actual climate actions (or in reality, the

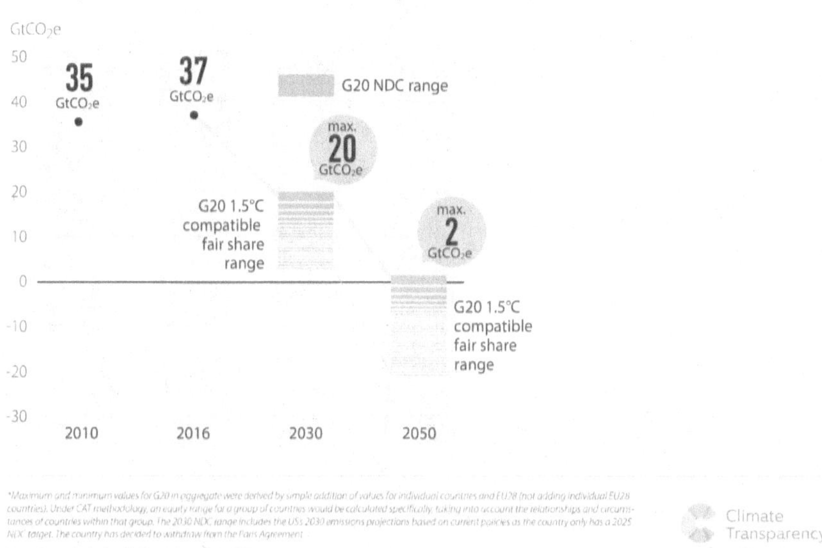

Figure 9. *Emissions gaps between what the G20 submitted NDCs (Nationally Determined Contributions) pledged and what is required by G20 as their 'Fair Share' of emission reductions, with timelines of 2030 and 2050, to comply with the 1.5°C goal.*

Source: Climate Transparency, "4. MitigationGap between current G20 GHG emissions excluding LULUCF and 1.5 compatible fair share 2030 and 2050 emission ranges", n.d.

lack thereof) say something very different, a classic case of double-speak. A few notable and well known recent examples are:

a) While hosting the UNFCCC climate conference, CoP-26, the British Prime Minister Boris Johnson was giving calls to the world to take drastic climate actions, to come to Glasgow with climate-saving plans, while his government was pushing hard to drill the North Sea (Cambo Oil field) for more climate-threatening petroleum (Capaldi, 2021).

b) After getting elected as the President of the United States (POTUS), Joe Biden made all the right noises about the climate crisis, and apparently made climate action one of his national and international policy pivots. He also brought the US back to the Paris Agreement. But at the same time, weeks before leaving for Glasgow CoP-26, he was negotiating with the OPEC (Organisation of Petroleum Exporting Countries) to raise their oil production, so that the US domestic prices of gasoline (Petrol) would remain low and American consumers could happily run their gas-guzzling SUVs thousands of miles at lower cost, and emit tons and tons of extra CO_2 individually (Stevans and Mui, 2021). Example of great climate action, really.

c) The world's biggest emitter, and by far the biggest coal consumer nation, China, has actually sharply increased its coal consumption post-COVID (Beals, 2021). This despite China's stated aim of soon capping its peak GHG emissions and reaching 'net-zero' emission status by 2060 (Myers, 2020), and its status as the world's largest Solar and Wind energy capacity producer and consumer, year after year. Some see this trend in several countries as COVID-recovery action.

d) The third largest CO_2 emitter country, India, also sharply increased its GHG emissions in 2021. This was aided by government incentives, despite the Indian PM playing 'climate champion' at Glasgow, where he delivered his 'pan-chamrit tattva' for climate action. An article in Nature, dated November 4, 2021, reports, 'India's carbon emissions are projected to increase by 12.6% this year, to 2.7 billion tonnes, which is around 7% of the global total and roughly equivalent to the emissions of the European Union' (Tollefson, 2021).

e) Global CO_2 emissions are also estimated to rise by as much as 4.9 per cent in 2021, after falling by nearly 5.4 per cent (other estimates go upto 6 per cent) in 2020, not because of benevolent climate action, but entirely due to the COVID-forced lockdowns globally (Press release, 2022).

As a short article in *Nature* reported during the first week of the Glasgow climate conference:

> The abrupt decline in global carbon dioxide emissions during the COVID-19 pandemic, caused by government-mandated lockdowns, will be all but erased by the end of this year, a consortium of scientists' reports this week. It predicts that carbon emissions from burning fossil fuels will rise to 36.4 billion tonnes — an increase of 4.9% — in 2021 compared with last year (see 'Pandemic rebound'). That's a faster recovery than many scientists expected. The rapid rebound, driven in part by the increasing demand for coal in China and India, suggests that emissions will begin to rise anew next year without substantial government efforts to bend the curve, the researchers warn. (BBC, 2021)

G20 FOSSIL FUEL FINANCING CONTINUES, EVEN WHILE CLAIMING CLIMATE ACTIONS

It is universally known that to drastically reduce the GHG emissions from fossil fuel extraction and burning, there are two clear action-lines (a third, possibly more important, is hardly talked about) that need to be followed. One is replacing today's fossil fuel based energy sources and supply chain with non-carbon energy. The related second action is sharply reducing and ultimately stopping any public financing of fossil fuel infrastructures, along with disincentivizing private financing of such infrastructure. The third option of reducing the gross primary energy (and material) consumption of high-consumption economies is so unpopular in these countries that it's hardly talked about or planned for. But despite many unequivocal warnings about continuing massive fossil fuel extraction and burning, and the resultant climate crisis arising out of this large 'mitigation/emissions gap', the G20 countries provided an average of USD 584 billion every year, on an average between 2017–2019, through tax expenditure, direct budgetary support, public finance, price support, etc., for the production and consumption of fossil fuels at home and abroad (Geddes, et al., 2020).

A fairly large part of these finances came from direct government support and public finances (Figure 10 below).

(Note : Figure numbers in the diagrams is of the original publication cited)

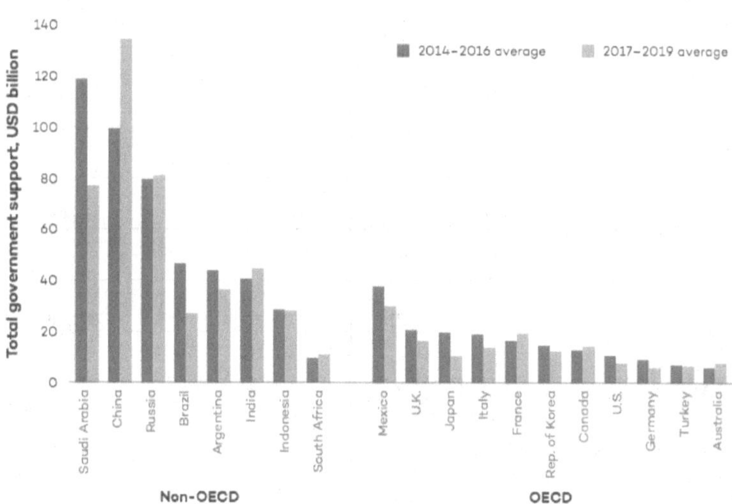

Figure 10. *G20 Government support to Fossil fuel sectors 2017-19.*

Source: Geddes et al., *Doubling Back and Doubling Down: G20 Scorecard on Fossil Fuel Funding*, 2020.

As G20 countries also hold overwhelmingly large share of control over global financial institutions, like the World Bank group, Asian Development Bank, Asian Infrastructure and Investment Bank, New Development Bank etc., their acts of commission need to be called out, as despite their modest claims of 'reaching Net-Zero emissions' by 2050—most developed nations target 2050, China targets 2060, and India, the latest G20 country to do so, declared 2070 at the Glasgow climate summit—they continue to endanger the life support systems on Earth. In spite of many commitments and pledges to end government support for fossil fuels and align their finance flows to be 'consistent with a pathway towards low greenhouse gas emissions and climate-resilient development' (UNFCCC, 2015) since the Copenhagen climate summit in 2009, the G20 governments continue to provide significant support to fossil fuels till date. There was a slight reduction in financial support to climate-destabilizing fossil fuel industries between 2014–16 and 2017–19, to the tune of 8–9 per cent, but the G20 countries have changed gear as a response to the pandemic, which caused economic slowdown. They have allocated at least USD 170 billion (likely significantly more) in public finance to fossil fuel-intensive sectors, between January 1 and August 12, 2020, in the name of recovery. Thus, the crucial role of public finance to move a major part of global economic activities away from climate-and-biodiversity threatening fossil fuels, have been subverted again.

It doesn't end there. Even though Solar Photo-Voltaic (PV) and onshore Wind power were now cheaper to produce per megawatt hour in most countries, the G20 governments kept giving large financial incentives to fossil fuel-based power (electricity) production (Figure 11 below).

If one looks at the types of incentives that the G20 governments continued to give to fossil fuel industries (Figure 12), they span a whole range of financial mechanisms.

Subsidies and other instruments were also used to promote the use of fossil fuels by the primary, intermediate, and end users of energy.

One would think that those G20 member countries with higher economic power or higher per capita incomes—the OECD members of the G20—would at least take the lead in moving away from supporting fossil fuels, and give much higher support to the transition into green energy. This was also enshrined in the accepted (at least in announcements) principle of CBDR-RC. That meant that the richer countries would do much more in pushing the transition from fossil fuels to non-carbon clean energy (not all 'non-carbon' energy sources can be called clean, but let's keep that aside for the time being), as they have more responsibility with regard to creating the climate change crisis, and also have more (financial, and technological) capacity to create and share real solutions.

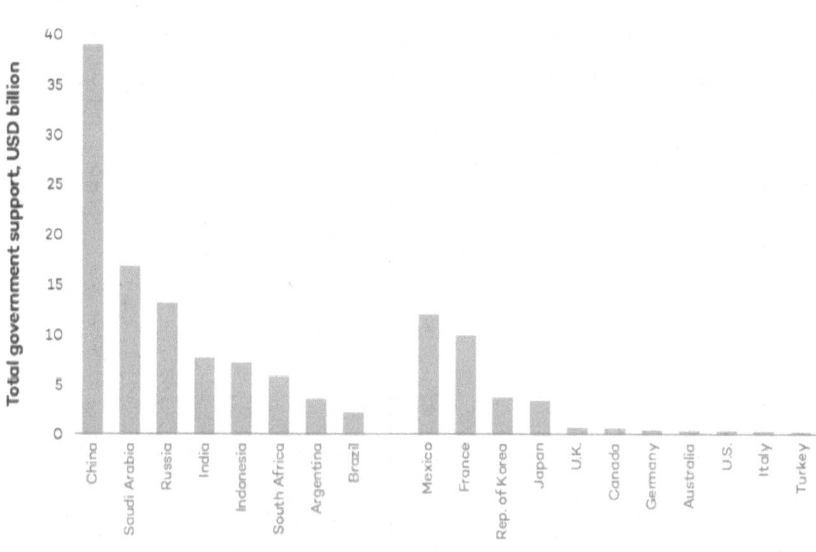

Figure 11. *G20 Government support to Fossil fuel-based power, 2017-19.*

Source: Geddes et al., *Doubling Back and Doubling Down: G20 scorecard on fossil fuel funding*, 2020.

Let's take a look (Figure 14) at the amount of G20 support to fossil fuels in the post-Paris period—in terms of per unit of GDP as well as absolute dollar values—by the richer OECD members and the comparatively poorer non-OECD members of the G20. This shows that the richer OECD members of G20 have actually spent much more public money per unit of GDP, to give support to the fossil fuel industries, in the period 2014–16 and also in the period 2017–19. So much for G20 rhetoric about climate action with justice (CBDR-RC be damned). Of course, this would not have been a cause for surprise if one was observing the G20 summit in Rome, Italy, just weeks before the Glasgow CoP-26. Despite some rhetorical announcements, there were hardly any commitments or new ambitions (Geddes et al., 2020).

It could have been very different, but: As we can see from all these numbers, figures, and negative climate actions of the G20 governments even in the post Paris Agreement period, most of them have actually promoted fossil fuel use, provided financial and policy incentives to fossil fuel industry, while making noise about the urgency of rapid and large climate actions. This happened in the periods 2014–16, 2017–19, and started again in 2021, after a dip during the pandemic hit 2020. As a result, the Earth is moving closer to catastrophic climate change

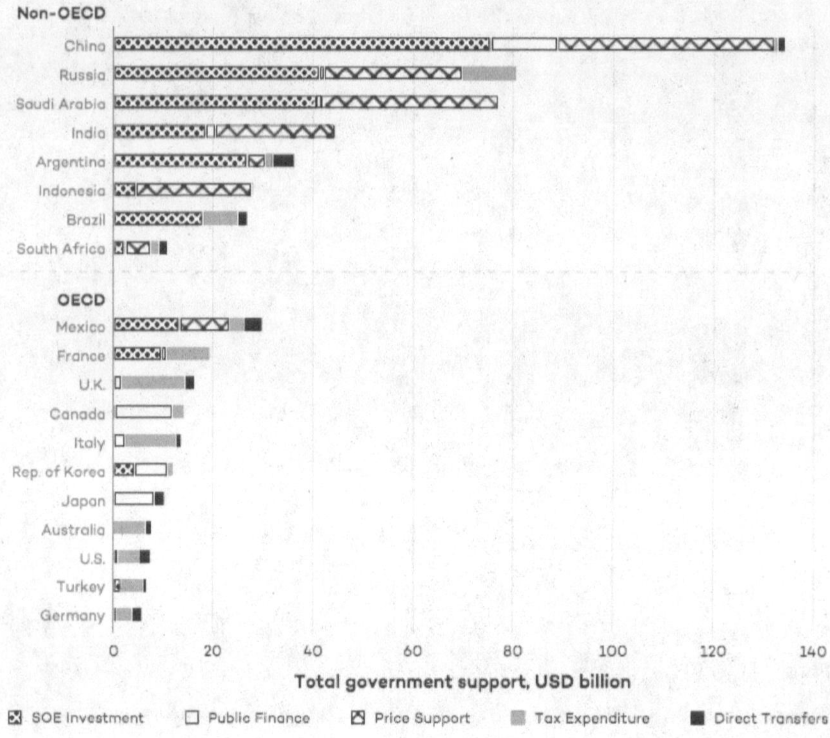

Figure 12. *Various types of Fossil fuel financing used by G20 governments.*

Source: Geddes et al., *Doubling Back and Doubling Down: G20 scorecard on fossil fuel funding,* 2020.

situations, with climate-extreme events rapidly increasing all across the globe. The first two volumes of IPCC Assessment Report 6 are out now—Working Group-1 report on the Physical Science Basis, and Working Group-2 report on impacts, adaptation, etc.—and both have clearly shown the extremely alarming situation that humanity and all living systems on Earth are facing. The G20 nations—the world's most powerful nations and the largest economies— could have directed the trillions of dollars they spent in promoting fossil fuels, to green sources. 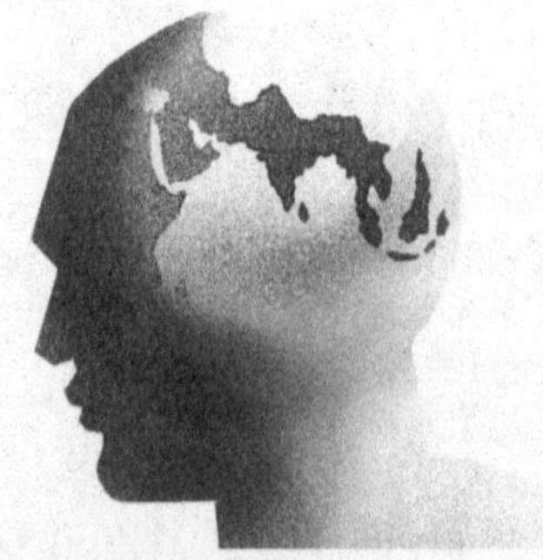 They could have just transitioned away from climate-threatening fossil fuels, and into distributed and appropriate renewable energy sources, energy savings, to create the shared circular economy they keep talking about. But perhaps that's too much of an expectation from a whole bunch of greedy, corrupt, deceiving, and corporate-controlled 'world leaders'.

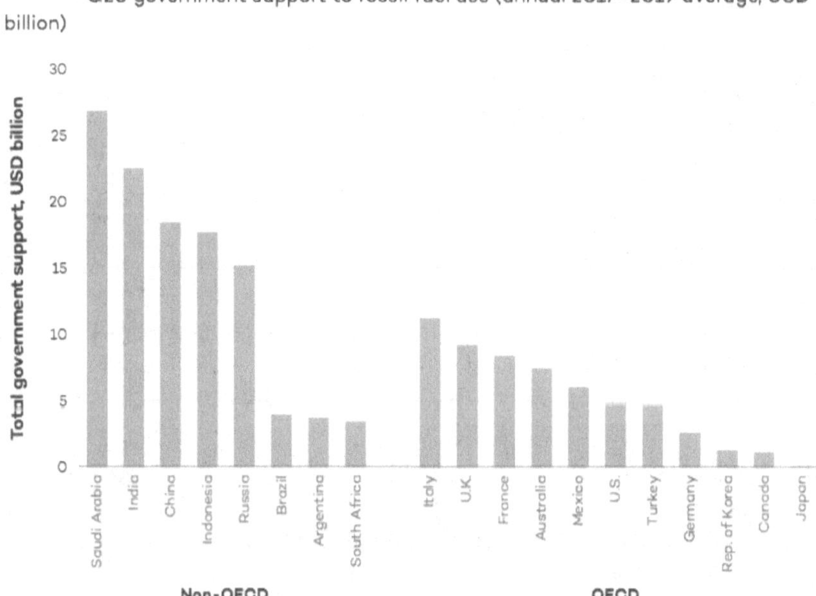

Figure 13. *G20 Government financial support for consumption of fossil fuels.*

Source: Geddes et al., *Doubling Back and Doubling Down: G20 scorecard on fossil fuel funding*, 2020.

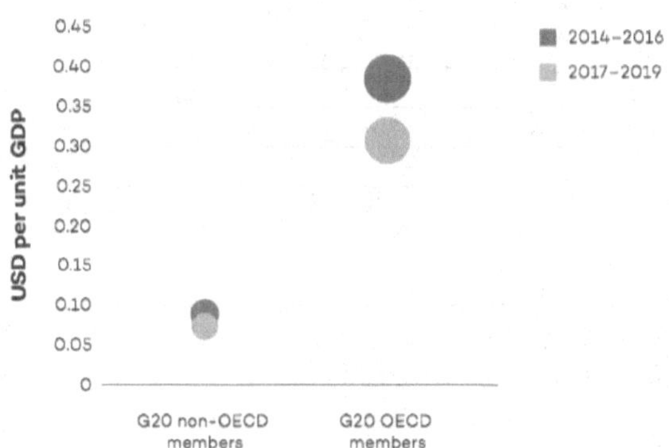

Figure 14. *G20 government support to fossil fuels – per unit of GDP and in absolute terms*

Source: Geddes et al., *Doubling Back and Doubling Down: G20 scorecard on fossil fuel funding*, 2020.

REFERENCES

BBC. 2021. G20 pledge climate action but make few commitments. October 31. https://www.bbc.com/news/world-59109186

Beals, R. K. 2021. Record coal burning in China, post-COVID recovery will feed a rebound in global carbon emissions: IEA. *Market Watch.* April 20. https://www.marketwatch.com/story/record-coal-burning-in-china-post-covid-rebound-will-feed-a-rebound-in-global-carbon-emissions-iea-11618921623

Boden, T.A., G. Marland, and R.J. Andres. 2011. Global, Regional, and National Fossil-Fuel CO2 Emissions. Carbon Dioxide Information Analysis Center, Oak Ridge National Laboratory. 2011. DOI: 10.3334/CDIAC/00001_V2011. Accessed at https://www.globalissues.org/article/231/climate-justice-and-equity.

Capaldi, P. 2021. Johnson's backing for the Cambo oilfield is unscientific and potentially disastrous. *The Guardian.* October 11. https://www.theguardian.com/commentisfree/2021/oct/11/johnson-cambo-oilfield-green-jobs-gas-fossil-fuel-workers-oil-gas

Climate Transparency. n.d. 4. Mitigation Gap between current G20 GHG emissions excluding LULUCF and 1.5 compatible fair share 2030 and 2050 emission ranges. https://www.climate-transparency.org/4-mitigation_gap-between-current-g20-ghg-emissions-excluding-lulucf-and-1-5-compatible-fair-share-2030-and-2050-emission-ranges

EPA. 2022. *U.S. Greenhouse Gas Emissions by Gas, 1990–2020.* "Climate Change Indicators: U.S. Greenhouse Gas Emissions." United States Environmental Protection Agency. Accessed at https://www.epa.gov/climate-indicators/climate-change-indicators-us-greenhouse-gas-emissions

European Commission. n.d. G20. https://ec.europa.eu/info/food-farming-fisheries/farming/international-cooperation/international-organisations/g20_en

G20 Germany. n.d. "PARTICIPANTS OF THE G20 SUMMIT IN HAMBURG IN 2017, G20 - a meeting at the highest level." https://www.g20germany.de/Webs/G20/EN/G20/Participants/participants_node.html

Geddes, A., Gerasimchuk, I., Viswanathan, B., Picciariello, A., Tucker, B., Doukas, A., Corkal, V., Mostaf, M., Roth, J., Suharsono, A., and I. Gençsü. 2020. *Doubling Back and Doubling Down: G20 Scorecard on Fossil Fuel Funding.* International Institute for Sustainable Development. https://www.iisd.org/system/files/2020-11/g20-scorecard-report.pdf

International Energy Agency. 2021. Total energy supply by source, G20 countries, 2019. https://www.iea.org/data-and-statistics/charts/total-energy-supply-by-source-g20-countries-2019

IPCC. 2018. "Summary for Policymakers." In: *Global Warming of 1.5°C. An IPCC Special Report on the impacts of global warming of 1.5°C above pre-industrial levels and related global greenhouse gas emission pathways, in the context of strengthening the global response to the threat of climate change, sustainable development, and efforts to eradicate poverty.* Edited by Masson-Delmotte, V., P. Zhai, H.-O. Pörtner, D. Roberts, J. Skea, P.R. Shukla, A. Pirani, W. Moufouma-Okia, C. Péan, R. Pidcock, S. Connors, J.B.R. Matthews, Y. Chen, X. Zhou, M.I. Gomis, E. Lonnoy, T. Maycock, M. Tignor, and T. Waterfield. Cambridge University Press. *World Meteorological Organization, Geneva, Switzerland, 32 pp.https://www.ipcc.ch/sr15/chapter/spm/*

G20 Foundation. n.d. What is the G20. Accessed at https://www.g20foundation.org/g20/what-is-the-g20

Myers, Steven Lee. 2020. China's Pledge to be Carbon Neutral by 2060: What it Means. *The New York Times.* September 23.

NOAA National Centers for Environmental Information. 2020. Monthly Global Climate Report for Annual 2019. January. Accessed at https://www.ncei.noaa.gov/access/monitoring/monthly-report/global/201913/supplemental/page-1.

OECD. n.d. G20 economies are pricing more carbon emissions but stronger globally more coherent policy action is needed to meet climate goals, says OECD. Accessed at https://www.oecd.org/tax/g20-economies-are-pricing-more-carbon-emissions-but-stronger-globally-more-coherent-policy-action-is-needed-to-meet-climate-goals-says-oecd.htm#:~:text=G20%20economies%20account%20for%20around,at%2097%25%20of%20emissions%20priced.

Press release. 2022. Global CO2 Emissions Rebounded to their Highest Level in History in 2021. *IEA.org.* March 8. Accessed at https://www.iea.org/news/global-co2-emissions-rebounded-to-their-highest-level-in-history-in-2021

Ritchie, Hannah, Roser, Max, and Pablo Rosado. 2020. *Annual CO₂ Emissions.* In "CO₂ and Greenhouse Gas Emissions." *OurWorldInData.org.* https://ourworldindata.org/co2-and-other-greenhouse-gas-emissions

Ritchie, Hannah, Roser, Max, and Pablo Rosado. 2020. *Annual total CO₂ emissions, by world region.* In "CO₂ and Greenhouse Gas Emissions." *OurWorldInData.org.* OurWorldInData.org/co2-and-other-greenhouse-gas-emissions

Stevans, P and Ylan Mui. 2021. White House calls on OPEC to boost oil production as gasoline prices rise. *CNBC.* August 11. https://www.cnbc.com/2021/08/11/as-gas-prices-rise-white-house-says-opec-action-is-simply-not-enough-calls-for-ftc-scrutiny.html

Storrow, B. 2018. Global CO2 Emissions Rise after Paris Climate Agreement Signed. *Scientific American*. March 24. https://www.scientificamerican.com/article/global-co2-emissions-rise-after-paris-climate-agreement-signed/#

Tollefson, J. 2021. Carbon emissions rapidly rebounded following COVID pandemic dip. *Nature*. November 4. https://doi.org/10.1038/d41586-021-03036-x

UNFCC. 2015. Paris Agreement. Article 2.1 C https://unfccc.int/sites/default/files/english_paris_agreement.pdf

2021 Union of Concerned Scientists. n.d. Data Global Carbon Project. Our World in Data.

SOS

G20 and Critical Maritime Infrastructure: A Framework towards Dialogue on Safety and Governance

Dokku Nagamalleswara Rao,
Dr. Manoj Babu Buraga and Kiran G. S. K.

The spectre of devastating attacks on Critical Maritime Infrastructure (CMI) installations and the subsequent catastrophic consequences isn't a cinematic sequence in a futuristic or sci-fi movie any more. These include, but are not limited to, the following military and commercial specifications: the threat to undersea cables and pipelines, container port facilities, navigation infrastructure, and marine electronic systems. Representative fears and growing concerns about a likely paralysis of global trade, security and communications with the breakdown of CMI in the ocean space have customarily featured in states' maritime strategies. This is because the ubiquity and interconnectedness of these structures have increasingly occupied a central place in contemporary military affairs, civil society and international political economy. Undersea cables acting as the backbone in the global digital connectivity, port infrastructure with its complex systems handling voluminous cargo to keep world trade moving, and marine systems and routes responsible for safe and secure critical oceanic operations all depict how CMI plays an important role in international politics and global security systems. With the Group of Twenty (G20) countries accounting for 90 per cent Gross World Product (GWP) (OECD and UNDP, 2019) and all members being Sea States—representing the world's largest twenty economies naturally depends on the ocean space to steer their natural capital, economic resources and environmental systems.

In short, functioning and resilient critical maritime infrastructures, more specifically, the service it provides, have become distinctively fundamental to the existence of modern society (Chauhan, 2019). Therefore, the safety and governance of CMI transpire to be prominently concerned with those maritime installations or nodes that are indispensable in the context of current and future global maritime trading and security systems. It is in this reconfigured context that this chapter attempts to look at the security measures of Critical Maritime Infrastructure from a G20 scope and calls for such mechanisms to be more active and institutionalized by facilitating dialogues, joint committees and working groups to contribute towards more rules-based maritime order and strengthen global and regional maritime governance frameworks.

This essay emphasizes that a dialogue or policy framework concerning CMI at an institutional level like G20 is important for several reasons. Broadly speaking, the significance and growing focus on the need for dialogue cannot be over-stated in the current securitized maritime space characterized by uncertainty and disorder. Amidst a sharp increase of attacks on these structures exemplified by the chemical explosion at the Beirut port, coupled with the apocalyptic mindset of the non-state and rogue actors, new rhetoric on how to safeguard these vi-tal maritime installations has started gaining prominence in the global security discourses (BBC, 2020). This new fascination and nosiness around the safety of Critical Maritime Infrastructure seem to suggest that it eluded our capture or appreciation previously. Moreover, the involvement and unpredictability of state and non-state actors, which compounds the risks to these structures, underscore the equation of what makes containing these malicious acts more challenging.

While not all attacks on CMI are of equal importance, i.e., not every threat poses a significant or similar security concern for nation-states, it is necessary to under-stand the context in which they operate and the range of mechanisms to prevent them. Because estimating where the next catastrophic threat that could jeopardize the world and modern societies will arise is not easy. But states and international organizations that seek to avoid such conflagration debacles should pay attention to the insecurities that encapsulate these infrastructures on the high seas. Though states are relatively tolerant of the 'kinetic effects' caused by such attacks, compared to the armed provocations, an important counterfactual question would be how long or to what extent such permissive attitudes will continue.

Despite the fact that these critical installations act as a pivot in almost every fac-et of global politics, attempts to contextualize and theorize their role in inter-national relations and security studies appear dormant (Bueger and Liebetrau, 2021). Rightly or wrongly, this may be because policymakers and scholars tend to consider maritime infrastructure as an exogenous variable in the structure of the international system. Nevertheless, when it enters or is considered part of the system, it has the ability to generate specific outcomes. For instance, neorealism estimates that hegemony over critical infrastructure affects the distribution of the power structure in the international system; similarly, neoliberalism reveals how states have increasingly becoming interdependent to avail these services, whereas social constructivism explains how they play a role in the construction of identi-ties. This shows that insulating Critical Maritime Infrastructure in the interna-tional system by characterizing them with adjectives like 'external' and 'essential' have failed to incorporate them in the broader social, political and economic discourses, suggesting a deterministic understanding of CMI in global politics (Goldthau, 2014). As a result, the transformative qualities of CMI and its role in the modern international system have not been captured adequately in main-stream International Relations theories.

Within the G20, surprisingly, maritime security at a summit level found much less prominence against potential for discussion, thus, neither have they instigated extensive dialogue nor has it resulted in a concrete policy framework so far. While there were sporadic references to the economic security of oceans and coastal areas, these were largely related to the peripheral maritime security concerns. Some of the G20's interventions into the maritime economy and its sustainability briefly started with precise and coordinated initiatives of 'The G20 Action plan on Marine Litter, 2017, and the 'B20[1]-G20 Special Dialogue - Unlocking Investment in Maritime Transportation Infrastructure for a more Sustainable Trade, 2019.'

In G20 summits and policy literature so far, there has been a distinct lack of summit-level discussions or a task force to address maritime security issues and the safety and governance of Critical Maritime Infrastructure. Therefore, this essay attempts to go some way towards remedying this omission. Indeed, G20 has the potential to steer an ecosystem of services concerning the Blue Economy.[2] Hence, the upcoming summits are to be seen as an opportune moment to (re)focus on oceans and strengthen their governance. Perhaps, encouraging G20 members to engage in Blue Diplomacy[3] actively could be one of the keys to unlock its potential to G20's agenda. The need for a maritime task force in G20 is becoming more imminent than ever. Thus, timely arrangements to frame appropriate policies and approaches that echo G20 members' national circumstances need recognition. Such a framework is expected to complement the G20's collective work, and individual members' contributions will yield strategic benefits. Moreover, we believe focusing on issues of global concern (commons), such as the safety of Critical Maritime Infrastructure, will anchor the G20's identity as a key international actor and help drive its core global economic agenda.

SIGNIFICANCE OF CMI IN G20 SCOPE

Spurred by the recent increase in attacks on critical maritime installations, such as conflicts at Libya's Ras Lanuf and Es Sider oil terminals, 2018; the ransomware attack on Colonial Pipeline, 2021; suicide attacks on shipping in Southeast Asia

---

[1] B20 (Business 20) is a business group within the G20 which organizes annual B20 summits since 2010. This arrangement, also known as the business voice of the G20, promotes collaboration between the businesses and policymakers.

[2] Blue Economy is concerned with promoting sustainable and inclusive growth of marine-based economic development. As a new paradigm for development, it aims to improve human well-being and social equity by focusing on better management of marine resources while reducing environmental risks and ecological inadequacies.

[3] 'Blue Diplomacy' or Blue Ocean Diplomacy is newly formed diplomatic spheres intertwined with economic interests, maritime strategy concerning river basin organizations, and sea and ocean international administrations. The concept is aimed at promoting institutional and legal capacity building, and financial and political coordination through the bilateral and multilateral agreements. It recommends diplomatic cadre to prepare for the Blue Economy, and interests coastal and Small Islands and Developing States (SIDS) for sustenance and sustainable development to cope with the international economic and security environment.

by the Abu Sayyaf Group (ASG); hijacked ships used as 'weapons' and water-borne improvised explosive devices (WBIED) used increasingly against vessels near to port infrastructure by Houthi Rebels in the Red Sea, gives further impetus of the involvement of non-state actors. Thus, the safety and reliability of Critical Maritime Infrastructure is emerging as one of the prominent issues in global security discourse to prevent 'foreseeable' attacks. It is a given that Critical Maritime Infrastructure has become so embedded and integral in the international system that the economic growth of the nations is invariably linked to the safety, capacity and efficiency of these structures, and out-and-out the G20 members are no exception. Further, with the rapid convergence of information and infra-structural technologies, it is only prudent for the G20 members to rethink the security standards to keep pace with non-state and rogue actors seeking to fur-ther their nefarious activities and exploit these vital global installations (Alcaidea and Llave, 2020). Besides, such attacks signify an epoch of intensifying maritime insecurity that impinges upon every nation and particularly hits hard at low- and middle-income countries.

The share of the 'Merchandise Trade-to-GDP' ratio acts as a basic indicator to mea-sure the economic value these installations bring to world trade. Global seaborne merchandise trade (both imports and exports) account for nearly 80 per cent by volume and 70 per cent by value, and the G20 countries' dependence on maritime trade is significantly high. Asia alone accounts for 62 per cent of global imports and 40 per cent of seaborne trade exports for 2019 (UNCTAD, 2018 and 2020). Interestingly, among them, the transition economies[4] such as China and Russia continue to record high growth surplus in trade, while India's exports and imports both increase along with its trade deficit. The UNCTAD's Maritime Transport 2020 report suggests that the world's merchant fleet is heavily dependent on Asia, and Asian companies own half of the world's fleet. For instance, in 2019, 93 per cent of shipbuilding happened in China, South Korea and Japan, and more than 90 per cent of ship recycling occurred in Asia (Bangladesh, India and Pakistan). Maritime merchandise trade, both goods and services, primarily depend on key and support infrastructure. Critical Maritime Infrastructure that supports goods-based trade is merchant shipping, ports and international maritime routes. Support sectors are a key part of the trade-in services, including telecommunication, defence, space, law enforcement and security apparatus and information and intelligence. Critical infrastructure within the service sectors makes for high-value targets being vul-nerable to both conventional and non-conventional threats. The above argument strengthens why the safety and governance of the Critical Maritime Infrastructure have become imperative for the global economy.

---

[4] Transitional economies are countries which undertake massive financial reforms of their economic systems/ institutions to transform from centrally planned economies towards a more market-cen-tric system. The term was popularized when South American nations, such as Brazil and Argentina, moved from military rule towards democratic governance in the 1980s. With globalization, the trend has been followed in various developing economies.

The idea behind the genesis of the G20 was to integrate G7 (Group of Seven) countries with other emerging economies and achieve nothing less than strong, sustainable, balanced and inclusive global development (Benson and Zürn, 2019). In the context of CMI, there are genuine concerns that such spaces are being transformed into more securitized zones. Ocean governance, in international politics, requires that those who trade and operate in the oceanic space do so within a safe environment ably supported by requisite laws and order. The threats to CMI, on the other hand, are dynamic and rapidly evolving. Unlike conventional threats, modern-day threats in the maritime domain are more non-conventional. With their incredibly easy access to critical infrastructure vulnerabilities, the cost they impute on the global economy and security is tremendous (Bueger and Edmunds, 2017).

The need to enhance economic and strategic interests in the maritime arena is motivated by the synergy between the 'United Nations Sustainable Development Goals' (SDGs), 2015 and G20's agenda of 'inclusive growth' and 'interrelated themes'. Such assumptions were also reinstated in the '2030 Agenda' (UNSDG, 2015), the global 'Development Cooperation' activity of diverse actors, and the Development Cooperation Forum of the UN. More specifically, the SDG14: 'Life below water' and the SDG9: 'Build resilient infrastructure, promote inclusive and sustainable industrialisation and foster innovation' virtually influence G20 projects of international financial stability, climate change mitigation, and sustainable development. The 2019 report of the Organisation for Economic Co-operation and Development (OECD) and the United Nations Development Programme (UNDP) on *G20 contribution to the 2030 Agenda* estimates that:

> [C]ollectively, G20 members account for around 85% of global gross domestic product (GDP), 75% of world trade, 80% of global carbon dioxide emissions (CO2) and 70% of global plastic production – as well as two-thirds of the world's population and more than half of the world's poor. (OECD and UNDP, 2019)

G20 members have been cognizant about their dominant position in the global economy and potential for future infrastructure investments in maritime space. The demand from developing economies and industry to facilitate further G20 dialogue concentrating actions towards the global ocean governance process by initiating dialogues, strategies, and regional cooperation on Ocean Economy have become noticeable. During the tenth G20 summit in Hamburg, Germany's G20 Presidency, 2017, a call from researchers around the world stressed for G20 to drive a 'sustainable ocean economy, innovation and growth' (G20 Insights, 2017). It mainly focused on seeking and integrating members' national Blue Economy Development Frameworks.

The safety and governance of Critical Maritime Infrastructure have been in flux. With a negligible amount of time and resources invested in addressing these concerns, the G20 members face challenges to make these systems fully resilient and governance more fool-proof. This essay argues that dialogues or task forces on Critical Maritime Infrastructure promoted and conducted at the G20 summit level are particularly important for two reasons: *One*, the dialogue or task force will help as a 'signature practice' of the G20 to address threats and challenges in safeguarding these maritime installations; *two*, these dialogues within G20 and with other international actors will help project G20 as a normative power and act as an influential instrument in handling maritime security threats.

CONSEQUENCES OF MARITIME CRITICAL INFRASTRUCTURE ACCIDENTS

Threats to order at sea are virtually different from threats faced over land, beyond traditional lines of comprehension. As most of these are conventionally driven security challenges, they are inextricably linked to homeland security. The challenges caused by threats to undersea cables and pipelines, container port facilities, navigational infrastructure and marine electronic systems account for one-third of security spending by maritime economies—the other two-thirds exhausted on the conventional internal and external defence over land. Besides, the conventional but incorrect perception has been that accidents caused by non-state actors, natural disasters and human and machine operational failures are solely threats for the respective industry or to the concerned state(s). In a deeply integrated state of globalized economic activity, intended and unintended accidents at sea unroll regional and global consequences. Such consequences include the price rise of energy resources, increase in the cost of transportation, price fluctuation of goods, and delay in some industrial works, depending on what the ships carry in a given time and route. For instance, the Ever Given container ship's recent Suez Canal blockage caused millions in revenue loss on one of the world's vital maritime routes (BBC, 2021).

Measuring the cost of disorder caused by accidents became less complex with the availability of various models of recovery and resilience. However, the anxiety around these threats puts intense pressure on the security apparatus, and mismanagement oftentimes causes instability in economic activity. The global actors fundamentally depend on established mechanisms and convergence of interest over protecting Critical Maritime Infrastructure, most of which depend on traditional practices, of which self-help has been a key module. In contrast, the availability of international assistance

to smaller blue economies appears to be influenced by the intensity of accidents and geographical factors.

To better understand the consequences of maritime critical infrastructure accidents, a list of causes of accidents is outlined under four themes: non–state actors, natural disasters, human and machine operational failures and structural issues in international relations. The former two are dynamic and can force devastating outcomes, which comes mainly with an element of surprise. The latter two human and machine operational failures and structural issues in international relations are challenges managed effectively with early preparedness measures and knowledge of best practices.

First, the accidents caused by violent non-state actors are generally themed under maritime criminality, further sub-categorized as maritime piracy, maritime terrorism and human and drug trafficking. The engineered accidents to CMI come from pirates, privateers, brigands, smugglers, maritime terrorists, maritime criminals indulged in piracy attacks on ships, ship ramming, armed robbery, hijacking, kidnapping-for-ransom, maritime-depredations, seaborne terrorist attacks on ports and ships, maritime transport of drugs, human trafficking, chemicals, firearms, weapons of mass destruction (WMD) and the new entry of cyberattacks.

In the past, violent groups, like Al Shabaab, Al Qaeda, Abu Sayyaf, Lashkar-e-Taiba, the Provisional Irish Republican Army (IRA), Palestinian groups including the Hamas, and the Liberation Tigers of Tamil Eelam (LTTE) have posed non-traditional maritime threats to Critical Maritime Infrastructure. The attack by Al Qaeda on USS Cole at Aden, October 2000, and the Mumbai terror attacks by Lashkar-e-Taiba in November 2008 were two major incidents where the attackers' use of seas shifted global and regional attention to vulnerability. The terrorist organizations of the Southern Philippines, Al Qaeda, Hamas, Hezbollah, Pakistani jihadi organizations, the LTTE, and the United Wa State Army of Myanmar, actively used oceans for drug traffic between areas of illicit opium production, e.g., Golden Crescent and Golden Triangle. For these terrorist groups, piracy has been a lucrative way of funding and used as an important political tool to weaken their adversaries' economies. Maritime terrorism and maritime piracy are two ways they jeopardize peace at sea. Formulating best practices to deter piracy and enhance the security of Critical Maritime Infrastructure in the Arabian Sea, the Indian Ocean, the Red Sea, and the Gulf of Aden are within the scope of the G20 contribution. Specifically, in the Indian Ocean, the areas of concern are the Gulf of Aden, off the coast of Somalia, the Gulf of Guinea, and the Sulu and the Sulawesi seas.

Alok Bansal (2010) argues that the maritime threat perceptions are steadily more centred around the non-state actors (armed groups). Alok's case focused explicitly on the Indian Ocean Region (IOR), specifically, with the background of the Mumbai terror attacks in November 2008, satisfying three conditions: the lack of major maritime power amongst IOR littorals, the region as 'home to most troubled maritime spots',[5] and non-state actors having significant maritime capabilities. Littoral states' capacities individually do not aid much because the capabilities of non-state actors are constantly expanding. The fundamental issue that underlies the threat is that non-state actors use maritime piracy in terrorist acts with impunity at high seas due to loose security cover. Therefore, such a security environment demands the 'need for cooperative maritime engagement amongst the maritime forces of the littoral states' (Bansal, 2010).

Second, concerning non-traditional threats apart from non-state actors, exposure to adverse environmental forces lead to maritime accidents. Forces that cause natural disasters at shore and sea include weather fronts triggering tropical floods, large squalls, sea-storms, 'derecho' storms, and tropical-revolving storms (TRS) such as cyclones, typhoons and hurricanes; climate change affects sea level change (SLC); and undersea earthquakes and volcanic eruption result in tsunamis. In recent years, the environmental discourse has increasingly identified climate change as an irreversible force with risks of extreme events and disasters. Meanwhile, some models precisely identified the impact of climate change concerning sea level change (SLC) along with construction gaps in port infrastructure increasing risks to infrastructures such as wharves, docks, piers and other maritime infrastructure (Sweeney and Becker, 2020). Besides, negligible structure design life of ports and internal SLC policy, design and planning documents warrant that most of the available port-related infrastructures today are incompatible and threaten the resilience of such ports against sea level change. At the same time, research by Sweeney and Becker revealed shocking findings that there had been a lack of regulatory design standards regarding SLC and port infrastructure's long service lives; on the contrary, those who have SLC policy, by and large, rely on uncertain SLC projections.

Third, the maritime accidents under human and machine operational failures link to the human lifestyle on land, and some independently occur at sea. Human actions on land can cause accidents at sea, including pollution through plastic pollution, chemical pollution, overfishing, coral reef damaged by unregulated deep-sea fishing and undersea mining, and exploration and pandemics. Machine-related accidents range from traffic congestion, ship collision, oil spills, chemical spills, oil refinery fires and explosions, chemical release, nuclear power plant damage with possible radiation contamination, airliner crashes in

---

[5] This region has the most troubled maritime spots with reference to non-traditional threats by non-state actors such as maritime terrorism and piracy, environmental threats and also traditional maritime conflicts between nation-states.

the sea and ferry disasters. The need to enhance G20 members' security and disaster mitigation levels could be based on risk assessments—limitations of terrorism, piracy attacks, traffic congestion, ship collision and oil spills. Magdalena Bogalecka (2020) developed a formula of 'Modeling-Identification-Prediction-Optimisation-Mitigation' to deal with the environmental consequences of CMI accidents. Bogalecka's overview was the product of research on ship accidents in the Baltic Sea and neighbouring waters. With modelling and identification of chemical release, it can assess consequences of transporting such chemicals for people, the environment and infrastructure.

Finally, the structural issues of international relations also cause violent incidents, such as differences in the code of conduct, differences over sovereign jurisdiction of Search and Rescue (SAR) regions, territorial sovereignty disputes, fishing rights disputes, seaborne migration, the difference in regulations for private security and small arms use, problems in identifying ships concerning real owners, the lack of policy emphasis, and gaps in security and governance of critical maritime infrastructure. These coastal hazards risk the resilience of ports and the shipping industry and have colossal effects on people, the environment, and infrastructure. For instance, few examples of gaps in Maritime Search and Rescue (M-SAR) operations are the Malaysian Airlines Flight 370 in 2014, the same year, the South Korean MV Sewol ferry disaster, and seaborne migration across the Mediterranean Sea. Gurpreet S. Khurana (2017) argued that the 'National Will' is a key requirement to 'enhance the effectiveness of existing mechanisms of maritime search and rescue (M-SAR)' and Humanitarian Assistance and Disaster Relief (HADR) in the Indo-Pacific region. The identified voids in coordinated responses of Humanitarian Assistance are 'attributed to either insufficient or absent "national will"'.

Similarly, the lack of G20's maritime dialogue is the lack of policy emphasis, but not because of the lack of converging collective motivation or geoeconomics interest, and they have been very much present. In the case of Humanitarian Assistance and Disaster Relief (HADR) operations, most risks are governance-related, which depict limits of present conventions and models of engagement. One of the considerations for disinterest in reforming resilient relief measures was the area of responsibility under the Search and Rescue Regions (SRRs) seen as large, which stems beyond their sovereign jurisdiction. The gap between M-SAR capacity and obligations falls short. International conventions have also imposed considerable additional obligations of establishing M-SAR services, rescue coordination centres (RCCs) and sub-structures on a 24/7 basis. Though small states cite a lack of capacity for non-accession as above, a deeper examination reveals real reasons for structural problems in international relations. In this study, the analysis limits the scope to three safety and governance issues of undersea cables, port and shipping infrastructure, and maritime routes.

LAURELS OF INSTITUTION BUILDING

Underlying the pivotal role of maritime institutions in the safety and governance of Critical Maritime Infrastructure, this section examines various maritime organizations that oversee the safety and governance of maritime infrastructure and institution building through tracking instruments, processes and progress. The initial motivations of establishing maritime institutions were to agree to set aside differences, create arms control arrangements and regulate military and economic activity. The shift in motivations to build institutions must be noted as the current trend suggests that the primary rationale for the proliferation of institutions and instruments is to cooperate to exploit global commons and increase economic productivity and prosperity.

The established systems and structures of the maritime domain are governed under international law—a set of provisions, rules and codes of conduct, where the process is typically measured within three governance domains: economic, political and humanitarian and progress understages of bilateral, regional and global interactions. The gains in this respect are mainly attributed to the International Law Commission's (ILC) relentless pursuance shaped into the *United Nations Convention on the Law of the Sea* (UNCLOS) 1982, an international treaty, considered the base of all maritime interactions concerning the territorial sea and the contiguous zone, the continental shelf and the high seas, fishing and marine conservation. The UNCLOS was a product of the incorporation of provisions from four treaties at the first *United Nations Conference on the Law of the Sea*, from February to April 1958: *the Convention on Territorial Sea and the Contiguous Zone* (CTS); *the Convention on the High Seas* (CHS); *the Convention on Fishing and Conservation of the Living Resources of the High Seas* (CFCLR); and *the Optional Protocol of Signature concerning the Compulsory Settlement of Disputes* (OPSD). The four Geneva Conventions are known as the 'traditional law of the sea'. The situation before and after the law of the sea was put in place was observed as the shift from a struggle in chaotic governance to a struggle for consistency and certainty. Thus, UNCLOS effectively became customary international maritime law despite some countries (the United States, Colombia, Israel and Venezuela) not adopting the all-encompassing conventions and protocols. Though the post-world war world has placed structural engagement models, many schemes in the maritime domain have been controversial and contested.

There has always been an issue of ambiguity regarding the application and implementation of certain provisions. Some understand the interest to refine maritime boundary delimitation methodologies as 'the search for predictability and certainty' (Hamid, 2019). The G20 authority to broker reliable and stable reform debilitates when some emerging economies and major powers fail to fulfil their commitments. For instance, the G20 structure has everything it needs to seize the opportunity of incentivizing and pushing dialogue on International Monetary Fund (IMF) reforms and adherence to UNCLOS. The ambiguity is caused by some provisions in the text that press for states' international obligations on contiguous zones fishing quotas and rights in high seas. The fact that the UNCLOS potentially undermines historical and territorial claims is the reason most coastal states cite it as a reason for not formalizing its mandate. Article 76 (1) of UNCLOS explains that 'coastal states are entitled to assert rights over a 200 nautical mile continental shelf provided that there are no overlapping claims via neighbouring states.'

Such a situation resulted from the earlier belief that the states had the right to determine the rules over the sea they control. In fact, such interpretations often favour particular states controlling what marine activities can be conducted at the expense of international law and small and less powerful states. This meant considerable uncertainty, not just about rules and laws in marine space but also introduced risks into maritime interactions. Thus, formulating ways to address these problems is the subject of intense debate in both policy and operation measures in the UN and other maritime organizations. This study aims to highlight gaps in universal maritime law, safety standards, and regulations that need G20's attention for reforms.

Institutions: most global institutions were the by-product of various international conflicts, which also applies to the maritime domain. By far, 'The Hague Conventions' or treaties adopted at the Peace Conferences held in The Hague, Netherlands, in 1899 and 1907 established various laws and customs of war; specific rules must be followed in the strict sense during hostilities. The institution-building process of maritime interactions roughly dates back to when the League of Nations set up a Committee of Experts in 1924 for the progressive codification of international law and subsequently the Conference for the Codification of International Law, 1930 at The Hague. The 'Territorial Waters' was one of three subjects agreed upon at the first conference, along with 'Nationality' and the 'Responsibility of States for Damage Caused in Their Territory to the Person or Property of Foreigners.'

The institutionalization of codifying international law is mainly led by the UN. The annual sessions of the United Nations General Assembly (UNGA) and the International Law Commission (ILC) interpret international law, and create new institutional mechanisms. The presidents of both organizations took revolutionary measures in codifying maritime law, of which, the UNGA Resolution 1105 (XI), February 1957, formally initiated maritime law. By far, the United Nations agencies and instruments regulate multilateral process at sea, of which the UNCLOS crafted three international maritime institutions: the International Tribunal for the Law of the Sea, the International Seabed Authority (ISA), and the Commission on the Limits of the Continental Shelf (CLCS). Of the three institutions, the work of CLCS is considered decisive as it clarifies and awards maritime zones when overlapping claims emerge between coastal states. Besides, the International Court of Justice (ICJ) is also responsible for passing judgements over disputes. The ISA regulates most mineral-related activities in Areas Beyond National Jurisdiction (ABNJ).

The International Maritime Organization (IMO) looks after the regulation of global shipping and sets the standards and requirements for safety, security and environmental performance. It checks operational efficiency, provides seafarers training, extends technical cooperation, intervenes in legal matters and enhances maritime security. This comprehensive focus of the IMO resulted in it being considered as 'the United Nations-at-sea'.

Though there is a difference in work culture between G20 and the IMO, both have subscribed to or strive for universal principles and practices and have a similar mechanism of working groups focusing on issues of international relevance. For instance, G20 working groups and IMO committees are engaged in the internal election of members to draft proposals and recommendations. Here, the framework needs to build consensus on the convergence between G20 and IMO mandates. This could be possible when G20 initiates internal dialogue and proposes collective recommendations before five committees of IMO. Such a proactive approach to assist and guide global maritime governance could strengthen the focus on the blue economy and be a boon to G20's profile.

Regional specific multilateral maritime interactions are also conducted through organizations and arrangements that are non-UN agencies. The Antarctic Treaty Secretariat, 2003, established by the Antarctic Treaty System 1958, has been perceived as a model of legal creativity and cooperation for regulating international relations in the region. There are positive implications of the evolution in this system for accommodating emergent law of the sea issues. However, it has considerable achievements in establishing conservation and scientific protocols, the application of provisions indicated competing regimes at the review stage. It appears that the legacy of multilateral challenges such as conflicting interests among members, the interplay of members and the evolution of a regime complex,[6] hail disagreements over proposals of bringing the Antarctic Treaty System under the framework of the United Nations. The unresolved general disagreements are regarding the use of military means for logistics functions, the ban on all types of atomic explosions, and the internationalization of Antarctic sovereignty. The condescending situation in implementing and enforcing both national laws and the law of the sea illustrates the challenge of 'constraints and complementarity' (Haward, 2009).

---

[6] The regime complex among international organisations is caused by an array of overlapping institutions and agreements that are supposed to govern a particular issue.

Much like the interplay of competing regimes of the Antarctic, the Arctic Council has been caught up between security and geopolitical issues. This happens despite its relevance to the changing times—climate change and the melting of the Arctic sea-ice has opened up new economic opportunities that offer accessibility of new waterways and large reserves of energy resources like oil, gas and minerals. Perhaps, International Seabed Authority (ISA) jurisdiction can be extended to the Arctic Ocean,[7] following recent interest in exploiting seabed resources. The pressing issue in this concern has been 'flag planting and finger pointing' concerning territorial claims in the Arctic and political geographies of the outer continental shelves (Dodds, 2010).

Instruments: the UNCLOS is treated as a principal instrument of maritime governance from the principles of *Mare Liberum*[8] and *Mare Clausum*.[9] The low ratification of the four treaties made at Geneva delayed the process by which various instruments were developed to push commonly agreed provisions in separate conventions. For instance, *the United Nations Fish Stocks Agreement* of 1995 evidently resembles the earlier CFCLR. The global maritime space is almost 70 per cent of the Earth, out of which the identified explored areas so far account for not more than 5 per cent. It is essential to understand the maritime rights of states to fully grasp why there are disputes and what activities are allowed in maritime space.

First, the UNCLOS text has defined maritime boundaries within the classification of maritime zones by dividing the Earth's water surface areas using physiographic or geopolitical criteria. They are internal waters, territorial sea (0–12 Nautical Miles [NM]), contiguous zone (12–24 NM), Exclusive Economic Zone (EEZ) (0–200 NM), continental shelf[10] and the high seas. The resources in maritime zones are very valuable. The authority of coastal states over these zones is important for the protection and security of the coastal state, global trade and

---

[7] Though ISA administers jurisdiction over the region surrounding the North Pole and the Arctic Ocean, its authority has been disputed by claimants. Thus, on certain portions of the region ISA lacks clear jurisdiction over seabed areas belonging to states which lay territorial claims in the Arctic. Canada, Denmark, Iceland, Norway, Russia and the United States have openly laid claims.

[8] *Mare Liberum* (in Latin) (1609) is an international law book titled *The Freedom of the Seas* (in English), authored by the Dutch jurist and philosopher Hugo Grotius. The legacy of this account is *the Right to Innocent passage* for travel and trade as the generally accepted principle of international waters, oceans, seas, and waters beyond national jurisdiction; a concept based on which UNCLOS Article 19 talks about rights and restrictions for a vessel to pass through the archipelagic and territorial waters of another state.

[9] *Mare clausum* (in Latin) (1635) is the term meaning 'closed sea' coined by John Selden in order to prove that certainly, in practice, the sea or any navigable body of water can come under the jurisdiction of a state; though states had *Mare clausum* policies declared before it was termed. In 1702, Cornelius Bynkershoek proposed a workable formula in *De dominio maris* limiting the distance of a cannon fired or the three-mile limit where a maritime state has jurisdiction.

[10] 'Continental shelf' to a marine nation, according to UNCLOS, cannot extend beyond 200 NM from the baseline; however, claims over legal continental shelf slightly differs for states with physical continental shelves and inhabited volcanic islands and uninhabitable islands, this extension is known as the continental margin, such an expanded continental shelf cannot exceed 350 miles.

marine environment and biodiversity. The conflicts over maritime rights have been significant disadvantages caused by the lack of data collection, lack of universal measures of marine environment protection provisions in UNCLOS and differences in the implementation of the law of the sea. There are three identified situations where applying the law of the sea challenged and caused maritime boundary disputes. *One*, coastal states were sharing waters with less than 400 NM. In this scenario, a median line must be identified under the equidistance principle. *Two*, an extension of the maritime zone (of territorial sea) with islands. *Three*, maritime zones from a disputed territory.

The internationally agreed delineation of these zones was defined with reference to the baseline of the national territory. The coastal states enjoy sovereignty over the internal, territorial, and archipelagic waters, including air space, seabed and subsoil, but should give innocent passage to ships. Thus, coastal states' boundaries give exclusive national rights and limits encompassing maritime features, mineral and biological resources. The baseline, for instance, was introduced to help straighten the coastline with a straight line across the mouth of indentations, thus considered as internal waters—an extension of national borders—and have the same legal status as on the land of the coastal state. As the baseline determines all other zones to help measure straight distances, the impending sea-level rise has legal implications for the baseline delimitations and maritime boundaries that are 'neither straightforward nor foreseeable' (Houghton et al., 2010).

Second, within the contiguous zone, coastal states may impose regulations to control maritime activities that infringe security in the territorial sea. In the Exclusive Economic Zone, the coastal state has sovereign rights to explore, exploit, manage and conserve living and non-living natural resources. Here, coastal states have the right to produce energy, build artificial islands, installations and structures, undertake scientific research, and protect and preserve the marine environment. The legal status of EEZ in the law of the sea leads to consensus remaining elusive due to contentious issues about the compatibility of national claims and law of the sea (Melchiorre and Plėta, 2018). Preventing uncertainty and defusing conflict can be vital in negotiating disputes over fisheries and military activities and intelligence gathering in the EEZ. Differences in identifying the continental shelf is a delimitation which causes disputes as it may vary when states claim extension slightly beyond the 200 NM boundary (see footnote 7). Any dispute settlement prospects in the law of the sea need 'a great deal of work to do' before reaching a satisfactory set of rules (Brown, 1977). Though such claims have to be supported by accurate marine mapping of geological features and geodetic data, the claim of an extended continental shelf up to 350 NM is justified. Besides, any such claim identifies the outer limit and cannot extend to deep seas. The practice of developing states stresses the 'without prejudice' principle on the CLCS recommendations in cases of disputed and unresolved maritime boundary delimitations (Kwiatkowska, 2013).

The progress can be measured as the consensus on the clear delimitation of maritime borders on paper and ground. This process helps govern EEZ waters and international waters, makes provision for the flag over the ship to determine law on board at international waters, and aids delimitation of the continental shelf according to the 'equitable principles/special circumstances' method. International bodies categorically clarify the applicability of UNCLOS over maritime areas, saying that it 'comprehensively' governs the rights of parties. However, some gracefully accepted, and others refused and criticized international bodies like the International Court of Justice (ICJ) and the Permanent Court of Arbitration (PCA). In this concern, the landmark rulings over maritime boundary disputes are the *North Sea Continental Shelf, Judgment, ICJ Report* in 1969, the *Cameroon v. Nigeria: Equatorial Guinea intervening, Judgment, ICJ Report* in 2002, the *Bay of Bengal Maritime Boundary Arbitration between Bangladesh and India*, 2009, and the *Arbitral Tribunal Ruling on the South China Sea by the Permanent Court of Arbitration* (PCA), 2016.

Third, the need for governance and safety of high seas or Areas Beyond National Jurisdiction (ABNJ) is convincing and complex. It is convincing because it gives the provision of marine activities beyond national jurisdiction. It has been his-

torically dynamically complex because of its remoteness and inaccessibility for conventional marine activities. The role of legal principles in identifying new pathways for ocean governance to deal with regulatory and implementation gaps is a dynamic process in areas beyond national jurisdiction (Houghton, 2014). The ABNJ accounts for around 64 per cent of the surfaces of oceans and is considered a global commons. The ABNJ is meant for everyone and no one—it is 'an ocean of surprises' with unexpected dynamics that may impact our ability to govern increasing interacting human use and present serious governance challenges (Merrie et al., 2014). The human activity in ABNJ has been supported by technological support and market opportunity, which drives the freedoms of high seas: navigations, fishing, lay cables and pipelines, and overflight. This area's conducive marine activities are establishing national arrangements for marine environment protection, laying submarine cables, renewable energy devices, and oil and gas platforms.

The national Environmental Impact Assessment Arrangements play a crucial role in increasing human activities, and the exchange and interoperability of the G20 states may be explored. The G20 can use the new interest in the need for special provisions to protect the high seas. The lack of legislation of universal environmental protection standards is the gap that requires G20 attention. The US, EU and India are individually attempting to frame and put into practise standards of regional measures. The Abidjan Convention (1984) among coastal countries of the West, Central and Southern African Region seeks to establish common standards applicable to members. It can offer various designs to ensure sustainable use of biodiversity on the high seas. The protection of biodiversity has particular importance to the UN. The dynamic nature of threats to biodiversity is intertwined with economic activity, such as fishing, exploitation of mineral resources, human activities, and bioprospecting for genetic resources that cause habitat degradation, pollution, climate change, climate engineering and ocean acidification. Furthermore, increased pressure requires strong management and stronger legislation in UNCLOS to protect biodiversity.

The key legal instrument for ensuring that ships comply with safety standards is the *International Convention for the Safety of Life at Sea* (SOLAS Convention), 1914. The customary international law for SAR stems from general search and rescue practices post the 1914 treaty of SOLAS in response to the 1912 Titanic disaster. Further, similar provisions were outlined in the Global Maritime Distress & Safety System (GMDSS) and the *International Convention on Maritime Search and Rescue* (M-SAR), 1979. IMO's Maritime Safety Committee separated oceans into 13 Search and Rescue Areas and Search and Rescue Regions. It also allocates and entrusts Search and Rescue Regions (SRRs) to specific countries concerned to meet the international obligation of SAR.

Further, the G20's political push for global economic reforms and governance matches the IMO 2020 instrument. The new interest regarding climate-sensitive reforms to the global economy is the convergence between the G20 and the IMO. The anxiety around quickly mitigating threats to climate change and the cost burden over the blue economy is one impending issue that must receive major focus.

Meanwhile, a set of international norms have been pushed through specific draft conventions such as the *Convention of Marine Research and Accountability*, the *Convention on Biological Diversity (CBD), 1993*, and the Nuclear-free zone (NWFZs) ban development, manufacturing, control, possession, testing, stationing or transporting of nuclear weapons in *airspace, territorial sea,* or *archipelago waters of the Parties.* All four, the UNCLOS, the SOLAS, the *International Aeronautical and Maritime SAR* (IAMSAR) and the *Convention on International Civil Aviation,* 1944, made it a requirement for states to establish an M-SAR system. It is a practice that recommends minimum SAR standards and collaborates to harmonize national maritime and aeronautical SARs. Notable achievements in coordination to share information, expertise and link their respective SAR systems, include the *Indian Ocean Rim Association (IORA) Memorandum of Understanding (MoU) on Coordination in SAR in the Indian Ocean Region (IOR)* 2014 by five member countries and the formulation of *the Asia-Pacific Regional SAR Plan,* 2015 (Khurana, 2017). Besides, establishing a dedicated *Study Group on the Harmoni-*

sation of Aeronautical and Maritime SAR (HAMSAR) by the Council for Security Cooperation in the Asia-Pacific (CSCAP) adds coordinated efforts.

As highlighted in this section, the institutional progress and convergence of global economic reforms and governance between maritime organizations and the G20 expose untapped scope. Thus, this section asserts that the institutions have a unique mandate with the changing nature of the global economy. To an extent, the G20 format can precisely aim to facilitate dialogue and address and build coordination on challenges to Critical Maritime Infrastructure.

BETWEEN SAFETY AND GOVERNANCE

The scope to improve the safety and governance of critical infrastructure demands a proactive approach to developing prevention, preparedness, and response and recovery strategies. Some of the scenarios discussed were terrorist attacks on undersea cables and pipelines, cyberattacks on port systems, ship collisions, an explosion in the industrial area of refineries, and a blast in petrochemical facilities. Concerning international politics over CMI, the policy and academic debates were focused on reforming systems and improving governance. The need to improve governance systems is driven by two factors, meeting the new demand of safety of CMI and combating ever-changing threats. Here the new requirements are centred around present changes in modes of business, technology and interest in new structures of operation. To secure the confidence of the CMI industry and their role in improving national economies, the construction and reconstruction of models of engagements are required. Such reforms need to take care of local priorities.

A critical review of the safety and governance of Critical Maritime Infrastructure systems has acknowledged that their resilience and operations take significant maritime security resources and efforts (John and Nwaoha, 2016). These include human, logistical, technological and financial resources. The concerned country's national resources govern the safety of these features within the shores. However, the need for comprehensive approaches to improving maritime governance 'will require collaborative approaches and coordinated efforts' by a wide range of economic and security actors, including governments, non-governmental organizations, security forces and industry (Sandoz, 2012).

It briefly touches on the international cooperation, governance structure, and legitimacy of the club. Why is safety and governance essential for disaster resilience and sustainable development? To the question of why the safety of Critical Maritime Infrastructure is important, the literature on the consequences of accidents has been focused on main models such as the process of events or accidents, connecting environmental threats and eventual environmental degradation. Following up on the accidents' economic cost also drives interest in critical maritime infrastructure, but few have focused on the domain of infrastructure and its technologies.

Case study

Submarine Cable Network: Submarine cables are often called the 'world's information superhighways' (CSIS, 2021). They are one of the service-based core maritime infrastructures whose safety is critical due to their extensive linkages in today's digital world. They deliver essential services responsible for the transmission of 95 per cent of global data. While this dependency allows us to navigate the digital transformation seamlessly and communicate and coordinate more efficiently, it has brought forth new vulnerabilities and security concerns. As transoceanic digital communications continued to grow in importance in modern societies and in the security of nation-states, state and non-state actors began to encroach on the maritime domain. Consequently, undersea cables have turned into a major technological battleground.

In this context, regardless of the many dangers they are exposed and subjected to, the threats to submarine cables are effectively siloed throughout the broader security discourses and even compartmentalized in maritime security studies. However, to contextualize the significance of submarine cables, these communication channels/nodes need to be seen as a part of a larger system or within security context—economic sectors, e.g., digital transactions; communication sector, e.g., for internet and 5G connectivity; or a specific purpose of international scientific cooperation. If the past maritime security incidents were anything to go by, attacks on submarine cables are likely to become more targeted, more unsettling, in addition to being more political and strategic. As a result, safety measures must pay attention to the protection, governance and full resiliency of the undersea cable infrastructure, and importantly, understand the security of these installations in the discourse of geopolitics and international relations.

While there exist international legal treaties like *the Convention for the Protection of Submarine Telegraph Cables, Geneva Convention on High Seas and Continental Shelf, International Regulations for Preventing Collisions at Sea*, and *United Nation Convention on the Law of Sea*, to govern and protect undersea cables from unruly actors, the safety of cables and their operations would need a certain degree of cooperation from international actors regarding handling the contingencies. The rationale behind this is to provide the international actors and industry stakeholders a common ground to formulate a plan of action to deter or counter such attacks on the cable infrastructure. Moreover, the multi-faceted nature of cable ownership necessitates delineating or clarifying responsibilities for submarine cables, both at state and non-state levels. While cooperation between submarine cable stakeholders regarding the safety of these installations will remain a major challenge, not because of political unwillingness to cooperate but because of the structural and operational responsibilities, which are often too complex and widely different. Add to this the varying domestic laws in different countries that are at times not clear enough, which further complicates their protection. This makes the role states play even more important in multilateral action and coordinated response to be examined critically.

Submarine cables work as a catalyst for transnational production networks and facilitate international economic activity. Against this backdrop, the global security community has witnessed how advanced threat actors have proven their ability to attack undersea cables by exploiting the inefficiencies in their governance. As such, given the importance of this Critical Maritime Infrastructure for global security, ensuring their complete resiliency must be a priority and challenge for the G20 member states. While some states have adopted few national measures, an actionable response or policy framework at a multilateral level remains limited and elusive. As such, international action backed by a multilateral setup like G20 stands to leverage policy coherence to ensure resilient and reliable submarine cable governance among the member states for the safe functioning of this global maritime common. For instance, intelligence sharing among G20 member states, risk assessments of cable projects and contingency measures in case of cable breaks could be explored.

Port Infrastructure: Though the safety and governance of physical maritime infrastructure have long been established, the developing trends in the adoption of new technologies and coordination methods have exposed some predatory activities at shores and high seas. The current trend demonstrates the major space of maritime operations within cyber and automation and control systems; thus, their safety and governance have been increasingly informationized and digitalized. As a result, most port systems linked to networked and autonomous systems like Rubber Tyred Gantries (RTGs), Ships to Shore (STS) cranes, vessel breathing systems, cargo handling, traffic control and safety and security systems, have experienced greater digitalization. The ease of doing operations in digital mode has made them equally vulnerable to terrorist cyberattacks for illegal data mining and financial thefts and ransoms (Gkousgkounis, 2016). Traditional cybersecurity systems like antivirus softwares installed on individual systems have a negligible role in protecting these Operation Technology (OT) networks—a vessel bridge navigation system (Electronic Chart Display and Information System - ECDIS), Dynamic Positioning (DP) system in the floating rig and the dock cranes. The cyber risks in the port facility have six vulnerable components or areas, namely Facility Access, Terminal Headquarters—for Data mining, Terminal Headquarters—to ransomware, Operation Technology (OT) system, Positioning, Navigating and Timing (PNT) and Vessels. As these technologies are integrated online, the core operational systems can be attacked directly by controlling infrastructure movement and effectively creating a massive backlog.

The performance of the operational networks was usually measured in an emergency state; thus, when it comes to cybersecurity breaches in ports, underreporting has been a common issue, as many OT systems at ports show them as errors, so perhaps, a reason for underreporting is being unaware of being attacked. The attacks were sometimes treated as issues within the system in OT systems and an approach of restarting the programme was followed. The new interest in data-driven and remote operations reduces the traditional approach of physically separating and converging IT and OT security systems (Murray, Johnstone and Valli, 2017). Although cyberattacks in IT systems can be easily identified, separating threats and errors in OT systems is challenging.

Further, most of the losses caused by cyberattacks have been accounted for as revenue loss rather than direct loss, which undermines the process of reporting, threat assessment and response. The misunderstanding has been that underreporting happens naturally due to market-driven effects—potential reputational risks or insurance problems. Nevertheless, cyberattacks certainly are manufactured, precisely targeted and preventable, and the maritime industry needs to improve ethical hacking capabilities (Chia, 2019). Another current trend has been cyber-induced environmental pollution, where the cost involves huge losses for the industry, national economies and the environment. A significant number of attacks target OT systems as they would not recover under most insurance policies. The significance of such incidents noted in one case highlights that the virus NotPetya resulted in USD 300 million loss to Maersk. The attacks took down half of the shipowners' network of an Australian shipbuilder Austal and the COSCO. The MSC (US-based gas pipeline operator and shipping company) Geneva HQ shut down for five days in a separate incident. There was a Cyberattack on Barcelona, San Diego in 2018; the US-based maritime facility's industrial control systems that monitor and control cargo transfer systems were infected with Ryuk ransomware in January 2020; the same year, in June, there was a cyber attack on Iran's Shahid Rajee port; in October 2020, there was a cyber attack by RedEchoon on India's power grid and ports, and in July 2021, the cyberattack on South Africa's state-owned Transnet's IT system disrupted key container terminals; these are examples where there is a threat of future attacks on OT systems.

Some studies argue that maritime professionals' 'lack of general knowledge in the field of maritime cybersecurity' and that it is 'necessary to increase training levels in the maritime sector and the port interface connection with the supply chain' (Alcaidea and Llavea, 2020). Israel's Naval Dome records that cyber attacks on maritime technology systems, i.e., cyber attacks on ports and related infrastructure of cyber commands, satellites, Navy and Coast Guard, energy and commerce industries, increased by 900 per cent from 2017 to 2020. A Lloyd's of London report estimated that when 15 Asian ports were to be hacked financially, the loss would reach above USD 110 billion.

International Maritime Routes: The international straits are extremely narrow water sections between two coastal states and have an extremely important role in global trade. The international traffic presses the importance of strait governance by two or more states. There is a high need for close cooperation, effective management and control of the straits between countries. There is a misconception between the legal regime of straits and the national security of the concerned states that the control has been understood from a narrow sense of sovereign rights rather than a right to control with the international obligation of providing innocent passage (Caminos and Cogliati-Bantz, 2014). The order at international straits requires two-way obligations for vessels and coastal states concerning security, piracy, safety and environmental protection. In principle, the vessels have the right to 'transit passage'; in addition, the relevant coastal states can intervene when a vessel conducts unrelated activities without permission. The governance is typically conducted under two modules: the Navigation Systems and the Traffic Separations Schemes.

The annual passage of ships in the Strait of Malacca accommodates 90,000, the Strait of Bab-el-Mandeb is 22,000; 18,829 ships pass through the Suez Canal, and 11,000 oil and LNG tankers cross the Strait of Hormuz. There are nine significant chokepoints in the Indian Ocean Region: the Suez Canal, Strait of Hormuz, Strait of Bab-el-Mandeb, Strait of Malacca, Lombok Strait, Sunda Strait, Six Degree Channel, Nine Degree Channel and the Cape of Good Hope. The vulnerability of the chokepoints implies lucrative maritime targets for terrorists and high chances of maritime accidents.

For instance, relatively small and narrow sea channels like the Gulf of Mannar have increased investments. Such a sharp rise of the ship-and-port infrastructure in recent years was led by geopolitically-motivated domestic investments, joint investments (between India and Sri Lanka), and external investments from China. In terms of geopolitical value, the security of maritime assets is a national concern notwithstanding a more global concern. Gaps in security and governance have greater ramifications for not just particular regions but global geo-economics. It implies that maritime trade in goods and services are much more integrated with global economic, political and social structures.

Though the perception over chokepoints traditionally revolves around vulnerability, they have been stabilized with widespread acceptance to customary navigation rules as codified in the *United Nations Convention on the Law of the Sea.* Adherence to a Traffic Separation Scheme (TSS) for transit passages reduces the risk of collision. However, tracing illegal activities can be tricky when international disputes or extended claims of maritime rights cause anxiety and impede passage. For instance, the Strait of Hormuz underlines challenges to strait governance. From the Strait of Malacca, the burden of environmental, safety, and security risks jointly shouldered by Indonesia, Malaysia, and Singapore derive varying economic benefits. Any disruptions in the Strait would negatively impact primary outsiders like Japan, China and Korea. The Strait has a Tripartite Technical Experts Group (TTEG) that develops technologies and processes to ensure undisrupted navigation, such as the Traffic Separation Scheme (TSS), the ship reporting system (STRAITREP) and the Marine Electronic Highway. Governance-based management of risks in increasingly stressed systems helps improve resilience and capacity aimed at accidents. Thus, the safety and governance of these passages also need more innovation.

The International Risk Governance Council (IRGC) launched a project on the risk governance of Maritime Global Critical Infrastructure (MGCI) in 2009. In collaboration with the Disaster Prevention Research Institute (DPRI) of Kyoto University in Japan, the project focused on the Straits of Malacca and Singapore. This Strait is one of the busiest shipping lanes globally, and all major regional powers have geoeconomics and geostrategic stakes, like the US, India, China, Japan and Australia. Of all, the Strait is the most congested passage in the world. The area is responsible for around 25 per cent of all world trade and half of the world's shipped crude oil. The security and governance in the area present a complex picture as it has huge proven reserves of energy resources and minerals yet to be exploited, and rich mangrove resources and marine and coastal biodiversity are at risk.

The capacity of interconnected infrastructures like international straits has been high in response to oil refinery fires and explosions. The Straits of Malacca and Singapore, the Suez and Panama Canals, reveal a relatively fair governance scheme. These fast-track response mechanisms are widely believed to be a required scheme to ensure stability in price changes and the increase of transportation costs from maritime accidents. As a result, the governance and security check of the Strait's traffic separation scheme (TSS) to avoid ship collisions between westbound and eastbound passage, navigational aid infrastructures to detect shallow water channel points and STRAITREP information system to identify ships' ownership and country, are deemed more effective than others (Kajitani et al., 2013).

G20'S MODEL FRAMEWORK OF MARITIME SAFETY AND GOVERNANCE

The informed assessments on the ways G20 can extend its platform to improve governing (global commons) maritime space have put forward several claims, most tuned to one tone—G20 that has long devoted itself to providing dialogue as part of its contributions to the global economic and development agenda can offer feasible options. G20 may explore a new dimension of multilateral approach with intricate patterns, rich in dialogue and unmatched arrangements across a wide range of existing and emerging forums. The convergence of interest within G20's formation brings together the world's major advanced and emerging economies, all of which are maritime economies. G20 is again the core focus of members strategizing against emerging challenges; their preparedness against threats has significantly transformed the extent of challenges they perceive. Thus, this study asserts that to a great extent, the G20 format has the potential to facilitate high-level dialogue and drive and facilitate cooperation among its members through expanded exchanges and sharing of experiences and information to address specific concerns over the safety and governance of Critical Maritime Infrastructure. This will boost coordinated performance and ensure members keep moving together along the road to sustainable growth and development.

As seen, unregulated activities and ambiguity in the laws of the sea cause the maritime threats to amplify and ravage in the high seas. To a great extent, this precarious situation can be attributed to the lack of coherent states' maritime strategies to ensure a safe and resilient CMI in the international system. Building coordination on challenges to Critical Maritime Infrastructure starts with building confidence. Some G20 members have been actively facilitated and contribute to sustaining the momentum in the Indo-Pacific with the Quadrilateral Security Dialogue (QUAD)—a strategic dialogue to secure a rules-based global order, freedom of navigation and a liberal trading system, and the recent AUKUS trilateral security pact between Australia, the United Kingdom and the United States. Apart from minilaterals, almost all individual G20 members officially formulated their maritime vision; some have articulated a clear foreign policy strategy with the Indo-Pacific, e.g., Australia, Germany, France, India, Indonesia, Japan, the United Kingdom, the United States and the European Union. Finally, yet importantly, India has used the opportunity of its chair of the UN Security Council Debate (2021) to introduce a holistic high-level open discussion on 'Enhancing Maritime Security: A Case for International Cooperation'.

Thus, the newfound interest in maritime geopolitics such as the Indo-Pacific momentum is an opportunity to catch up with the trend. The upcoming G20 summits present an opportunity for exploring ways to foster and harness a resolution-based approach by reflecting on its members' concerns. Lastly, considering the sensitivity and criticality of these infrastructures, the need for the G20's observation to focus on identifying and building on existing multilateral institutions and processes over safety and governance of Critical Maritime Infrastructure becomes vital.

This study emphasizes a model G20 maritime framework that should assist the members of the G20 in coping with emerging maritime security and the blue economic issues. G20 policies have the potential to cause transboundary and multi-sector impacts, so establishing a G20 Maritime Working Group is necessary. Institutionalizing assistance programmes to resist and recover from CMI accidents show the end of inadequate preparedness on the horizon. The central role of CMI in maritime economic security converges with G20's global economic agenda, which has been discussed below its full potential. The study's analysis on consequences of threats to CMI estimates that considerable space is open for G20 to push robust safety and governance mechanisms. The developing economies and the industry desire G20 to advocate key modules of investments and growth reforms that can be realized.

Regarding the need to reform the law of the sea, specifically on universal rules of engagement and the code of conduct in the international straits, the G20 CMI arrangement has the potential to facilitate and steer dialogue. The convergence between the G20 core economic philosophy and global sustainable development agenda opens scope to untapped domains. Specific to maritime security, G20's approach should advocate and recommend reforms to maritime multilateralism in IMO and other regional organizations. In specific, multilateral dialogue shall focus on detailing a universal code of conduct on levels of engagement about how to deal with non-traditional security threats. It must take local priorities and threat assessments of the specific cases. Such a process in strategic terms may aim to drive regional efforts to (re)build countries' maritime economies in sensitive coastal areas, such as the Coast of Somalia and others.

The three identified areas that require G20 attention are safety and governance of undersea, over the sea and land-based support infrastructures. The three CMIs that need G20's intervention to push the multilateral resilience of supply chains are undersea cable infrastructure, ports and international maritime straits governance. Apart from conventional threats, the emerging threats to the above are attacks on surveillance and tracking infrastructure of CMI of those systems connected to cyber, automation and control systems.

The action plan of G20 should focus on three things: support capacity building programmes among regional maritime arrangements to build the confidence of small states; facilitate a security dialogue to enhance confidence-building comprising naval chiefs and national security bodies of maritime nations; advocate an integrated governance infrastructure combining all major straits and chokepoints.

The action plan of Capacity Building Measures (CBM) shall aim at process-driven security dialogue on Critical Maritime Infrastructures, including merchandized goods and services. In comparison, the set of action plans should focus on integrated international law enforcement mechanisms governing undersea cable infrastructure, major straits and chokepoints. These targets are more synchronized with the G20's guiding principles of international cooperation towards global economic reforms and governance. Reflecting on the influence of maritime infrastructure on the most significant aspects of the global economic and financial agenda and its due process needs focus. The following recommendations, to an extent, improve the G20's profile and are conducive to its core economic reform agenda.

In reforming safety and governance provisions of the law of the sea:

- G20 dialogue on maritime security facilitates strategic and tactical decisions at the reforms level by enabling members to consider the full spectrum of risks. Where safety and governance of CMI can become its area of responsibility.
- G20 policies should continue to focus on delivering transboundary and multi-sector impact and accommodate the Blue Economy.
- The dire need for cooperative maritime engagement among the maritime forces of the littoral states concerning non-state actors' involvement in maritime piracy and maritime terrorism should be recognized.

Action plan on improving maritime security:

- An action plan to facilitate operational decisions and strategic guidance by rolling up risk assessments could work best when targets follow the hierarchy among the group, regional, national and finally field levels.
- A situational intervention of adaptive responses is required, which varies with geographic factors.
- The main activities of the G20 Maritime Working Group should resonate with the general consultative status.
- There should be support for setting up an integrated marine environment assessment programme.

Critical Maritime Infrastructure:

- Responding to the shipping industry's urge to improve cyber vigilance, a G20-driven platform for collective cyber intelligence sharing command would foster resilience. The need for maritime cyber risk management programmes can be encouraged among members.
- A G20 (Maritime) Intel Coordination Centre may be launched with an active team that assists users by providing training focusing on guidelines and review processes.
- Similar to the US's Container Security Initiative (CSI), a G20 Container Security Initiative may be launched to coordinate and share G20 members' intelligence to identify containers that pose a risk.
- Similar to Think Tanks 20 (T20), a dialogue could be initiated between G20 members' National Maritime Think Tanks (NMT20).

REFERENCES

Adler, Richard M., and Jeff Fuller. 2007. "An Integrated Framework for Assessing and Mitigating Risks to Maritime Critical Infrastructure." *2007 IEEE Conference on Technologies for Homeland Security* 252–257.

Alcaidea, Juan Ignacio, and Ruth Garcia Llave. 2020. "Critical Infrastructures Cybersecurity and the Maritime Sector." *Transportation Research Procedia* 45: 547–554.

Andrew Merrie et al. 2014. "An Ocean of Surprises – Trends in Human Use, Unexpected Dynamics and Governance Challenges in Areas Beyond National Jurisdiction." *Global Environmental Change* 27: 19–31.

Bansal, Alok. 2010. "Maritime Threat Perceptions Non-State Actors in the Indian Ocean Region." *Maritime Affairs: Journal of the National Maritime Foundation of India* 6 (1): 10–27.

BBC. 2020. "Beirut Explosion: What We Know So Far." *The British Broadcasting Corporation (BBC)*. Accessed July 2021, 22. https://www.bbc.com/news/world-middle-east-53668493.

BBC. 2021. "The cost of the Suez Canal blockage". *British Broadcasting Corporation. https://www.bbc.com/news/business-56559073*

Benson, Robert, and Michael Zürn. 2019. "Untapped Potential: How the G20 Can Strengthen Global Governance." *South African Journal Of International Affairs* 26 (4): 549–562.

Bogalecka, Magdalena. 2020. *Consequences of Maritime Critical Infrastructure Accidents, Environmental Impacts: Modeling—Identification—Prediction—Optimisation—Mitigation.* Amsterdam: Elsevier.

Brown, E. D. 1977. "The Continental Shelf and the Exclusive Economic Zone: The Problem of Delimitation at UNCLOS III." *Maritime Policy and Management* (4) 6: 377–408.

Bueger, Christian, and Timothy Edmunds. 2017. "Beyond Seablindness: A New Agenda for Maritime Security Studies." *International Affairs* 93 (6): 1293–1311.

Bueger, Christian, and Tobias Liebetrau. 2021. "Protecting Hidden Infrastructure: The Security Politics of the Global Submarine Data Cable Network." *Contemporary Security Policy* 42 (3): 391–413.

Caminos, Hugo, and Vincent P. Cogliati-Bantz. 2014. *The Legal Regime of Straits: Contemporary Challenges and Solutions.* UK: Cambridge University Press.

Chauhan, Pradeep. 2019. "Physical Protection of India's Critical Maritime Infrastructure: Part 1." *The National Maritime Foundation of India.* Accessed

August 2021, 10. https://maritimeindia.org/physical-protection-of-indias-critical-maritime-infrastructure-part-1/.

Chia, Raymond Yh. 2019. "The Need for Ethical Hacking in the Maritime Industry." *The Society of Naval Architects and Marine Engineers Singapore 38th Annual Journal.*

Cole, Bernard D. 2013. *Asian Maritime Strategies – Navigating Troubled Waters.* Annapolis: Naval Institute Press.

Davenport, Tara. 2012. "Submarine Communications Cables and Law of the Sea: Problems in Law and Practice." *Ocean Development & International Law* 43 (3): 201–242.

Dodds, Klaus. 2010. "Flag Planting and Finger Pointing: The Law of the Sea, the Arctic and the Political Geographies of the Outer Continental Shelf." *Political Geography* 29 (2): 63–73.

Fiott., Daniel. 2021. "Naval Gazing? – The Strategic Compass and the Eu's Maritime Presence." *European Union Institute for Security Studies*, Brief, 1–8.

G20 Insights. 2017. *Sustainable Ocean Economy, Innovation and Growth: A G20 Initiative for the 7th Largest Economy in the World.* Policy Briefs.

Gkousgkounis, Georgios. 2016. *Assessing Terrorist Cyber-Risks and the Potential Use of Terrorist Cyber-Threats in the Maritime Sector.* Master of Arts Dissertation, Greece: University of the Peloponnese.

Goldthau, Andreas. 2014. "Rethinking the Governance of Energy Infrastructure: Scale, Decentralization and Polycentrism." *Energy Research and Social Science* 1: 134–140.

Hamid, Abdul Ghafur. 2019. "Refining Maritime Boundary Delimitation Methodology: The Search for Predictability and Certainty." *IIUM Law Journal* 27 (1): 35-61.

Haward, Marcus. 2009. "Chapter Xi. The Law Of The Sea Convention And The Antarctic Treaty System: Constraints Or Complementarity?" In *Maritime Boundary Disputes, Settlement Processes, And The Law Of The Sea*, edited by Jon M. Van Dyke, 231–251. Brill.

Houghton et al. 2010. "Maritime Boundaries in A Rising Sea." *Nature Geoscience* 3: 813–816.

Houghton, Katherine J. 2014. "Identifying New Pathways for Ocean Governance: The Role of Legal Principles in Areas Beyond National Jurisdiction." *Marine Policy* 49: 118–126.

Khurana, Gurpreet S. 2017. "Maritime Search and Rescue and Disaster Relief in the Indo-Pacific: The Need for "National Will"." *Maritime Affairs: Journal of the National Maritime Foundation of India* 13 (2): 23–36.

Koga, Kei. 2018. "ASEAN's Evolving Institutional Strategy: Managing Great Power Politics in South China Sea Disputes." *The Chinese Journal of International Politics* 11 (1): 49–80.

Kumar, Amit. 2012. "Maritime History of India: An Overview." *Maritime Affairs* 8 (1): 93–115.

Kwiatkowska, Barbara. 2013. "Submissions to the UN Commission on the Limits of the Continental Shelf: The Practice of Developing States in Cases of Disputed and Unresolved Maritime Boundary Delimitations or Other Land or Maritime Disputes. Part One." *The International Journal of Marine And Coastal Law* 28 (2): 219–341.

Leigh, Kathy. 1992. "Liability For Damage ToThe Global Commons." *Australian Year Book Of International Law* 129–156.

Melchiorre, Tiziana, and Tomas Plėta. 2018. "Military Activities in the Exclusive Economic Zone: A Contentious Issue of the International Law of the Sea." *Journal of Security & Sustainability Issues* 8 (20): 127–142.

Menzel, Anja. 2018. "Institutional Adoption and Maritime Crime Governance: The Djibouti Code of Conduct." *Journal of the Indian Ocean Region* 14 (2): 152–169.

Morcos, Pierre, and Colin Wall. 2021. "Invisible and Vital: Undersea Cables and Transatlantic Security." *Center for Strategic and International Studies (CSIS).* https://www.csis.org/analysis/invisible-and-vital-undersea-cables-and-transatlantic-security/.

Murray, G., M. N. Johnstone, and C. Valli. 2017. "The Convergence of IT and OT in Critical Infrastructure." Edited by C. Valli (eds). *The Proceedings Of 15th Australian Information Security Management Conference.* Perth: Edith Cowan University. 149–155.

Nezamuddin et al. 2020. *Impact Of Sea-Level Rise and Extreme Events on Infrastructure Development in Global Trade and Logistics Supply Chain.* Policy Briefs, G20 Insights.

Nwaoha, T. C., and A. John. 2016. "Safety Critical Maritime Infrastructure Systems Resilience: A Critical Review." *International Journal of Maritime Engineering* 158 (A3): A209-A218.

OECD and UNDP. 2019. *G20 Contribution to the 2030 Agenda: Progress and Way Forward.* The Organisation for Economic Co-operation and Development (OECD) and the United Nations Development Programme (UNDP).

Sandoz, John F. 2012. *Maritime Security Sector Reform.* US Institute Of Peace, pp. 1–12.

Sloggett, Dave. 2014. *The Anarchic Sea: Maritime Security in the 21st Century.* New Delhi: Pentagon Press.

Sweeney, Benjamin, and Austin Becker. 2020. "Considering Future Sea Level Change in Maritime Infrastructure Design: A Survey of US Engineers." *American Society of Civil Engineers, J. Waterway, Port, Coastal, Ocean Eng* 146 (4): 1–12. doi: 04020019.

UNCTAD. 2018 and 2020. *Review of Maritime Transport.* The United Nations Conference on Trade and Development.

UNSDG. 2015. "Transforming our world: the 2030 Agenda for Sustainable Development." *The High-level Political Forum on Sustainable Development.* United Nations.

Wagner, Eric. 1995. "Submarine Cables And Protections Provided By The Law Of The Sea." *Marine Policy* 19 (2): 127–136.

Williams, Laura C. 2017. "An Ocean Between Us: The Implications Of Inconsistencies Between The Navigational Laws Of Coastal Arctic Council Nations And The United Nations Convention On The Law Of The Sea For Arctic Navigation." *Vanderbilt Law Review* 70 (1): 379–411.

Wingrove, Martyn. 2021. "Cyber Security to Be Developed For Critical Maritime Infrastructure." *Riviera - News Content Hub.* https://www.rivieramm.com/ news-content-hub/news-content-hub/cyber-security-to-be-developed-for-critical-maritime-infra.

Yoshio Kajitani et al. 2013. "Economic Impacts Caused By the Failure of A Maritime Global Critical Infrastructure—A Case Study of Chemical Facility Explosion in the Straits of Malacca and Singapore." *Journal of Transportation Security* 4: 1–25.

Afterword

India's Non-Substantive G20 Hosting During a Global Leadership Void

By Patrick Bond

With 80 per cent of global GDP, 75 per cent of world trade, 60 per cent of the people and just over half the world's land, the G20 group remains the world's premier elite club of state leaders and multilateral officials. But the body has degenerated: steadily since peak power in 2009, rapidly since the 2014 conflict between Russia and the West over Ukraine, and spectacularly since Vladimir Putin's 2022 invasion of Ukraine. So, when India hosts the G20 in 2023, especially at Narendra Modi's heads-of-state summit in New Delhi on September 9–10, there are sure to be further frictions and even, potentially, a fatal splintering.

As just one reflection of the difficulties Modi will face, consider how in the eight months before the Bali G20 in November 2022, the massive local and global costs of Putin's latest invasion of Ukraine could simply not be mitigated. Notwithstanding energetic diplomatic efforts by the Indonesian host, President Joko Widodo, there were no prospects for peace (Al Jazeera, 2022). After Putin's September losses of substantial ground that his army had taken in the country's northeast during the March offensive, he used October-November to wreck most of Ukraine's electricity and drinking water systems in time for a brutal winter—and then skipped an uncomfortable face-to-face confrontation with his Western counterparts at the G20, rendering the body irrelevant in addressing the most immediate crisis of the day.

The Indian G20 summit will (likely) follow the 2023 BRICS+ meeting in South Africa. (At the time of writing, there was no announcement on the latter's date.) There, assuming host President Cyril Ramaphosa survives impeachment proceedings begun in December 2022, he and foreign minister Naledi Pandor are anxious to continue building up their own substantial international influence, which is already by far the greatest within Africa. Only African Union 2022 chairperson Macky Sall and Rwandan dictator Paul Kagame (both guests at Bali) come close. Ramaphosa's personal petty corruption—associated with cash held at a residence—pales next to the massive illicit financial flows he facilitated in the business sector (Bond, 2018). But if he manages to hold on to power in bruising intra-party conflicts, his second (2024–29) term in office promises even greater international stature.

Likewise, Modi became far more powerful on the global stage in 2022, in part by keeping his shoes planted in several places at once: playing the Western-imperial G7 bloc off against the rising BRICS, and making military deals with the other Quad (US-UK-Australia) powers against China, as Sino-Indian border conflicts and myriad other tensions continue to flare. However, no amount of Modi's fleet-footedness and fortitude can raise the G20 to the challenge of overcoming structural breakdown.

To illustrate, the most obvious limitation that both Ramaphosa and Modi faced, while closely collaborating at the World Trade Organization (WTO) to lobby for Intellectual Property (IP) waivers on COVID-19 vaccines and treatments (starting in October 2020), was global capitalism's self-destructive tendencies. Western Big Pharma corporations and allied politicians—especially from Britain and Germany—simply rejected the notion of a genuine global public good (indeed, one already massively subsidized by Western, Chinese and Russian governments) even during a pandemic that killed 15 million people and caused a global recession (Inman, 2021).

Yet on the other hand, by mid-2023, even if the Russian invasion has not been resolved, conditions will be even more propitious for Modi, while all around him, multilateralism is crashing and his own society and environment suffer acutely. That will leave the Indian prime minister in an embarrassing situation, in which constipated global power relations prevent breakthroughs on the major problems of our era. Like the global corporate sector's World Economic Forum, there is no shortage of aspirations and even (what can at first blush be considered) forward-looking multilateral projects. However, it doesn't take long to unpack some of the most extreme flaws, starting with Modi's own articulation of an agenda blinded to geopolitical and domestic *realpolitik*.

A METHOD TO MADNESS? TALKING LEFT, WALKING RIGHT

The vision for India's G20 presidency, 'Vasudhaiva Kutumbakam' ('One Earth One Family One Future') will be, Modi claimed in Indonesia, 'inclusive, ambitious, decisive and action-oriented.' In an article under his name published on the day his G20 presidency began (December 1, 2022), 'India's G20 presidency: creating healing, harmony, hope, and working to promote a universal sense of oneness', Modi claimed, 'The previous 17 presidencies of the G20 delivered significant results, for ensuring macro-economic stability, rationalizing international taxation, and relieving debt-burden on countries, among many other outcomes' (Press Information Bureau, 2022).

He asked, 'Can the G20 go further still? Can we catalyze a fundamental mindset shift to benefit humanity as a whole?' His line of argument revealed stunning hypocrisy, given what he has done to India since his proto-fascist reign began in 2014, or indeed dating to the 2002 communal violence in Gujarat that he notoriously flamed:

> Some may argue that confrontation and greed are just human nature. I disagree. If humans were inherently selfish, what would explain the lasting appeal of so many spiritual traditions that advocate the fundamental oneness of us all? One such tradition, popular in India, sees all living beings, and even inanimate things, as composed of the same five basic elements – the panch tatva of earth, water, fire, air and space. (Press Information Bureau, 2022)

And there was more dissembling:

> We have tried to make national development not an exercise in top-down governance, but rather a citizen-led "people's movement". As the mother of democracy, India's national consensus is forged not by diktat but by blending millions of free voices into one harmonious melody… Our citizen-centric governance model takes care of even our most marginalized citizens while nurturing the creative genius of our talented youth. (ibid.)

From fibbing about current realities, to making unfulfillable promises about a future world premised on Big Data's power:

> Fortunately, today's technology also gives us the means to address problems on a humanity-wide scale. The massive virtual worlds that we inhabit today demonstrate the scalability of digital technologies… We have leveraged technology to create digital public goods that are open, inclusive and interoperable… These have delivered revolutionary progress in fields as varied as social protection, financial inclusion, and electronic payments. (ibid.)

In reality, India's financial inclusion strategy includes highly-deregulated microfinance, with the result that excess debt levels left farmers and farmworkers committing suicide at just as rapid a rate (more than 10,000 annually) in the early 2020s as in 2014. Even a World Bank study by Arvind Panagariya in 2008 acknowledged that among suicide victims, there is a 'greater debt burden and greater reliance on informal sources of credit' (Panagariya, 2008). And after all, Modi's main intervention in rural finance destroyed 86 per cent of his country's currency in late 2016, with devastating consequences for those in distant areas.

Such framings by Modi represent a conventional tech-centric discourse among devotees of the World Economic Forum, where a Fourth Industrial Revolution was proclaimed in 2016, one capable of solving all of earth's problems (World Economic Forum, n.d.). Likewise, it's no surprise that the most incorrigible crisis India is contributing to—climate catastrophe—also gets a nod: 'For healing our planet, we will encourage sustainable and environment-friendly lifestyles based on India's tradition of trusteeship towards nature' (Press Information Bureau, 2022).

In reality, under Modi, India has witnessed one of the world's fastest-rising greenhouse gas emissions rates, from 40 billion to 54 billion tonnes from 2014–20. The 'trusteeship towards nature' is unconvincing when Modi—in alliance with China's Xi and the United States' Biden regimes—opposed language in the Glasgow 2021 United Nations climate summit calling for a 'phase out' of coal, insisting on a 'phase down' (WION Web Team, 2021).

Modi brags that 'India's experiences can provide insights into possible global solutions…' He says, 'During our G20 presidency, we shall present India's experiences, learnings and models as possible templates for others, particularly the developing world.' Thank goodness we have here a book, with all the information required within its pages, to serve as a vital antidote.

THE G20'S CONSTIPATION OF THE BRAIN, AND DIARRHEA OF THE SUMMIT DECLARATION

The key managers of the process, G20 'Sherpa' Amitabh Kant and chief G20 coordinator Harsh Vardhan, are meant to assure continuity with Widodo's quasi-successful meeting in Bali (HT Correspondent, 2022). But the G20 fusion of imperialist and sub-imperialist powers has the opposite mandate, in reality: maintain exclusivity, reduce expectations for solving global crises, beat about the bush with pleasing rhetoric, but then do very little aside from trying to manage a world economy beset with capitalist crises.

This formula was first observed in 1998 at the time of the emerging markets' economic meltdown, and it was then rebooted in 2008 for the global financial crisis. The 2020 coordination of quantitative easing to prevent a full global economic crash was impressive, but the subsequent financial market bubbling and then fiscal austerity has undermined social stability in scores of countries suffering new debt crises. In 2022-23, the central crises affecting the world's citizenries include climate, economic volatility, energy costs and hunger, what with the potential mass starvation of several hundred million people due to food and fertilizer shortages and price hikes.

The climate-management failure that occurred simultaneously in Sharm El-Sheikh at the United Nations Framework Convention on Climate Change's 27th annual gathering is revealing. The G20 again offered sympathetic rhetoric:

Mindful of our leadership role, we reaffirm our steadfast commitments, in pursuit of the objective of UNFCCC, to tackle climate change by strengthening the full and effective implementation of the Paris Agreement and its temperature goal, reflecting equity and the principle of common but differentiated responsibilities and respective capabilities in light of different national circumstances… We recall and further urge developed countries to fulfil their commitments to deliver on the goal of jointly mobilizing USD 100 billion per year urgently by 2020 and through to 2025 in the context of meaningful mitigation action and transparency on implementation (G20 Bali Leaders' Declaration, 2022).

The grant-equivalent amount of that broken 2009 promise was only $24 billion, according to Oxfam. But the most important point, in spite of a Loss & Damage fund being introduced in Egypt, was the ongoing refusal of any G20 economy to acknowledge its own economic liability. (South Africa's environment minister fought hard so China would not be named-and-shamed as a climate debtor.) The 'polluter pays' principle found in many G20 statements of environmental management foundational principles, was simply in default by these emitters. Of the 16 leading historic greenhouse gas emitters (from both fossil fuels and land changes), all (aside from Ukraine) were G20 members (Evans, 2021).

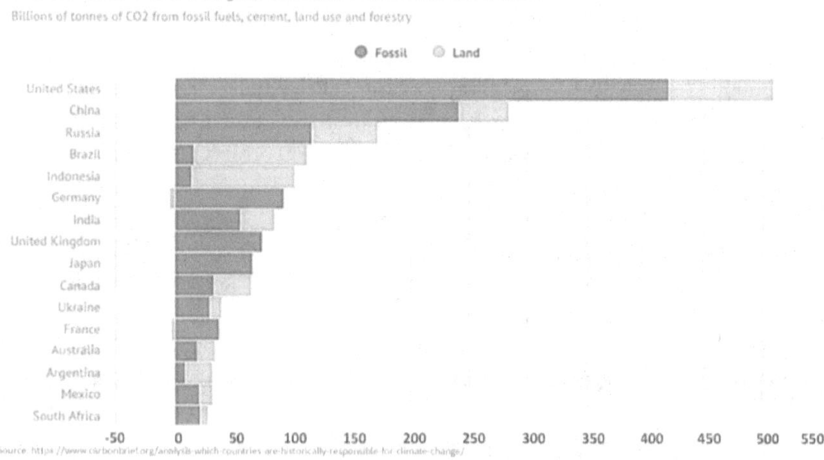

Figure 1.

Source: Simon Evans, Analysis, Which countries are historically responsible for climate change?, Carbon Brief, 2021.

Figure 2.

Source: Bond, Glasgow COP26 and Beyond: Climate Justice Advocacy in the Glasgow Agreement, 2021.

JAW-JAW AND WAR-WAR

Ultimately, the most profound failure of the G20 in Bali—and probably will be in New Delhi in 2023 too—was its reflection of geopolitical tensions. The overwhelming problem was the inability of any force on earth to settle the war that Putin started in February 2022 by invading Ukraine—or, to air Moscow's rationale, that the West's eastward expansion of NATO is responsible for (against early-1990s promises made by G7 leaders to Putin's predecessors). Putin has long fumed about the 2014 US State Department assistance to pro-western Ukrainians who overthrew his allies in Kyiv. And centrist Western leaders have likewise accused Putin of meddling in their elections, including in 2016 in the United States, and in his support for fascistic movements including those in France and Italy.

The NATO threat was, to Western leaders, a red herring argument, since by invading Ukraine, Putin provoked Finland and Sweden to join the military alliance and in any case, the Ukrainian leadership had in early February 2022 committed *not* to apply to join NATO. And there was certainly evidence from Putin's own speeches that his initial invasion strategy—such as the ill-fated march of tanks from Belarus to Kyiv—reflected an extraordinarily arrogant desire to recreate Peter the Great's empire.

In this context, the G20 could only be considered an impossible terrain for diplomacy, yet *Economic Times* deputy editor Pranab Dahl Samanta argued that India's leadership was responsible for face-saving phraseology regarding Russia and Ukraine. In the final communique, Modi's officials apparently copied the way in which the BRICS handled its own many contradictions at the June 2022 virtual meeting hosted by Xi Jinping: 'We reiterated our national positions as expressed in other fora, including the UN Security Council and the UN General Assembly.' As the declaration continued,

> Most members strongly condemned the war in Ukraine and stressed it is causing immense human suffering and exacerbating existing fragilities in the global economy – constraining growth, increasing inflation, disrupting supply chains, heightening energy and food insecurity, and elevating financial stability risks. There were other views and different assessments of the situation and sanctions. Recognizing that the G20 is not the forum to resolve security issues, we acknowledge that security issues can have significant consequences for the global economy. (G20 Bali Leaders' Declaration, 2022)

This vacuous approach merely confirms *status quo* thinking, allowing the jaw-jaw to cover for war-war whose implications stretch far beyond eastern and southern Ukraine. Yet, this seems to be the best the G20 can do, what with the Moscow-Beijing authoritarian commitment to a limited version of counter-hegemonic militarism bumping up against resurgent US expansionism. In a November 2022 discussion, 'Using Marxism to Understand the Ukraine War,' City University of New York political economist David Harvey argued for G20 intervention against 'this very unjust war,' given the stalemated balance of forces:

> it could be brought to an end by the G20 pressuring the two leading powers in the world – which are China and the United States – to actually make sure that this comes to an end. But my fear is that the United States doesn't want it to come to an end. I really think that actually it sees this possibility as a moment in which it can reassert its hegemony… Ukraine has about a big chunk of the global grain trade. And actually that in itself, by the way, may be one of the reasons why this will come to an end, because shortage of food grains and food security around the world is becoming a big issue. And the G20 folk are beginning to say, 'Hey, listen this is getting dangerous for all of us and so something has to be done to bring it to an end.' (Democracy at Work, 2022)

What has become clear, though, is that within the G20, both great-power and middle-power geopolitical loyalties are not set in stone. For example, Putin expected support from his New Delhi and Beijing counterparts at a Shanghai Cooperation Organisation (SCO) conference in Samarkand, Uzbekistan in September 2022, as a result of the dramatic increase in discounted oil and gas sales to India. Yet Modi nevertheless remarked that now was 'not a time for war,' and Putin was embarrassed to have to publicly explain himself to Modi and Xi regarding his army's defeats on the eastern front, the disconnected gas supplies to Europe, and the likelihood of ongoing upheavals in global markets (Agence France-Presse, 2022).

Then, at the G20's November 2022 meeting in Bali, Putin retreated from a potential in-person showdown, instead deploying his foreign minister Sergey Lavrov to make a brief, bitter appearance instead. This was not the first time, for when G20 central bank governors and finance ministers met in April, those from the US, United Kingdom and Canada walked out when a Russian representative was allowed in. The subsequent BRICS and SCO meetings were, hence, ever more important for Putin and Xi to profess the need for a non-US dollar system to handle international payment settlements as well as trade more generally.

With Putin's war and ongoing military and economic pressure placed on Xi by the Biden Administration, the delinking of the West from the East appeared to be rapidly accelerating. As a result, the geopolitical tension overwhelmed a long list of Indonesian efforts to broaden G20 summit declaration language: sustainable development, energy, food and fertilizer supply chains, biodiversity loss, carbon neutrality, vaccine technology transfer, sharing of the digital economy, tourism, cross-border payments, financial stability, multilateral trade, infrastructure building, care for migrants, anti-money laundering and empowerment of women, among more than 50 points.

In declaration rhetoric promoting 'G20 Action for Strong and Inclusive Recovery,' the authors from Indonesia had obviously learned the framing language preferred in multilateralism, but there was no intention at all to deliver, in this classic talk-left walk-right dance (C20 Indonesia 2022 Civil, n.d.).

SOUTH AFRICA TAKES A BRICS+ BATON—TO UNSEAT THE G20?

Looking ahead, the SCO momentum towards an alternative strategy to Western domination may well come in the days and weeks before the G20 meet in New Delhi, as the BRICS are anticipated to summit in South Africa under President Ramaphosa's leadership. What can be expected? Ramaphosa's own roots in left traditions—1970s student radicalism, the mineworkers union which he led into a general strike in 1987 and the early-1990s liberation movement (when he was secretary general of the ANC)—are distant memories.

Since he lost the critical vote of confidence he required from other party leaders to become Nelson Mandela's deputy in 1994, Ramaphosa veered into big business where he accumulated an estimated USD 650 million million until he became Deputy President in 2014. If McDonalds or Coca-Cola needed a franchisee, it was Ramaphosa. If a mining house—Lonmin, known as the 'unacceptable face of capitalism'—wanted lethal state support to end a wildcat strike, it was Ramaphosa who emailed the police minister, resulting in the 2012 Marikana Massacre 24 hours later (Bond, 2018).

But Ramaphosa and Pandor have strong training in radical rhetoric, so more broad-based statements are anticipated, as well as occasional efforts to assert justice at the global scale. Though unsuccessful in mid-2022, Ramaphosa and Modi were the two leading proponents of a waiver on COVID-19 vaccine IP. Regrettably they pretended that their defeat was a victory. Instead of addressing waivers forthrightly, they allowed the G20 summit to promise a (relatively stingy) USD 1.4 billion fund for future vaccines and medicines, with this soaring but ultimately meaningless Declaration rhetoric:

> We recognize that the extensive COVID-19 immunization is a global public good and we will advance our effort to ensure timely, equitable and universal access to safe, affordable, quality and effective vaccines, therapeutics and diagnostics… We support the WHO mRNA Vaccine Technology Transfer hub as well as all as the spokes in all regions of the world with the objective of sharing technology and technical know-how on voluntary and mutually agreed terms. (G20 Bali Leaders' Declaration, 2022)

Likewise, following a decision at the 2018 BRICS summit (which Ramaphosa led), a Vaccine Centre was meant to have been established in host-city Johannesburg. Yet, due mainly to bureaucratic bumbling on South Africa's part, by 2022 it still had not been (aside from a vague commitment to notional 'virtual' collaboration).

A poignant contrast could be recalled to much more fluid power relations at the 2001 WTO summit in Doha. There, in spite of South Africans suffering a president (Thabo Mbeki) who was accurately accused by scientists of killing 350,000 compatriots through his AIDS denialism and refusal to roll out medicines, Cape Town-based Treatment Action Campaign health-rights activists (most living with HIV) led a global campaign for waivers on Anti-Retroviral medicines. They won, and when finally delivered at home through the public sector, that access to a genuine global public good raised life expectancy from 52 to 65 from 2004–19 (Bond, 2020).

Power relations were far more adverse in 2020–22 when Ramaphosa and Modi made a similar call for urgent access to generically-produced (not brand-name)

COVID-19 vaccines. Their failure meant that in South Africa, health profession-als attribute 150,000 of the country's 300,000 excess deaths to the roll out delay. Although from mid-2021, leaders of the United States (Joe Biden) and France (Emmanuel Macron) were gradually won over to the waiver demand, it can, nev-ertheless, reasonably be argued that the South African and Indian leaders were not aggressive enough in their lobbying of other G20 rulers. Where, especially, was their name-and-shame of Angela Merkel and Boris Johnson, who were the main IP-waiver blockers?

There are other mishaps that must be recorded, so as not to be repeated. Pandor's first UN statement after the invasion in late February was a demand that Putin's troops leave Ukraine, but on March 1, the ruling party was given a major donation (more than USD 670,000) by pro-Putin oligarch Victor Vekselberg, and from then on, South Africa U-turned and expressed official neutrality. It was the only such contribution recorded in the first quarter of 2022; Vekselberg owns 49 per cent of the fourth largest manganese mining house, with other shares owned by the main ANC-linked investment com-pany (van Rensburg, 2022).

RESISTANCE WAS FUTILE IN BALI, BUT IN INDIA WILL BE FERTILE

There is always hope that by engaging in critical analysis and activism that are sufficiently persuasive, a bottom-up internationalism can be forged, causing the global elites to wake up and become nervous. Potential uprisings lie around every corner, but as political risk consultancy Verisk Maplecroft assessed matters in a September 2022, report, '68 countries have experienced a significant deteriora-tion in civil unrest score since 2020, compared to 30 with a significant improve-ment' (Verisk Maplecroft, n.d.).

Perhaps the most notable of the social uprisings was Black Lives Matter, which began in the US in mid-2020, catalyzed by police violence. But in another re-port in March 2020, before COVID-19 got underway, a conservative Washington think tank—the Centre for Strategic and International Studies—labeled the prior decade 'The Age of Mass Protests' and graphed an impressive uptick in 'civilian anti-government protests'(Haig, Schmidt and Brannen, 2020). To be sure, the pe-riod after 2016—when elections that approved Brexit and took Donald Trump into the White House—included far more right-wing protesters.

The question is whether such unrest—especially if caused by soaring prices that affect access to vital basic needs—can move beyond the 'IMF Riot' (which like popcorn rises and falls too quickly to make a durable impact). Transcending the specific attacks on immediate sources of society's grievances requires an inte-gration of structural and ideological components of struggles, in a manner that

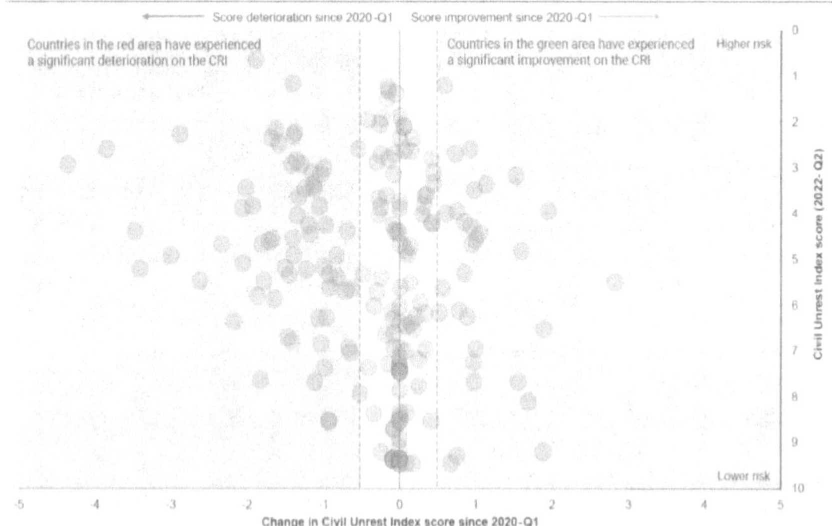

Figure 3. Global civil unrest has spiked since the outbreak of the COVID-19 pandemic

Source: Kinnear and Blanco, Cost of living crisis inflames civil unrest risks in emerging markets, 2022.

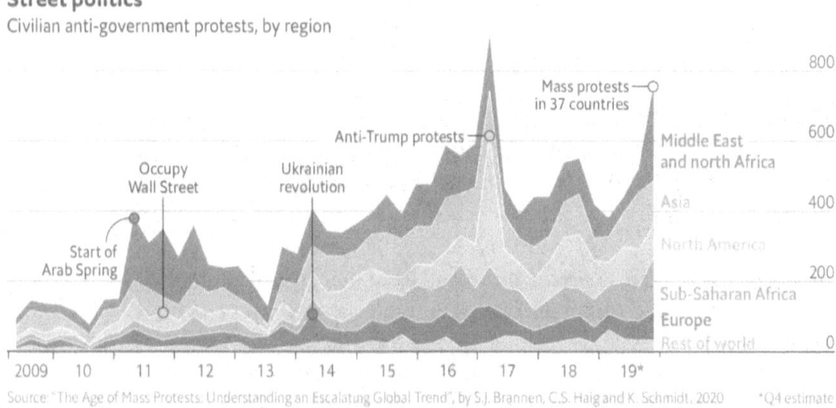

Figure 4. Street Politics: Civilian Anti-government Protests, by Region

Source: The Economist, Political protests have become more widespread and more frequent, 2020.

draws in more allies and reaches further for social change. Sometimes opportunities provided by major international events, such as a G20 summit (or most famously, the 1999 Seattle WTO Summit), permit solidarities to emerge. In 2022, in part due to major differences among those with influence in leftwing groups, such opportunities have been very hard to find. The People's BRICS occasionally suffer from such differences, for example in 2021 during India's hosting, over how the voice of Chinese independent leftists should be heard.

And as another example of difficulties in representing dissent, in September 2022 the G20 host country witnessed impressive protests against fuel price hikes, following demonstrations against a vegetable-oil price increase several months earlier and major social unrest in 2019–20. To track the impact, consider the civil-society 'C20' process, one which occasionally gives rise to radical demands that flow through to G20 Sherpas, where typically they are smiled at but ignored. The C20 structure faded somewhat in recent years due to COVID-19, and appeared to suffer cooptation by the time several hundred mainly-NGO workers met in Indonesia in October 2022. Yet a C20 Working Group on Education, Digitalization and Civic Space issued a policy brief with this absolutely valid critique of the host regime:

> Amid the vast protest from the people in 2020, the Indonesian government passed the controversial Job Creation Bill into law containing a revision to a total of 79 laws without adequate public consultation. A similar pattern was previously observed once the government and parliament hurriedly amend- ed the Anti-Corruption Law in 2019 that weakened the nation's fight against corruption, resulting in days of civil unrest in Jakarta and many other cities. Not only did such inadequate public participation downgrade the most essential good governance principles, but it also made the policy making process a fully exclusive domain of political elites. (C20 Indonesia 2022 Civil, n.d.)

Vigorous 'tree-shaker' outsider activism of this sort means the job of the insider 'jam-maker' (who might have acquired some sort of polite access to the G20 halls) is to find the ideal fruits that have been loosened, so that a division of labour between radicals and reformers emerges. Often this is an exceptionally difficult process, especially given the ideological differences and strategic approach of protesters, who tend to prefer the full-fledged delegitimization of elites. But there is far too little such discussion between radical social movements and reformist NGOs that seek entry to G20 and similar processes.

However, in 2017, when Hamburg, Germany was the host city for the G20, a model for both street-heat—i.e., tens of thousands of demonstrators—and a major alternative-summit conference drew the C20 into constructive debates with local social movements with a more transformative agenda than mere tweaking of summit declarations or even of multilateral institutions, policies and processes (G20 Hamburg, n.d.).

The 2023 BRICS counter-summit that no doubt arises from India's vibrant activism will offer one test. Before that, the BRICS+ summit in South Africa will also allow critique of the alternative, even if there are presently too many divisions in the progressive movement to make any meaningful progress.

The leader of the largest trade union, for example, the National Union of Metalworkers of South Africa, shifted radically in 2022 by endorsing not only Putin's invasion (on grounds NATO was mainly in the wrong), but then suggesting Ramaphosa put pressure on the BRICS to do more on Russia's behalf. Likewise, the same union—once active in the People's BRICS when hosted by Brazilians in 2019—allowed a former (pro-coal, pro-nuclear) head of the electricity company to assist with energy policy drafting, resulting in a dramatic turn from its prior decade promoting eco-socialism, to essentially backing climate denialism.

Hence, just as in 2013 when hundreds protested the BRICS summit at Durban's convention centre (after first stopping to demonstrate at the US Consulate) and 2018 when Johannesburg activists protested at the BRICS Bank and the next day at the BRICS summit, the 2023 'brics-from-below' will need maximum solidarity from, especially, Indians and Brazilians who invariably have the most free and uninhibited uncivil society movements and radical intellectual supporters. And we are all acutely aware of those progressive Chinese and Russian dissidents whose capacity to join in debate, much less in protest, is curtailed by their respective dictatorships.

The alternative, bottom-up summits have been hosted in recent years—both in person and virtually—by the People's BRICS network. Like the 2016 in-person People's BRICS event in Goa, this has resulted in profound exchanges between activists and their allies, for whom we are all extremely grateful.

And now, thanks to the progressive CSOs in India whose ideas are so well articulated and produced in the pages of this compendium, we can pose a question, namely: will the same bottom-up solidarity and genuine speaking of truth-to-the-powerless (and not to-the-powerful—as preferred by vain, petit-bourgeois scholars) expand in 2023, through G20 critiques by Indian activists and writers? This book sets a bar high for the rest of us who have similar aspirations.

REFERENCES

Agence France-Presse. 2022. Now is 'not a time for war', India's Modi tells Russia's Putin who vows to 'end this as soon as possible'. *South China Morning Post.* September 16. https://www.scmp.com/news/asia/south-asia/article/3192827/indias-modi-tells-russias-putin-now-not-time-war

Al Jazeera. 2022. Indonesia's Widodo calls on G20 to work to 'end the war'. November. https://www.aljazeera.com/news/2022/11/15/indonesias-widodo-calls-on-g20-to-work-to-end-the-war

Bond, Patrick. 2018. For South Africa's New President, 'Black Economic Empowerment' Is All About Personal Enrichment. *The Nation.* February 27. https://www.thenation.com/article/archive/for-south-africas-new-president-black-economic-empowerment-is-all-about-personal-enrichment/

Bond, Patrick. 2020. Covid-19 attacks the down-and-out in ultra-unequal South Africa. *International Viewpoint.* April 8. https://internationalviewpoint.org/spip.php?article6516

Bond, Patrick. 2021. Glasgow COP26 and Beyond: Climate Justice Advocacy in the Glasgow Agreement. *The Bullet.* https://socialistproject.ca/2021/07/glasgow-cop26-and-beyond/

C20 Indonesia 2022 Civil. n.d. *Policy Brief. C20 Education, Digitalization, and Civic Space Working Group CIVIC SPACE SUB-WORKING GROUP.* https://pshk.or.id/dokumen/8960

Democracy at Work. 2022. "Using Marxism to Understand the Ukraine War - Richard Wolff & David Harvey". *Youtube.* November 26. 21:15. https://www.youtube.com/watch?v=NEZP_RzT2Dk

Evans, Simon. 2021. Analysis, Which countries are historically responsible for climate change?. *Carbon Brief.* https://www.carbonbrief.org/analysis-which-countries-are-historically-responsible-for-climate-change/

G20 Bali Leaders' Declaration. 2022. The White House. November 16. https://www.whitehouse.gov/briefing-room/statements-releases/2022/11/16/g20-bali-leaders-declaration/

G20 Hamburg. n.d. Information Portal on the Protests against the 2017 G20 Summit in Hamburg. https://www.g20hamburg.org/

Haig, Christian Stirling, Schmidt, Katherine, and Samuel Brannen. 2020. *The Age of Mass Protests: Understanding an Escalating Global Trend.* Centre for Strategic & International Studies. https://www.csis.org/analysis/age-mass-protests-understanding-escalating-global-trend

HT Correspondent. 2022. G20 Members briefed on priorities for India's Presidency. *Hindustan Times.* November 27. https://www.hindustantimes.com/

india-news/g20-members-briefed-on-priorities-for-india-s-presidency-101669489630941.html

Inman, Phillip. 2021. Drop Covid vaccine patent rules to save lives in poorest countries, UK and Germany told. *The Guardian.* June 12. https://www.theguardian.com/world/2021/jun/12/drop-covid-vaccine-patent-rules-to-save-lives-in-worlds-poorest-countries-britain-and-germany-told

Kinnear, Hamish, and Jimena Blanco. 2022. Cost of living crisis inflames civil unrest risks in emerging markets. *Verisk Maplecroft.* May 11. https://www.maplecroft.com/insights/analysis/cost-of-living-crisis-inflames-civil-unrest-risks-in-emerging-markets/

Panagariya, Arvind. 2008. *India: The Emerging Giant.* New York: Oxford University Press. p. 153,

Press Information Bureau. 2022. "Today, India commences its G20 Presidency". Press Release. Government of India. December 1. Accessed at https://pib.gov.in/PressReleseDetailm.aspx?PRID=1880141

van Rensburg, Dewald. 2022. amaBhungane | The ANC's manganese 'gold' mine, the windfalls, and the Russian oligarch. *News24.* May 10. https://www.news24.com/fin24/companies/amabhungane-the-ancs-manganese-gold-mine-the-windfalls-and-the-russian-oligarch-20220510-2

Verisk Maplecroft. n.d. *Political Risk Outlook 2022.* https://storage.pardot.com/456202/16558274111rZddzalY/Verisk_Maplecroft_Political_Risk_Outlook_2022.pdf

The Economist. 2020. Political protests have become more widespread and more frequent. May 10. https://www.economist.com/graphic-detail/2020/03/10/political-protests-have-become-more-widespread-and-more-frequent

World Economic Forum. n.d. "The Fourth Industrial Revolution, by Klaus Schwab." https://www.weforum.org/about/the-fourth-industrial-revolution-by-klaus-schwab

WION Web Team. 2021. COP26: US, China promoted 'coal phase down' concept. Then why is India getting disproportionate blame for it?. *WION.* November 15. Accessed at https://www.wionews.com/world/cop26-us-china-promoted-coal-phase-down-concept-then-why-is-india-getting-disproportionate-blame-for-it-429295.

Contributors

Sonal Raghuvanshi is a heterodox political economist and is currently working and helping build the New Political Economy Initiative at the Indian Institute of Technology, Bombay. Her research is broadly centered around the role of finance in development, macroeconomic policy in developing economies, structural explanations for global inequalities, and the political economy of development and climate change. She is also a Research and Strategy lead at Economist for Future International and has been engaged in critically assessing the economics discipline and advocating for curriculum change with the Rethinking Economics Network.

Soumik Lahiri is an Art Director, Graphic Designer and Illustrator who has worked with popular publications such as *National Geographic Traveller* and *Conde Nast Traveller India*. He began his design journey at a socio-political journal called *Kindle*, in Calcutta, where he established himself as an editorial designer and illustrator with a keen sensibility towards design in journalism. He has also designed and art-directed a political strategy board game, Shasn. He collaborates extensively with writers, filmmakers, editors, video content creators, motion graphic artists, production designers, product designers and game designers. The cross pollination of ideas and mediums in storytelling is what intrigues him the most. His work can be found on his website www.soumiklahiridesign.com and under the Instagram handle 'lahiri_moshai'.

Prabhat Patnaik is an Indian Marxist economist and political commentator. He taught at the Centre for Economic Studies and Planning in the School of Social Sciences at Jawaharlal Nehru University in New Delhi, from 1974, until his retirement in 2010. He was also the Vice-Chairman of the Kerala State Planning Board (2006–2011) and was part of a four-member high-power task force of the United Nations to recommend reform measures for the global financial system along with Joseph Stiglitz, Francois Houtart and Pedro Paez.

Patrick Bond is a political economist, political ecologist and scholar of social mobilization. Currently a professor at the Department of Sociology, University of Johannesburg in South Africa, he has also served as a Professor at the Western Cape School of Government (2020-21) and was a Distinguished Professor of Political Economy at the University of the Witwatersrand School of Governance (2015-2019). His publications covering global geopolitics include, *Elite Transition: From Apartthied to neoliberalism in South Africa, Against*

Global Apartheid: South Africa meets the World Bank, IMF and international finance, Talk Left, Walk Right:South Africa's frustrated global reforms, Politics of Climate Justice: Paralysis above, movement below and *BRICS: An anti-capitalist critique*. He works closely with anti-privatisation movements in South African and African environment, labour, social and community movements.

Anushka M. is a lawyer by qualification. She has also pursued the Master's in Social Science of the Internet. She is interested in the political economy of technology and its use in developing countries.

Vibhuti Patel has retired as a professor from the Tata Institute of Social Sciences and SNDT Women's University, Mumbai. Her areas of specialization have been Gender Economics, Women's Studies, Human Rights and Social Movements. She has authored Women's Challenges of the New Millennium (2002), co-authored Reaching for Half the Sky (1985), Indian Women Change and Challenge (1985) and Status Report for ICSSR- Critical Evaluation of Women's Studies Research during 1947-1988 (1989). She has edited two books, namely, Discourse on Women and Empowerment (2009), and Girls and Girlhoods at the Threshold of Youth and Gender (2010). She is a co-editor of a series of 15 volumes, including Empowering Women Worldwide by The Women Press, Delhi and Gendered Inequalities in Paid and Unpaid Work of Women in India by Springer (2022). Over the last four decades, her work has focused on issues of intersectionality—where gender, development and social justice meet.

Prativa Shaw is an economist with research interests in Sustainable Development, International Trade & Investment and Regional Cooperation. She has worked with the Ministry of Finance, Government of India, Research and Information System for Developing Countries (RIS), New Delhi and PHD Chamber of Commerce and Industry, New Delhi. In 2018-19, she was chosen for the prestigious fellowship, IDE-JETRO-IDEAS, under the Institute of Developing Economics and Japan External Trade Organisation, Japan, and completed her diploma in International Studies.

2030 Agenda and India: Moving from Quantity to Quality - Exploring Convergence and Transcendence, a book she has co-edited and co-authored, was published by the Springer book series, South Asia Economic and Policy Studies.

Elizabeth Edison has completed her Master's degree in Development and Labour Studies from the Centre for Informal Sector and Labour Studies, Jawaharlal Nehru University, New Delhi. Her research interests include understanding development paradigms, gender, and migration studies. Her latest publication looks into home based work within the larger capitalist circuit.

Dokku Nagamalleswara Rao is a Research Assistant at the Center for Land and Warfare Studies (CLAWS) and a Doctoral Fellow (Ph.D.) at Shandong University, P.R. China. Rao has obtained his M.Phil. in the Chinese Studies Division from the Centre for East Asian Studies (CEAS), School of International Studies (SIS), Jawaharlal Nehru University (JNU); his Masters in Politics and International Relations, and his PG Diploma in Human Rights from Pondicherry University. Rao has also worked as a Research Intern with the Chennai Center for China Studies (C3S).

Dr. Manoj Babu Buraga is an Associate Fellow at the National Maritime Foundation, New Delhi and former Research Fellow, at the University of Lausanne, Switzerland and Université of Paris 13, France. He received his PhD in Politics and International Relations with a specialization in European Studies from Pondicherry University His current research focuses on EU-India Maritime Security, India-France in the Indo-Pacific, and Minilateralism in the Indo-Pacific.

Kiran G. S. K. is a Doctoral student at the Department of Humanities and Social Sciences, the Indian Institute of Technology (IIT), Guwahati. He is a Junior Research Fellowship recipient from the Ministry of Human Resource Development (MHRD). He pursued his M.Phil. from the Indian Institute of Technology, Hyderabad and his Masters from the Centre for South Asian Studies (SAF), Pondicherry University. At IIT Guwahati, Kiran's research mainly focuses on maritime security, maritime capacity-building measures, and sub-regional studies.

Beni Chugh manages the research at the Future of Finance Initiative (Dvara Research). Her work focuses on identifying systemic stability and consumer protection concerns in digital finance. Beni also studies digitisation of social protection, to identify vulnerabilities for marginalized citizens. At the initiative, her work also focuses on designing and implementing citizen centric, digital social protection delivery platforms.

Sagari R. Ramdas is a veterinary scientist, a member of the Food Sovereignty Alliance, India, and is learning to be an agro-ecological food-farmer. She is a Popular Educator at the Kudali Learning Centre in Telangana, India, where she designs and facilitates transformative popular education processes on Social justice, Food Sovereignty and Buen Vivir, with Bahujan (Dalit-OBC-Muslim) and Adivasi youth and women. Through the alliance, she works closely with landless small and marginal farming communities, by organizing for food sovereignty. She writes on her interests concerning social justice, food sovereignty, livestock and ecological governance. She is an Honorary Research Fellow at the Centre for Agroecology, Water and Resilience (CAWR), Coventry University, UK. She is a founder and former director of Anthra, an organization of women veterinary scientists.

Aditi Anand is a policy researcher with work focused on how to make governance structures more inclusive for vulnerable communities. She is currently the National Coordinator of Wada Na Todo Abhiyan (WNTA), where she engages with several multiple-stakeholder approaches at the national and global level to enhance the relevance of Sustainable Development Goals for vulnerable communities and uphold the 'Leave No One Behind' agenda.

Anirban Bhattacharya is a researcher, activist and political commentator. He did his PhD on Labour History from Jawaharlal Nehru University, New Delhi. Presently, he is the Team Lead, National Finance at the Centre for Financial Accountability, New Delhi.

Soumya Dutta is an educator, author and activist working on Climate, Energy & related ecological issues. He has written extensively, has been involved with training large numbers of activists, teachers and students and has given lectures in universities across the globe on these issues. Soumya Dutta has spoken in many UNFCCC and SDG side events, and has analysed and intervened in several state plans on Climate Change. Soumya has also engaged-written-spoken on development finance issues. He has also written extensively on and trained over 1000 high school science teachers on innovative science teaching and low cost research methodologies.